Communications in Computer and Information S(

AF213088

Commenced Publication in 2007
Founding and Former Series Editors:
Alfredo Cuzzocrea, Dominik Ślęzak, and Xiaokang Yang

More information about this series at http://www.springer.com/series/7899

Colin Allison · Leonel Morgado
Johanna Pirker · Dennis Beck
Jonathon Richter · Christian Gütl (Eds.)

Immersive Learning Research Network

Second International Conference, iLRN 2016
Santa Barbara, CA, USA, June 27 – July 1, 2016
Proceedings

Springer

Editors
Colin Allison
University of St Andrews
St Andrews
UK

Dennis Beck
University of Arkansas
Fayetteville, AR
USA

Leonel Morgado
INESC TEC and Universidade Aberta
Coimbra
Portugal

Jonathon Richter
Salish Kootenai College
Pablo, MT
USA

Johanna Pirker
Inst for Info System & Comp System
Graz University of Technology
Graz
Austria

Christian Gütl
Inst for Info System & Comp System
Graz University of Technology
Graz
Austria

ISSN 1865-0929 ISSN 1865-0937 (electronic)
Communications in Computer and Information Science
ISBN 978-3-319-41768-4 ISBN 978-3-319-41769-1 (eBook)
DOI 10.1007/978-3-319-41769-1

Library of Congress Control Number: 2016943385

Printed on acid-free paper

This Springer imprint is published by Springer Nature
The registered company is Springer International Publishing AG Switzerland

iLRN 2016 Preface

The iLRN conference is in its 2nd iteration reporting high quality results in immersive learning research. It is organized by the Immersive Learning Research Network (iLRN), an international organization of developers, educators, and research professionals collaborating to develop the scientific, technical, and applied potential of immersive learning. Effective immersive learning experiences are created within multiple media using myriad techniques and employing a wealth of knowledge that spans many disciplines wherein immersive learning and training may be relevant. The vision of iLRN is to seek out, innovate, and share the evidence and potential for immersive learning. One way of doing this is by hosting a worldwide conference of immersive scholars from across the disciplines, beginning in 2015 in Prague, Czech Republic. These conferences are designed to support and create opportunities for ILRN members to meet and share in collaborative contexts and build their professional immersive learning research and development capacities, and share practical experiences in various scientific tracks and other presentation formats. But more than this, they were devised as an incubator during which iLRN members can collaboratively develop a comprehensive research and outreach agenda that encompasses the breadth and scope of learning potentialities, affordances and challenges of immersive learning environments.

2016 marks the 2nd Annual iLRN conference, hosted at the University of California at Santa Barbara, a beautiful and sunny place near the beach, amidst a busy network of immersive technology corporations, non-profits, entertainment and tourist attractions, and other learning and research institutions in the California area. It's a setting where we hope to better define "immersion" and what that means across our connected interdisciplinary focus. We hope to highlight what "immersive" learning means to a number of focused disciplinary areas. We hope to immerse ourselves in a number of designed experiences to compare and contrast what capabilities they bring – and what things they disallow or take away.

This year's special focus is set on the concept of "The Versatilist". Creating effective learning experiences using immersive technologies requires the coordination of multiple types of special expertise and effort. Artists, programmers, developers, content specialists and evaluators must work together. Creating immersive experiences is getting easier everyday, but doing them well so people learn effectively is much harder. People engaged in the production of high quality immersive learning experiences, thus, must be a specialist in one or more disciplines with the ability to appreciate and work effectively from the lens of other specialties. There's a call for immersive learning professionals to be "versatilists".

As such, this conference is focused on providing opportunities for individuals from a wide variety of areas to share their information across the fields involved with the research, development, implementation and practical experiences, and business of immersive learning. The conference format was designed to gather submissions to the main track focusing on the conference theme, while the six special tracks, workshops, and two publication outlets were planned to draw more interest from diverse communities of scholars and practitioners based on discipline, methodology, or technology type. Two stimulating keynotes and six invited Featured Speakers from academia and research-sponsored industry complement the technical program. We showcase and discuss all of this scholarly and embodied experience through our podcast, *The Versatilist*, with our host and 2016 ILRN general co-chair, Dr. Patrick O'Shea. The podcast is one great way for us to explore the scope and depth of this exciting emerging interdisciplinary field.

Like the inaugural conference, iLRN 2016 is an important forum for immersive learning research. The call for papers resulted in a total of 45 submissions from around the world. Every submission has undergone a rigorous review by at least two members of the program committee to keep high scientific and quality standards. The editorial board decided based on the reviewers' comments to accept 16 full papers for the Springer Proceedings, which is an acceptance rate of 36 percent. The full papers are arranged into two parts of the proceedings, the main track and the special tracks. The accepted papers' authors are from: Austria, Australia, England, Portugal, Scotland, Germany, U.S.A. (California, Illinois, Massachusetts, Montana, Oregon, North Carolina).

We would like to thank all who contributed to the success of this conference, in particular the members of the iLRN committee (and the additional reviewers) for carefully reviewing the contributions and selecting a high quality program. Our general co-chairs Christian Gütl and Patrick O'Shea did a perfect job in organizing and coordinating the conference details. Colin Allison and Leonel Morgado did an incredible job as PC co-chairs, handling the development of a wonderful program, and Johanna Pirker for doing the same for the special tracks. Dennis Beck and Amal Shehadeh took over the tedious job to prepare this volume. And of course, we would like to especially thank Jonathon Richter, iLRN executive director, for taking care of the local arrangements and many other aspects in the organization of the conference.

The following people performed admirably in their roles as special track co-chairs:

- Dennis Beck and Yvonne Earnshaw – K-12 and School Tech
- Giuliana Dettori – Self-regulated learning in immersive environments
- Vic Callaghan, Michael Gardner, Jonathon Richter – Future Education Special Track.
- Markos Mentzelopoulos, Daphne Economou, Vassiliki Bouki, Aristidis Protopsaltis, Ioannis Doumanis – Cognitive Serious Gaming Special Track
- Kirstin Miller, Marsha Goldberg, Steven R Poe, and Kevin Shrapnell – EcoCities Special Track
- Johanna Pirker, Foaad Khosmood, Britte H. Cheng, Maroof Fakhri, Zoë J. Wood – Immersive and Engaging Educational Experiences Special Track.

We hope that you enjoy reading the content of these proceedings. Browse the papers, reflect on the interdisciplinary connections and applications, contact the authors to continue discussions, and continue to advance iLRN's immersive learning agenda by becoming a versatilist - able to apply a depth of skill to a progressively widening scope of immersive learning situations and experiences, equally at ease with technical issues as with disciplinary strategies and content.

June 2016

Jonathon Richter
Christian Gütl
Patrick O'Shea
Dennis Beck
Amal Shehadeh

iLRN 2016 Main Conference Preface

ILRN 2016 is the second annual international conference of the Immersive Learning Network. It follows on from the inaugural conference held in Prague in July 2015. The topic is becoming increasingly relevant as the power and affordability of suitable computers, mobile devices, network connectivity and interface technologies has made virtual and augmented reality environments more accessible than ever before. ILRN's mission is to stimulate the use of, and share knowledge about, these exciting technologies as they are applied effectively in education and learning scenarios. This requires both fundamental and applied research. ILRN aims to develop a comprehensive research and outreach agenda that encompasses the breadth and scope of all the learning potentialities, affordances and challenges of immersive learning environments. To achieve this, the ILRN has invited scientists, practitioners, organizations, and innovators across all disciplines to report on their research in the ILRN 2016 international conference. Twenty-three papers were received for this event and after a rigorous reviewing process eight were selected as full papers for this Springer publication (35% acceptance rate). The authors of these papers hail from Austria, Australia, England, Germany, Portugal, Scotland, and in the United States, North Carolina and Oregon.

Papers in the main conference report on the use of immersive learning environments to address a variety of educational challenges. Self-regulated learning is the subject of study by Pedros et al., who recommend best practices for supporting students who are transitioning into advanced learning scenarios where they must become more independent and self-reflective. Gutl et al. describe a multi-user virtual world based on Open Wonderland used to support a pedagogical model, which combines immersive collaboration with an exploratory teaching approach for the archaeological domain. Fabola and Miller report on experiences using a variety of novel user interfaces which allow school children to access a sophisticated OpenSim-based immersive model of a 14th century cathedral. Moissinac et al. describe an immersive environment – Rippleville - for teaching teenagers how to avoid obesity. O'Shea and Elliot explore the capabilities of augmented reality apps for iOS and Android devices and asses them in terms of educational usability and value. The user experience (UX) in a VLE is the focus of research by Janssen et al. who used the widely used Minecraft platform for their experiments. Bakri and Allison investigate the evolving support for accessing immersive environments via standard web browsers and address the question of the likelihood of the 3D Web and virtual worlds converging. Eferre et al. review features of a learning analytics tool that is part of an e-learning multimodal dialogue system, which, in turn, is part of an immersive environment to support different learning scenarios.

We hope you will find this collection of papers informative and engaging. We encourage you to join ILRN and participate in future events.

June 2016

Colin Allison
Leonel Morgado

iLRN 2016 Special Tracks Preface

The field of immersive digital learning environments has been an extremely successful and emerging topic of interest. One of the grand challenges of this complex and growing research field is its interdisciplinary and broad nature. Immersive learning consists of a wide range of research interests and fields and enables collaboration between researchers and practitioners from different disciplines. Continuing on our successful experience at iLRN 2015, we have introduced special tracks as forum for quality scientific research in focused areas. The mission of these focused tracks is to bring together specialists from diverse areas to enable an interdisciplinary collaboration and exchange of knowledge.

Thus, we invited specialists from different research fields to submit focused special tracks to this conference to highlight various areas of immersive learning. iLRN 2016 features four special tracks covering topics:

- The special track "K-12 and School Tech" is chaired by Dennis Beck and Yvonne Earnshaw. The goal of this track is to discuss current, relevant, and situated immersive learning research in the primary and secondary classroom.
- The track "The Future of Education" explores visions of possible ways how immersive-reality technologies might change future education. The track is chaired by Vic Callaghan, Michael Gardner, and Jonathon Richter.
- In the track "Cognitive Serious Gaming" the track chairs Markos Mentzelopoulos, Daphne Economou, Vassiliki Bouki, Aristidis Protopsaltis, and Ioannis Doumanis explore how cognitive principles can be applied to improve the training effectiveness in serious games.
- In the track "Immersive and Engaging Educational Experiences" the track chairs Johanna Pirker, Foaad Khosmood, Britte H. Cheng, Maroof Fakhri, and Zoë J. Wood discuss how educational environments can be designed, developed, and analyzed with focus on immersion and engagement.

Twenty-two submissions were received by the Special Tracks and six were chosen as full papers to be published in the Springer proceedings for an overall acceptance rate of 28%. Authors submitted contributions from England, Ireland, and in the United States – Arkansas, California, Illinois, Montana, and Ohio.

We would like to express our gratitude to all chairs and reviewers of the special tracks and their engagement and commitment to make the tracks an integral part of the main conference by providing a broad variety of high-quality presentations with an in-depth overview of different research topics related to immersive learning. We cordially thank each and every person who contributed toward making the special tracks to such an integral and successful part of the main conference.

June 2016

Johanna Pirker
Ken Hudson

Conference Organization

iLRN Executive Director

Jonathon Richter | Salish Kootenai College, USA

General Chair

Patrick O'Shea | Appalachian State University, USA

General Chair

Christian Gütl | Graz University of Technology, Austria

Vice-Chair

Michael Gardner | University of Essex, UK

Program Co-chair

Colin Allison | University of St Andrews, UK

Program Co-chair

Leonel Morgado | INESC TEC and Universidade Aberta, Portugal

Special Track Co-chair

Ken Hudson | Stealth mode startup, Ontario, Canada

Special Track Co-chair

Johanna Pirker | Graz University of Technology, Austria

Workshops Co-chair

Scott Warren | University of North Texas, USA

Workshops Co-chair

Rainer Malaka | University Bremen, Germany

Publicity and Public Relations Chair

Anasol Peña–Rios University of Essex, UK

Publications Co-chair

Dennis Beck University of Arkansas, USA

Publications Co-chair

Amal Shehadeh Graz University of Technology, Austria

Local Chair

Jatila Van Der Veen University of California - Santa Barbara, USA

North America Co-chair

Jennifer B. Elliott University of North Carolina, USA

South America Co-chair

Lynn Alves UFBA, Brazil

South America Co-chair

Andreas Pester Carinthia University of Applied Sciences, Austria

South America Co-chair

Roger Tavares UFRN, Brazil

Asia Pacific Co-chair

Henry Been-Lirn Duh University of Tasmania, Australia

Europa Co-chair

Francesco Gabellone CNR IBAM Lecce, Italy

Europa Co-chair

Fotis Liarokapis Masaryk University, Czech Republic

Middle East Co-chair

Mohammad Al-Smadi	Jordan University of Science and Technology, Irbid, Jordan

Middle East Co-chair

Samir Elseoud	American University, Egypt

Africa Chair

Mathy Vanbuel	Audiovisual Technologies, Informatics & Telecommunications, Belgium

iLRN Advisory Board

Jon Dorbolo	Oregon State University, USA
Francois Garnier	École Nationale Supériore des Arts Décoratifs, France
Beatrice Hasler	Interdisciplinary Center Herzliya, Israel
Pasi Mattila	Center for Internet Excellence, Finland
Carlos Delgado-Kloos	Universidad Carlos III de Madrid, Spain

Program Committee

Abelardo Pardo	The University of Sydney, Australia
Alan Miller	University of St Andrews, UK
Alexander Nussbaumer	Graz University of Technology, Austria
Allan Fowler	Kennesaw State University, USA
Alok Mishra	Atilim University, Turkey
Anasol Peña-Ríos	University of Essex, UK
Anders Drachen	Game Analytics, Denmark
Andreas Schmeil	University of Lugano (USI), Switzerland
Annika Wiklund-Engblom	Åbo Akademi University, Finland
Aurelie Herbet	ENSAD, France
Béatrice Hasler	University of Barcelona, Spain
Bruno Joho	Lucerne University of Applied Science and Arts, Switzerland
Christian Gütl	Graz University of Technology, Austria
Christothea Herodotou	The Open University, UK
Colin Allison	University of St Andrews, UK
Daniel Livingstone	Digital Design Studio, Glasgow School of Art, UK
David Lowe	The University of Sydney, Australia
Demetrios Sampson	University of Piraeus, Greece
Dennis Beck	University of Arkansas, USA
Dominic Kao	Massachusetts Institute of Technology, USA

Erik Champion	Curtin University, Australia
Erik Harpstead	Carnegie Mellon University, USA
Ferial Khaddage	Deakin University, Australia
Foaad Khosmood	California Polytechnic State University, USA
Fridolin Wild	The Open University, UK
Guenter Wallner	University of Applied Arts Vienna, Austria
Ignazio Passero	Università degli Studi di Salerno, Italy
Indika Perera	University of Moratuwa, Sri Lanka
Jannicke Baalsrud Hauge	University of Bremen, Germany
Jochen Kuhn	University of Kaiserslautern, Germany
Johanna Pirker	Graz University of Technology, Austria
John Cook	University of West of England, UK
John Venable	Curtin University of Technology, Austria
Jonathon Richter	University of Oregon, USA
Jose Zagal	DePaul University, USA
Justin Ehrlich	Western Illinois University, USA
Kai Erenli	UAS bfi Vienna, Austria
Leonel Morgado	INESC TEC/Universidade Aberta, Portugal
Lisa Gjedde	Aalborg Universitet, Denmark
Marcus Specht	Open University of the Netherlands, Netherlands
Margit Höfler	University of Graz, Austria
María Blanca Ibáñez	Universidad Carlos III de Madrid, Spain
Markos Mentzelopoulos	University of Westminster, UK
Mary Webb	King's College London, UK
Max North	Southern Polytechnic State University, USA
Michael Derntl	RWTH Aachen University, Germany
Michael Gardner	University of Essex, UK
Mikhail Fominykh	Europlan UK Ltd, UK
Milos Kravcik	RWTH Aachen University, Germany
Mohammad Al-Smadi	Jordan University of Science and Technology, Jordan
Monique Janneck	Fachhochschule Lübeck, Germany
Narayanan Kulathuramaiyer	Universiti Malaysia Sarawak, Malaysia
Panagiotis Bamidis	Aristotle University of Thessaloniki, Greece
Patrick O'Shea	Appalachian State University, USA
Rainer Malaka	University of Bremen, Germany
Ralf Klamma	RWTH Aachen University, Germany
Scott Warren	University of North Texas, USA
Stefanie Lindstaedt	Graz University of Technology, Austria
Stephanie Linek	ZBW Leibniz Information Centre for Economics, Germany
Stylianos Mystakidis	University of Patras, Greece
Timo Koskela	University of Oulu/CIE, Finland
Tobias Schreck	Graz University of Technology, Austria
Wolfgang Slany	Graz University of Technology, Austria

Special Track on K-12 and School Technology

Special Track Chairs

Dennis Beck	University of Arkansas at Fayetteville, USA
Yvonne Earnshaw	University of North Texas

Program Committee

Scott Warren	University of North Texas, USA
Jonathon Richter	Salish Kootenai College, USA
Matthew Schmidt	University of Cincinnati, USA
Dennis Beck	University of Arkansas, USA
Yvonne Earnshaw	University of North Texas, USA

Special Track on The Future of Education

Special Track Chairs

Vic Callaghan	University of Essex, UK
Michael Gardner	University of Essex, UK
Jonathon Richter	Salish Kootenai College, USA

Program Committee

Chantel Dan Chen	University of Essex, UK
Jennifer O'Connor	National University of Ireland, Galway, Ireland
Susi Daryanti	Universitas Gadjah Mada, Indonesia
Dr Simon Egerton	University of Monash, Malaysia
Dr Gary Graham	Leeds University, UK
Dr Anita Greenhill	Manchester University
Prof Roger Hawkins	University of Essex, UK
Brian David Johnson	Arizona State University, Phoenix, USA
Dr Anasol Peña-Rios	British Telecom, UK
Dr Carlos Sanchez-Lozano	Bogota, Colombia
Dr Fang Wang	Brunel University, UK
Prof Minjuan Wang	San Diego State University, USA
Hsuan-Yi Wu	National Taiwan University
Dr Victor Zamudio	Instiuto Tecnologico de Leon, Mexico
Dr Shumei Zhang	Shijiazhuang University, China
Dr Ping Zheng	Canterbury Christ Church University, UK

Special Track on Cognitive Serious Gaming (CSG)

Special Track Chairs

Markos Mentzelopoulos	University of Westminster, UK
Daphne Economou	University of Westminster, UK
Vassiliki Bouki	University of Westminster, UK

Aristidis Protopsaltis	Friedrich-Alexander-Universität, Germany
Ioannis Doumanis	CTVC Ltd, UK

Program Committee

Mark Baldwin	University of Westminster, UK
Tom Boyle	London Metropolitan University, UK
Paul Brna	University of Edinburgh, UK
Charalampos Karagiannidis	University of Thessaly, Volos, Greece
Petros Lameras	Serious Games Institute, UK
Panagiotis Petridis	Aston University, UK
Thrasyvoulos Tsiatsos	Aristotle University of Thessaloniki, Greece

Special Track on Immersive and Engaging Educational Experiences

Special Track Chairs

Johanna Pirker	Graz University of Technology, Austria
Foaad Khosmood	California Polytechnic State University, CA
Britte H. Cheng	SRI International, CA
Maroof Fakhri	Labster, Denmark
Zoë J. Wood	California Polytechnic State University, CA

Program Committee

Allan Fowler	Kennesaw State University
Brian Mcdonald	Glasgow Caledonian University, UK
Dominic Kao	Massachusetts Institute of Technology, MA
Kai Erenli	UAS bfi Vienna, Austria
Ralf Klamma	Aachen University, DE
Ryan Locke	Abertay University, UK
Volker Settgast	Fraunhofer Austria, Austria

Sponsors

Graz University of Technology, Institute for Information Systems and Computer Media

Contents

Virtual Worlds

Exploratory and Collaborative Learning Experience in Immersive Environments

Implementation and Findings from an Archaeological Domain

Christian Gütl[1,2(✉)], Lisa Maria Tomes[1], Johanna Pirker[1], and Vanessa Chang[2]

[1] IICM, Graz University of Technology, Graz, Austria
{cguetl, jpirker}@iicm.edu, lisa.tomes@gmail.com
[2] SoIS and Curtin Teaching and Learning, Curtin University, Perth, WA, Australia
{cguetl, Vanessa.Chang}@curtin.edu.au

Abstract. This paper describes a multi-user learning environment in a virtual world setting. An exploratory and collaborative learning using an educational scavenger hunt metaphor form the basis for student learning and engagement in virtual world. The learning experience is based on the following elements: exploration – students explore the learning content on their own, and build a knowledge base. Cooperation and Collaboration – students cooperate and collaborate to uncover information, share findings, and gain knowledge and skills. Discussion and Reflection – students discuss and solve problems together, and exercise reflective learning. Based on this idea, three main contributions are provided in this paper: Firstly, a pedagogical model which combines immersive, online, and virtual collaboration with an exploratory teaching approach. Secondly, the learning tasks and interactions are incorporated by a flexible to use set of tools in the virtual world Open Wonderland. Finally, an experimentation study evaluating the virtual world in the learning domain Egyptology.

Keywords: Exploratory learning · Collaborative learning · Immersive · Virtual world learning environments · Game-like learning design

1 Introduction

"I like the idea of finding information. The statues were interesting and the learning goal is fulfilled! Fun learning! Moreover, the constant communication was great!" The above student feedback is from an experience encountered in the 3D immersive and virtual world. The aim of the learning is to explore and learn in a fun and engaging virtual environment. Apart from the 'fun' element, the student singled out the importance of communication in the learning process. In this paper, an exploratory virtual learning in multi-user virtual worlds with learning activities focusing on communication and collaboration in the archeological domain is presented.

C. Allison et al. (Eds.): iLRN 2016, CCIS 621, pp. 3–16, 2016.
DOI: 10.1007/978-3-319-41769-1_1

Models encompassing engaging learning pedagogies and motivational strategies to achieve learning outcomes are integral in modern teaching and learning settings (Nasir and Hand 2008; Roschelle et al. 2007; Pirker et al. 2014). Intrinsic motivation can support students in self-directed learning (Hartnett et al. 2011). Recent learning approaches to motivate students include the use of game elements to facilitate learning, exploratory learning to capture the interest of learners; collaborative learning for learners to engage with and connect; all with the intent to distill enjoyment and to inspire learners who want to learn (Pirker and Gütl 2015). In recent years, the increase in the number of online courses has allowed learning to be more accessible; however the dichotomy of this poses both challenges and opportunities. Although the reach is far and wide, many such online courses are purely traditional e-learning or distance learning courses. The attraction to this is that the traditional e-learning environment allows users to work quicker and independently from remote locations (Clark and Mayer 2011). The downfall of this is the difficulty to organize learners to share, discuss, debate, engage and learn collaboratively. Virtual worlds (VW) have learning tools that provide several advantages. In the form of multi-user environments they support the use of different communication channels and collaboration technologies. Users are in control of their learning target when immersed in a VW environment. In a multi-user platform, users have the opportunity to meet with other learners, to work collaborative to solve problems, receive immediate feedback, and work in an engaging environment. Depending on the design of the learning content, a VW environment may have exploratory and experimental components. The exploratory component may include game-like guided interactive exercises for learners to discover and achieve mastery level of a defined domain. In this regard, learners have the opportunity to learn and apply concepts in a much more natural and less stressful setting (Reinmann-Rothmeier and Mandl 1994). The experimental component may include a suite of visualizations or simulations for learners to mimic and apply the subject domain (Guetl 2010; Pirker et al. 2012). As learning is scaffolded, learners will have the autonomy to make choices, work with other learners, participate and contribute in learning activities. Consequently, it makes sense to explore the VW capabilities as an ideal e-learning tool to support game-based, exploratory, and collaborative learning scenarios. But how well do VWs support exploratory and collaborative learning settings? How well does such virtual exploratory learning work to engage and motivate users?

The aim of this paper is to describe the implementation of an exploratory learning setup in the multi-user avatar-based virtual world environment Open Wonderland by adopting the educational scavenger hunt metaphor and assess the usability as well as the ability to engage and immerse users. Three main contributions are described in this paper. First, a pedagogical model which combines online and virtual collaboration with an exploratory teaching approach is proposed. The second contribution is the integration of this model in an immersive virtual world. Finally, a user study evaluating the virtual world on the factors of usability, immersion, and user motivation is presented. The remainder of this paper is structured as follows: first, a background work on pedagogical approaches and technologies is given which involve collaborative and exploratory strategies. Second, a conceptual approach on how to engage users in a virtual environment with different learning activities is provided. An introduction of a collaborative and exploratory virtual world scenario implemented in Open Wonderland is proffered. A VW learning environment of an Egyptian myth is provided, followed by a description of the evaluation and findings, and recommendations for future work.

2 Background and Related Work

This section gives an overview of the teaching concepts and the implementation related to the learning setup introduced in this paper.

Collaborative learning is a student-centered teaching method that can be used in classroom or online learning. Collaboration comes naturally to human beings because of our evolution (Johnson and Johnson 1991). Through collaboration, learning outcomes are enriched by discovering, sharing and negotiating knowledge (Dillenbourg 1999). There are many ways for collaborative learning to take place but also certain prerequisites are needed for collaborative work to happen. First of all, a form of interdependence has to be created. Johnson and Johnson (1991) emphasized in this context whereby *"the first requirement for an effectively structured cooperative lesson is that students believe that they sink or swim together. […] While the essence of cooperative learning is positive interdependence, other essential components include individual accountability […] and group skills"*. In this regard, being collaborative is highly dependent on one's cooperation and social skills. Another important aspect is the individual accountability when learners are collaborating to work together to solve problems (Hron and Friedrich 2003). *Exploratory learning*, also known as *discovery learning*, is a form of active learning where students have to construct their own knowledge from unstructured information or materials usually provided by an instructor. The advantages of this approach include a deeper understanding of the learning material due to self-discovery and a higher autonomy of the learner resulting in an increased awareness and high intrinsic motivation (Bruner 1961). Njoo and De Jong (1993) identified computer simulations as well suited for exploratory learning *"[…] because they can hide a model that has to be discovered by the learner"*. But the learning approach is not without controversy. Students' negative perception is caused by misunderstandings and certain errors that they would make. To overcome this, an enhanced approach is to provide the students with basic information before allowing them to explore in more detail (Marzano 2011). *Scavenger hunts* used in educational contexts is becoming increasingly popular. Although it is argued that scavenger hunt is not an ideal teaching concept, it is very popular because of the game-like character and the ability to motivate students. Most of the time, the goal of a scavenger hunt is to bring together certain objects or information in order to answer a set of questions. The educational value can be increased if several people are required to work together to share and discuss ideas (Klopfer et al. 2005).

Unlike other technologies used in distance learning settings, *virtual worlds (VW)* can provide a feeling of immersion with multiple communication and interaction channels. VWs are collaborative forms of immersive virtual learning environments. The multi-user virtual platform also provides a sense of group awareness (Gütl 2010). Consequently VW can support exploratory and collaborative learning settings for various subject domains, such as learning languages (Ibanez et al. 2011; Berns et al. 2013), natural science or engineering (Pirker et al. 2012), and history (Manuelian 2013;

Jacobson and Gillam n.d.). An example for exploratory learning in a VW is the 'infection control game', where students play different hospital staff roles and exercise different hygiene procedures (Jarvis et al. 2007). In the context of the work presented in this paper, *Giza3D* from Harvard University (Manuelian 2013) is an environment set up with an aim to familiarize students with ancient Egypt. The 3D model of the Giza plateau is historically accurate and can be used in classrooms and for scientific research. In the ancient Egypt 3D environment students can move around freely, look at objects and buildings from different angles. The limitation here is that the environment does not support multi-user access and collaborative learning. A second example, the *Egyptian Oracle*, is a mixed reality experience in which the audience can see a projection of a religious ceremony in a virtual Egyptian temple but also with real actors and a digital puppeteer to interact with the audience (Jacobson and Gillam n.d.). In order to enhance learning experiences in subjects like Egyptology, and provide students with an engaging learning environment, we propose an educational scavenger hunt metaphor in an immersive learning environment. In the next section the proposed pedagogical model to combine collaborative and exploratory learning to create VW is provided.

3 Conceptual Approach

The goal of the design process was the development of a constructivist pedagogical model to support self-directed and engaging learning in a learner-centric and collaborative virtual world (VW). The aim of this model is to be used in different multi-user virtual setups and subjects domain. This should not be limited to one specific technology or subject discipline.

To design a virtual experience with exploratory and collaborative character which also focuses on learning achievements by peer or group communication and reflection, we focus on providing the following elements for the learning process:

1. *Exploration*. The users have the possibility to experience and explore the learning content on their own, gather information, and build a knowledge base. This stage of knowledge acquisition allows the learners to control their learning.
2. *Cooperation and Collaboration*. Students are engaged to cooperate and collaborate in order to uncover information, share findings, and gain knowledge and skills.
3. *Discussion and Reflection*. Interactions in the form of discussions to solve problems and reflect on the knowledge gained.

Figure 1 illustrates the pedagogical model to learn in an exploratory and collaborative way which can be mapped as an iterative cycle. The learning experience starts in the first step with an *Exploration* task, which is also seen as the basic step of the learning experience. This is followed by the *Cooperation and Collaboration* to work on knowledge building tasks. Learners are engaged to share information and to gain insights and knowledge. This allows the learners to expand their knowledge and deepen their understanding. In the last step, the *Discussion and Reflection* task, the students can discuss issues and problems together and reflect on the content, and organize themselves for further iteration. Integrated in an immersive environment, this approach can be mapped to an educational Scavenger Hunt metaphor with a focus on collaboration and social experiences.

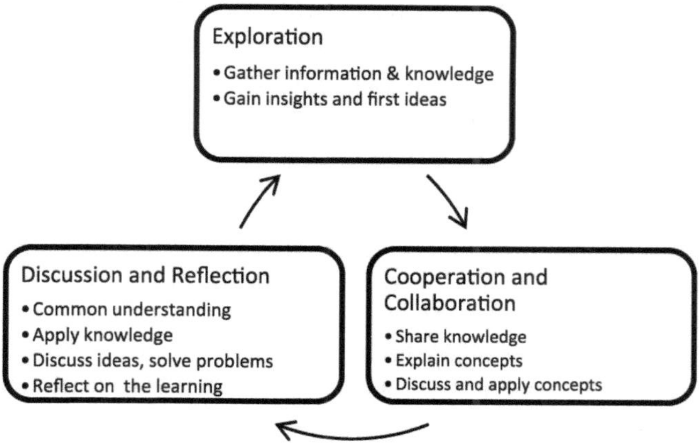

Fig. 1. Pedagogical model for exploratory and collaborative learning

Based on these activities, different functional requirements can be identified. To support the pedagogical model, an online environment should provide social interactions and communication tools. This includes the ability to interact and socialize with other users. Tools such as text or voice chat and the visual appearance of customizable avatars and the ability for these avatars to interact with each other are available in the environment. Other tools to support collaboration can be developed and included to share and transfer knowledge. Collaborative virtual world toolkits also allow users to drag and drop content such as pictures or documents into the worlds to share information. Other learning tools, such as whiteboards enable brainstorming and information to be gathered for discussion. To support exploratory experiences, an environment should be provided to allow users the freedom to support their own exploration of the learning content and interactions within the environment.

Since the use of VWs often requires users to learn how to interact with the software tool and the 3D environment, the world should be designed in an engaging and user-friendly way to help users overcome initial barriers, avoid early dropouts and feeling of frustration. Thus, such online environments should be designed with usability and user engagement in mind. Additionally, they should also attract users with a focus on immersion and game-like design with autonomy to explore independently and collaboratively. In the next section, a VW, which is designed based on this pedagogical model with a focus on immersion, engagement, and collaboration is presented.

4 Virtual World

The Virtual Egypt World (VEW) was implemented with the open source avatar-based multi-user virtual world platform *Open Wonderland (OWL)*[1]. OWL was built for educational and business purposes and offers a range of tools to support group work

[1] http://openwonderland.org/.

and collaborative tasks (Open Wonderland 2015). Due to its collaborative character, the educational design, its extensibility and a range of tools supporting collaborative and explorative tasks OWL was chosen as toolkit to built the VEW in. In this work, the following built-in tools were used: the *User list* which shows all users who are currently online, the *Textchat* for communication with one or more other users, and the *Stickynote* module which adds a yellow pad to the world on which text can be written. Additionally, four modules described below have been developed or adapted to enable the learning experience outlined in Sect. 3 but also to be used in a flexible way in other learning settings.

First, the *Chat Bot* module adds chat functionality to a non-personal character (NPC) character or any other object in the world. Students can talk to this character using predefined question and answer options. The chat bot implementation builds on previous work from Riedmann (2014). Second, the *Item module* allows teachers to annotate any object in the world with information in the form of text and image. Students can uncover this information by hovering over the object with their mouse cursors. To indicate that an object is annotated with information, rotating red and yellow dots appear automatically around the object. It is also possible for students to add the information to their object inventory to be used later. To enforce collaboration, a teacher can define and assign roles which enable students to uncover information only from selected objects. Quizzes were built as interaction activity where students have to work together and share their respective information in order to work out the answers to the questions. Third, the *Item board* provides students with a tool to exchange information during and after their learning. Students can select objects from their inventory and add them to the item board to share with the other students. This enables a compilation of all uncovered information in one place. Fourth, the *Quiz module* enables a teacher to define multiple choice questions which is aligned to the learning outcomes. Once a student is in proximity range of an object provided with the Quiz functionality, a set of questions are generated and students can take the test. If the student passes the quiz, the student will be teleported to another VW or to another level continuing the course of learning.

The extension of OWL by these new functionalities was easy to develop given the modular architecture. The open source VW building platform was written in Java and is extensible by programmers and content providers. The main installation includes the important core functions, such as authentication, networking, content management, and client rendering. New features and functionalities can also be added by modules. This is realized by uploading the respective Java archive to the server (Kaplan and Yankelovich 2011).

5 A Showcase of the Archeological Domain

The learning experience follows the pedagogical concept outlined in Sect. 3, and is implemented based on the virtual platform described in Sect. 4. In the *Virtual Egypt World (VEW)* students learn about the Osiris Myth which is a story from ancient Egyptian mythology. It tells the story of the murder of King Osiris by his brother Seth, and the subsequent fight with Osiris' son Horus for the throne (Assmann 2001).

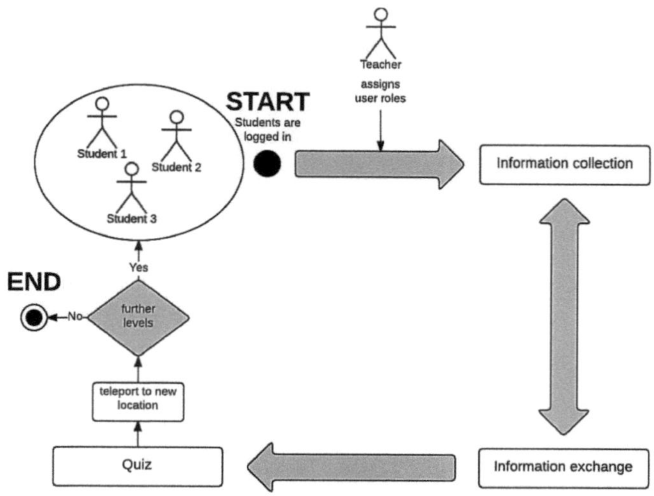

Fig. 2. Learning process in the *VEW*

The Open Source 3D models from Google 3D Warehouse (3DW 2015) were used for creating the virtual world.

Figure 2 shows an overview of the learning process in the VEW. First, students log into the virtual world and become visible to the teacher. In the next step, the teacher forms the groups and assigns the following roles to the students: *Adventurer, Scientist, Priest, and Historian*. Information that is visible for the students is defined at this stage. The four roles were especially designed for the Egyptian scenario and may need to be adapted for other learning subjects. This is followed by the learning exploration tasks where students uncover and collect as much information as possible. In parallel with exploring information about the Osiris Myth, students can also share their knowledge by using the *item board* and *text or voice chat*. If a student does not know who to contact regarding a specific piece of information, a hint will be shown in the inventory containing the name of the student who has already obtained the information. Finally, if the students believe that they have collected and learned all the necessary information, they can take the quiz. If the student answers all questions correctly, they will be teleported to another world to the next level of learning until all the levels were completed. At the heart of the VEW is a pyramid that students can explore. An NPC themed as an Egyptian nomad character, as shown in Fig. 3a, stands at the entrance of the pyramid. This feature is realized with our chat bot module. Students can talk to the NPC in a guided dialog following a question and answer structure according to a pre-defined set of knowledge base. Students can receive hints on how and where to find relevant information. The pyramid has three levels. Each level is built like a maze, with level 1 occupying the largest floor space followed by two smaller levels in accordance to the pyramid-shaped structure. In order to reach the top level, the students have to find their way through the mazes on the first two floors. Each upper level is also accessible via a ramp. The parts of the Osiris myth are hidden in five statues of Egyptian deities which were distributed in the pyramid. The item module was used to

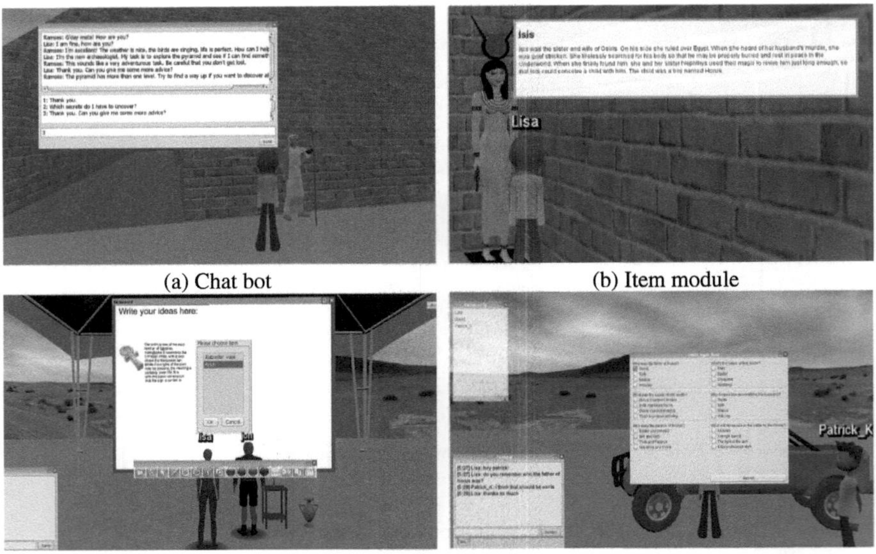

(a) Chat bot (b) Item module

(c) Item board (d) Quiz module

Fig. 3. Selected places of the *Virtual Egypt World (VEW)*

attach the learning content. Figure 3b shows the statute of Isis which provides information relevant in the context of the Osiris myth. Three additional objects were hidden in a total of five Egyptian statues but the information in the three objects is not connected to the Osiris myth.

Outside the pyramid, students can find the 'archaeologists tent' with the Item board where they can meet after exploring the pyramid and share the information they have found (see Fig. 3c). The place where the students can take the quiz is symbolized by the all-terrain vehicle (see Fig. 3d). The truck was chosen as an analogy to 'drive away' after having learned everything about the Osiris myth. If the final quiz is successfully completed, the student will be teleported to a world where the student will receive information on the successful completion of the learning tasks.

6 Evaluation and Findings

6.1 Evaluation Objective and Setup

The aim of this evaluation is to learn about students' perception of the pedagogical approach and the prototype. It is envisaged that the results from this study will inform a flexible solution that is applicable for a wider range of subject domains. Thus the evaluation focuses on the following dimensions: (1) Motivation, (2) Immersion, (3) Usability, (4) Perception of knowledge acquisition.

The chosen research method combines quantitative and qualitative methods including a pre- and post-questionnaire, interviews, recording of participants' activities, and observation. Participants were able to answer questions in German or English. In the

Table 1. Overview of tasks for the study participants

Task number	Time	Description
Task 1	4 min	Explore the virtual world to get used to control the avatar
Task 2	4 min	Familiarize themselves with the communication tools (voice and text chat)
Task 3	2 min	Review the user role assigned to each of the participant in the group
Task 4	15 min	Explore the pyramid, find objects and uncover hidden information based on the individual roles
Task 5	15 min	Share information with the other group members using the Item Board and communication tools
Task 6	5 min	Take the quiz (multiple choice questions) about concepts learned in task 4 and 5

first case, the answers were translated for this paper. The experimentation took place in a controlled environment with a small group of students ranging between two and four students. In this experiment, the prototype was limited to the avatar representation's interaction in the VW as well as voice and text chat (due to technical restriction in the experimentation environment Skype voice chat was used rather the native one of the platform). A pre-defined script of tasks was used for the experiment. Each participant was placed in a separate room during the experimentation. The procedure including the planned time schedule of the experimentation follows the following steps: (1) Welcome and overview of experimentation - 5 min, (2) Pre-questionnaire - 5 min, (3) Brief training using the virtual world - 5 min, (4) Learning experience in virtual world - 45 min, (5) Post questionnaire - 10 min. The learning activities and learning tasks with the allocated time frames used for the study are given in Table 1.

The prototype is developed based on Open Wonderland and the implemented Egypt virtual world focuses on the Osiris myth. The pre-test includes questions about demographic data, knowledge of the subject domain, computer literacy skills, gaming skills, and virtual world usage. The post questionnaire covers general questions regarding perceptions about the learning experience and design aspects as well as the virtual world and the tools. For the specific focus of this experimentation, the motivational aspects are measured by the flow state scale (Jackson and Marsh 1996), immersion are measured based on a 32-question immersion scale by Jennett et al. (2008), and the usability are measured by the System Usability Scale (SUS) after Brooke (1996). The questionnaires use a five point Likert scale with an open-ended section. The experimentation activities were recorded by video camera and transcribed. Motivational and immersion scale as well as SUS are represented in a scale from 0 to 100. A more detailed description of the study details, but also results is available in Tomes (2015).

6.2 Evaluation Results and Findings

The participants were recruited within the social network group of university students. Eighteen students participated in the evaluation, 13 (72.2 %) of them were male. All of the participants were students in various fields. The participants aged between 20 and 31 with a mean value of M = 25.50 (SD = 3.15). Group formation was based on the availability of the participants within a one week timeframe. The group size varies between two and four students, with four groups of students with three members, one with two members and a final group with four members.

None of the 18 students have pre-knowledge in the subjects of Egyptology, three had heard of the Osiris myth but cannot recall the exact details about it. In terms of computer literacy, the majority of participants rate themselves either as expert or advanced user, resulting with a mean of 4.28 (SD = 1.02). The students rated themselves higher with a mean of 4.39 (SD = 0.78) when asked about their internet skills.

When it comes to immersive learning environments, the participants rated their experiences in virtual worlds quite low with an average of only 3.83 (SD = 1.10), despite their advanced skills in using computers. The rate of proficiency of virtual worlds did not rate well with a mean score of 1.94 (SD = 1.00). Participants reported to have some experiences in the context of gaming and collaborative work. Notably, none of the participants have had any experience with simulations. Although the participants had not reported extensive experiences in using virtual worlds, they see the potential for them in using such settings, especially in geographical dispersed environment, play-like environment, repetitive training of hazardous, risky and dangerous situations.

The findings of the learning experience itself reveal ambivalent attitudes. On the positive side, comments include: *"I like the idea of finding information. The statues were interesting and the learning goal is fulfilled! Fun learning! Moreover, the constant communication was great!"* On the negative side the technical maturity and graphical representation were raised: *"nice idea, but with technical issues that interfere with the experience"*; *"Bad graphics"; "Graphics could be improved"*.

In terms of the contextualized virtual worlds and tools, the students liked the pyramid and the maze-like structure to find objects and uncover information. Some of the comments included *"The riddle was nice, and I liked that teamwork was required to do the final quiz."* Two students found the character in front of the pyramid (chat bot) an important component offering hints and conveying a *"sense of adventures"*. Besides the issues of the graphical appearance, cumbersome controls are raised as a serious issue: *"The controls were not good, especially inside the pyramid. Every time I turned I could only see a wall."* In terms of the learning experience, the students found the *Item board* as relatively important (M = 3.39; SD = 1.20), and rated the Quiz component even higher (M = 3.94; SD = 1.26). In terms of the virtual world's support for collaboration, the students found the VEW easy to use and they were well supported (M = 4.11; SD = 1.23). The learning task was also perceived as enjoyable and fun (M 4.00, SD 0.97): *"I actually found it very funny. It had something adventurous." "It was fun. But you also had to be concentrated. It wasn't just for fun, but rather you have to be focused in the learning tasks."* On the nominal scale between 0 and 100, the motivational measure scored fairly average with a mean of M = 63.68 and a standard deviation SD = 13.47. Navigational problems and intuitive control featured for the avatars and tool interaction might have interfered with the learning flow. In contrast, the positive attitude for group work in the setting as well as the feeling of providing value to the group for finishing the task have positively influenced the result. The game-based character of the setting is also seen on the positive side: *"I liked that you have to search for the information and that every piece of it was hidden separately in one of the statues."* With regard to immersion, the measure between 0 and 100 scored lower with a mean of 50.66 (SD = 11.42) than the motivational aspect. The graphic representation might have had a negative impact in this context: *"graphics looked a bit stale, not all that realistic or inviting to exploration"*. Also the participants do not agree of having a feeling of 'being part' of the virtual world and gave a fairly low rating with a value of M = 1.76 (SD = 0.90). In terms of usability, the SUS value was acceptable with an average of 65.28 (SD = 17.70). In particular the small amount of time participants were required to learn to use the system has been mentioned as a positive effect. The technical problems were some of the negative as with issues relating to the control tools and the avatar in the smaller maze. The following statements may illustrate this: *"We often got stuck with our avatars on a wall. One time I even left the pyramid unintentionally." "I never know whether I would be able to move when a window in the world was open. Sometimes I could and sometimes I couldn't." "Using the Whiteboard was not very intuitive."* The participants' perceptions regarding the knowledge acquisition bear both positive and negatives aspects. This is reflected by the responses about the overall perception of the learning experience of the Osiris myth to expand knowledge by a slightly positive attitude by a mean value of M = 3.06 (SD = 1.43). Even more critical are the opinions on how they would consider this kind of virtual world for learning activities. A selection of the response might shade more light with this aspect: *"I see it as learning opportunity 'in between' but not for targeted learning." "It is probably better suited for a younger audience, e.g. for primary school children, primary school children because you can represent things graphically." "Whether you can learn well with such worlds depends on your personal learning preferences. I'm certainly not the type who can learn well with such information."*

7 Conclusions and Further Work

Although the educational scavenger hunt approach based on exploration and collaboration concepts as well the prototype implementation has shown potential in modern learning settings, there is room for improvement. In terms of immersion and realism of the virtual places, more accurate and appealing 3D models need to be used for improved learning and student engagement. From the experimentation, the students had commented on positive learning experiences with a majority of the students who had enjoyed learning in the environment. In particular the freedom of exploring (the explorative learning design) and the integrated game design elements were perceived well. However, usability and technical issues influenced the experiment. Some students had voiced their frustrations with the control and navigation features in the maze. It is acknowledged that with the identified usability issues, the control interfaces and panels of the tools will need to be improved. From this study, it can be summed up that the students liked the game-based learning design. The students also liked the ability to have a sense of achievement with the teleported feature to move up to the next level.

While the virtual world toolkit Open Wonderland is definitely a good tool to quickly and easily create collaborative worlds, it lacks game design features. OWL is designed to support the creation of VWs with a strong focus on collaborative aspects, but is limited in the support of adaptable graphical representations (e.g. customizable user interfaces) or game-like environment interactions (e.g. stories, specific game mechanics). Thus, future experiments could focus on the implementation of this scenario in tools, which enable a stronger focus on graphics, environment interactions, different forms of navigation, and more mechanics inspired by game design. This makes comparisons between similar integrations in other virtual world toolkits (e.g. Second Life) or in game engines (e.g. Unity) to promising areas of interest for future work. In order to get a better understanding and a stronger representation of the learning process and achievement of the learning outcomes in such a virtual world it is recommended that experiments with a larger group of students and different types of learners (e.g. younger or older) and users (VW novices or experts) will be conducted and also to examine the actual benefit of such immersive learning scenarios in comparison to more traditional formats, such as physical or text-based learning. As already highlighted by similar studies, (Pirker et al. 2013) a user- (/learner-) centric design of such learning environments is essential and different usability heuristics should be considered for designing such virtual worlds. A more fine-grained user evaluation with focus on various specific usability and technical issues can further improve the understanding what works and what can be still improved to make virtual worlds to more user-friendly and valuable tools for learners. Following these improvements, it is hoped that the applicability of this study and the new learning environment can be used and replicated in other subject domains.

Acknowledgment. This paper is part of research resulting of visiting academic activities of Lisa Maria Tomes and Christian Gütl at the School of Information Systems. The visits were supported and sponsored by School of Information Systems and Curtin Business School, Curtin University, and Institute for Information Systems and Computer Media (IICM) at Graz University of Technology. The authors would like to thank the anonymous reviewers for their valuable suggestions to improve the quality of this paper.

References

3DW: Warehouse Website, Google (2015). http://sketchup.google.com/3dwarehouse/. Accessed Feb 20 2015

Assmann, J.: The Search for God in Ancient Egypt. Cornell University Press, London (2001)

Berns, A., Gonzalez-Pardo, A., Camacho, D.: Game-like language learning in 3-D virtual environments. Comput. Educ. **60**(1), 210–220 (2013)

Brooke, J.: SUS-A quick and dirty usability scale. Usability Eval. Ind. **189**(194), 4–7 (1996)

Bruner, J.S.: The act of discovery. Harv. Educ. Rev. **31**, 21–32 (1961)

Clark, R.C., Mayer, R.E.: E-learning and the Science of Instruction: Proven Guidelines for Consumers and Designers of Multimedia Learning. Wiley, New York (2011)

Dillenbourg, P.: Collaborative Learning: Cognitive and Computational Approaches Advances in Learning and Instruction Series. ERIC, New York (1999)

Gütl, C.: The support of virtual 3D worlds for enhancing collaboration in learning settings. Techniques for fostering collaboration in online learning communities: Theoretical and practical perspectives, 278–299 (2010)

Hartnett, M., George, A.S., Dron, J.: Examining motivation in online distance learning environments: complex multifaceted and situation-dependent. IRRODL **12**(6), 21–38 (2011)
Hron, A., Friedrich, H.F.: A review of web-based collaborative learning: factors beyond technology. J. Comput. Assist. Learn. **19**(1), 70–79 (2003)
Ibanez, M., Kloos, C.D., Leony, D., Rueda, J.J.G., Maroto, D.: Learning a foreign language in a mixed-reality environment. Internet Comput. IEEE **15**(6), 44–47 (2011)
Jackson, S.A., Marsh, H.W.: Development and validation of a scale to measure optimal experience: The flow state scale. J. Sport Exerc. Psychol. **18**, 17–35 (1996)
Jacobson, J., Gillam, R.: The egyptian oracle; recreating egyptian religious ceremony in mixed reality (n.d.). http://publicvr.org/publications/JOCCH-7.pdf. (unpublished)
Jarvis, S., Smith, S., Hallam, C., Knight, J.: Preliminary findings from research on the causes of failure to adhere to infection control in two trusts. Oral presentation. Health protection (2007)
Jennett, C., et al.: Measuring and defining the experience of immersion in games. Int. J. Hum.-Comput. Stud. **66**(9), 641–661 (2008). ISSN: 1071-5819. doi:http://dx.doi.org/10.1016/j.ijhcs.2008.04.004
Johnson, D.W., Johnson, R.T.: Learning Together and Alone: Cooperative, Competitive, and Individualistic Learning, 3rd edn. Allyn and Bacon, Boston (1991)
Kaplan, J., Yankelovich, N.: Open wonderland: An extensible virtual world architecture. Internet Comput. IEEE **15**(5), 38–45 (2011)
Klopfer, E., Perry, J., Squire, K., Jan, M.F., Steinkuehler, C.: Mystery at the museum: a collaborative game for museum education. In: Proceedings of the Computer Support for Collaborative Learning: Learning 2005: The Next 10 years! pp. 316–320. International Society of the Learning Sciences, May 2005
Manuelian, P.D.: Giza 3D: digital archaeology and scholarly access to the Giza pyramids: the Giza project at Harvard university. In: 2013 Digital Heritage International Congress (DigitalHeritage 2013). IEEE (2013)
Marzano, R.J.: Art and science of teaching. The perils and promises of discovery learning. Educ. Leadersh. **69**(1), 86 (2011)
Nasir, N.I.S., Hand, V.: From the court to the classroom: Opportunities for engagement, learning, and identity in basketball and classroom mathematics. J. Learn. Sci. **17**(2), 143–179 (2008)
Njoo, M., De Jong, T.: Exploratory learning with a computer simulation for control theory: learning processes and instructional support. J. Res. Sci. Teach. **30**(8), 821–844 (1993)
Open Wonderland: Open Wonderland official Website (2015). http://openwonderland.org/. Accessed 20 Feb 2015
Pirker, J., Berger, S., Guetl, C., Belcher, J., Bailey, P.H.: Understanding physical concepts using an immersive virtual learning environment. In: Proceedings of the 2nd European Immersive Education Summit, Paris, pp. 183–191 (2012)
Pirker, J., Riffnaller-Schiefer, M., Gütl, C.: Motivational active learning: engaging university students in computer science education. In: Proceedings of Innovation and Technology in Computer Science Education, pp. 297–302. ACM, June 2014
Pirker, J., Gütl, C.: In: Reiners, T., Wood, L.C. (eds.) Gamification in Education and Business, pp. 253–275. Springer International Publishing, Switzerland (2015)
Pirker, J., Gütl, C., Belcher, J.W., Bailey, P.H.: Design and evaluation of a learner-centric immersive virtual learning environment for physics education. In: Holzinger, A., Ziefle, M., Hitz, M., Debevc, M. (eds.) SouthCHI 2013. LNCS, vol. 7946, pp. 551–561. Springer, Heidelberg (2013)
Reinmann-Rothmeier, G., Mandl, H.: Wissensvermittlung: Ansätze zur Förderung des Wissenserwerbs (1994)
Riedmann, P.: Realistic immersive virtual agent-based learning environment (RIVALE). Master's thesis, Graz University of Technology (2014)

Roschelle, J., Tatar, D., Chaudhury, S.R., Dimitriadis, Y., Patton, C., DiGiano, C.: Ink, improvisation, and interactive engagement: Learning with tablets. IEEE Comput. **40**(9), 42–48 (2007)

Tomes, L.M.: Exploratory and social learning in 3D virtual worlds. Master's thesis, Graz University of Technology (2015)

Strategies to Design a Mixed-Reality Immersive Environment and Influence Teen Health Behaviors

Béatrice Moissinac(✉), Kimmy Hescock, Jon Dorbolo, Siew Sun Wong, and Melinda Manore

Technology Across the Curriculum & College of Public Health and Human Sciences, Oregon State University, Corvallis, OR 97331, USA
{beatrice.moissinac,kimmy.hescock,jon.dorbolo, siewsun.wong,melinda.manore}@oregonstate.edu

Abstract. The influence of combined experiential learning through face-to-face instruction and immersive environment (IE) on health behavior change has not been examined extensively. The goal of the WAVE ~ Ripples for Change Childhood Obesity Prevention project was to determine the effectiveness of teaching nutrition and physical activity knowledge with an IE designed to reinforce these healthy behaviors (i.e. Rippleville), and if it could improve overall diet and physical activity. Participant engagement was crucial for the participant's exposure to the decision-making process and data collection. This paper describes the strategies implemented in Rippleville to maximize participation and to engage a remote and scattered teenage population into an IE, including our mixed-reality models, as well as learning, engagement, and programming strategies.

1 Introduction

As young adults transition from high school to college or the work environment, they demonstrate negative health behavior [14]. The Oregon State University WAVE ~ Ripples for Change Childhood Obesity Prevention project was an interdisciplinary project examining whether health behaviors can be influenced using face-to-face instruction in the physical world paired with an immersive environment (IE) called Rippleville. The project aimed to alleviate the negative transition behavior in adolescents by the introduction of PAN-FCS knowledge (Physical Activity, Nutrition, and Family and Consumer Sciences). Moreover, the WAVE project hypothesized that applying knowledge through an IE, such as Rippleville, could improve the learning outcomes and further influence behavioral change. This hypothesis is grounded in research showing that IE may cause change in a person's subjective experiences, body states, and physical space behaviors. Interaction within IEs has been shown to induce subjective experiences such as nicotine and alcohol cravings [1, 3, 5] and fears such as aerophobia [9] and acrophobia [12]. It has demonstrated effects on body states such as blood pressure [13] and body mass index [6]. Simulated exercise activity in IEs correlates to increased physical activity in the physical space [2]. Individuals who exercised

C. Allison et al. (Eds.): iLRN 2016, CCIS 621, pp. 17–28, 2016.
DOI: 10.1007/978-3-319-41769-1_2

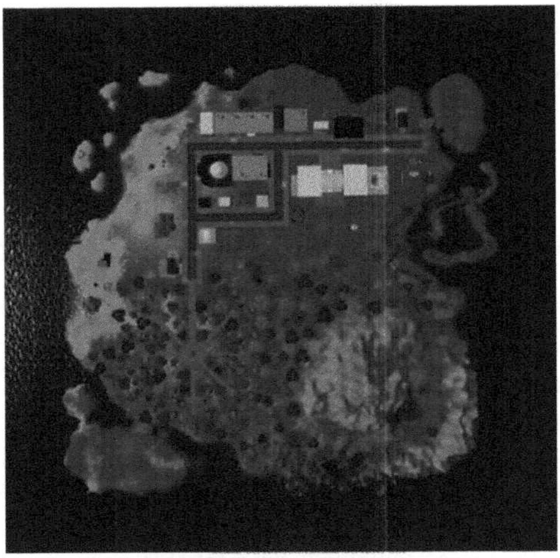

Fig. 1. Aerial view of Rippleville

super powers in an IE exhibited greater altruistic behavior in the physical space [8]. In this work, we present Rippleville, an island (Fig. 1) implemented on the OpenSimulator (OS) which is an open source version of Second Life. For this study, the participants had their own avatar living on the island, which they controlled from a third person perspective. The WAVE project's participants were healthy adolescent soccer players, geographically scattered among nine high schools in two non-neighboring school districts. The ability to answer our research questions lied into the engagement of these adolescents in Rippleville. This paper presents our work on strategies to engage a remote and scattered teenage population into an IE. Section 2 presents Rippleville's learning objectives. Section 3 describes our mixed-reality strategy, then Sects. 4, 5, and 6 present our learning, engagement, and programming strategies respectively.

2 Learning Objectives

2.1 The WAVE Study

The goal of the WAVE ~ Ripples for Change Childhood Obesity Prevention project was to develop, evaluate, and compare the effectiveness of physical world face-to-face instruction and reinforcement via experiences in an IE. The curriculum integrated two years of PAN-FCS (Physical Activity, Nutrition, and Family and Consumer Sciences) intervention for obesity prevention, and was administered to adolescent soccer players (n = 500). Rippleville was the IE designed to reinforce the PAN-FCS, and administered only to the intervention group (n = 320).

2.2 Rippleville's Learning Objectives

First, the WAVE face-to-face learning objectives focused on teaching sport nutrition skills to high school soccer players. These learning objectives were then reinforced through an IE, Rippleville. The learning objectives were concentrated around the following key areas: (1) Knowing pre, during, and post-exercise hydration, fuel needs, as well as how to choose foods and beverages to meet these needs, (2) Recognizing the symptoms of exercise fatigue, (3) Balancing school and sport with appropriate food and fluid selection, (4) Understanding the component of body weight composition and image, and (5) Staying well (e.g. injury prevention).

3 Immersive Strategies

Participants were occasional computer users. Except for a few video game users, most were not familiar with IEs. Thus, Rippleville had the inherent risk of being perceived as foreign and counter-intuitive. We mitigated this risk by creating a mixed-reality model.

IE are defined by two criteria: synchronicity and reality. The synchronicity defines when the participants must be logged in for the simulation to function. If the simulation requires participants to be logged in at the same time, then this simulation is fully synchronous. If there is no such requirement to provide a complete immersive experience, then the simulation is asynchronous. In the case of Rippleville, the high number of participants (n = 320) required the creation of an asynchronous environment, since it would be extremely hard to coordinate all logging in at the same time. The asynchronous environment allows a participant to log in and experience the simulation at any time. If several participants were logged in at the same time, they could still interact with each other. However, this age group is not attracted to asynchronous designs (if one logs in and sees no one else, one is likely to never come back). Thus, a mixed-reality model was developed to address this issue. The reality of the simulation defines how an IE is grounded to the physical world. This was a strategy used to help participants identify with their avatar and increase engagement. In the case of Rippleville, the mixed-reality strategy had the IE transferred into the physical world. For example, orientation events (Sect. 5) occurred in the high schools, with the team and coach present. The participants received newsletters based on the narrative of

(a) Taco Buzz (b) Winter event

Fig. 2. Elements of Rippleville

Rippleville, and were invited to synchronous events (i.e. Halloween costume contest, New Year's fireworks, Fig. 2(b)).

4 Learning Strategies

In this section, we describe the learning strategies used to achieve the learning objectives presented in Sect. 2. First, we developed quests to entice the participants into practicing the sport nutrition knowledge and skills they learned in the classroom. Second, we designed real-time feedback for the participants to evaluate their performance, how their decisions were impacting overall health, and their ability to continue the quest. The feedback was given in real-time using a heads-up display called *RippleTracker*. Third, several hundreds of food and beverage items normally available to adolescent were provided in three frameworks: convenience/grocery stores, fast food/ restaurants, and food booths.

4.1 Quests

Rippleville was not designed to present educational content, but to reinforce decision-making process via actual practice. The participants exhausted their avatar during a quest, running and jumping, and thus must refuel during and after the quest. To entice the participants into immersive physical activity, we designed five quests to be played by the participants in any order, any number of times, and at any moment. This allowed for regular and realistic practice of planning before, during, and after the effort. The quests were started by selecting their poster from the *Activity Kiosk* (Fig. 3(c)) on the main square. Briefly, the quests and their learning objectives were:

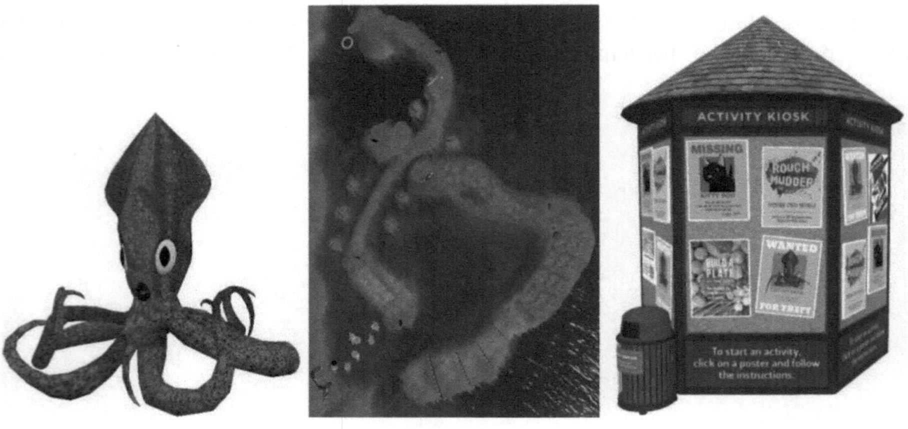

(a) Kraken (b) Aerial view of the Rough Mudder (c) Activity Kiosk

Fig. 3. Elements of Rippleville

Missing Cat: Help a Rippleville citizen to locate her cat; Tour of Rippleville.
Mischievous Kraken: A clue hunting adventure with the Kraken (Fig. 3(a)), Rippleville's high school mascot and mischievous creature; applying good hydration behaviors.
Rough Mudder: Fantastic obstacle course race (Fig. 3(b)).
Shopping on a Budget: Groceries store race-shopping under constraints.
Pizza Jeopardy: Choose the best food option presented.

Reward System: The participants received a reward when completing a quest. The reward was dependent on their "health level" at the end of the quest based on the *RippleTracker*'s criteria. Reward differed per quest, reflecting the inherent difficulty of the quest (i.e. "Rough Mudder" was "worth" more than the "Missing Cat"). The reward was divided into two parts: (1) points, which accumulated throughout the simulation and were an indicator of the participation and quality of choices made, and (2) virtual currency, which could be spent on food and articles for the avatar. Each participant was associated with their physical soccer team, and the accumulated score was displayed in order on the *Leader Board.*

4.2 RippleTracker

The *RippleTracker* (Fig. 4) was a heads-up display on the participant's screen, which reflected the current health condition of the avatar. The parameters were hydration, added sugar consumed, minutes of physical activity[1] and average *Diet Quality*. Each parameter had a gauge divided in three levels: good (green), average (yellow), and bad (red). A pointer slid on each gauge to mark the level of the parameter, and a smiley face above the pointer reinforced the meaning of the color. The center of the *RippleTracker* had a large smiley face, which represented the overall health of the avatar.

Fig. 4. Rippleville tracker (Color figure online)

Simulating Human Physiology: The depletion or gain of each value reflects the virtual physical activity and virtual alimentation of the avatar, using the participant's physiological data as well as human physiology. These changes were real-time feedback.

[1] It's important to note that OpenSimulator allowed only two speed of physical activity: walking and running. Thus, the performance of the participants was their ability to stay fueled and hydrated within proper nutritional guideline.

However, time was wrapped in Rippleville to accelerate the effects of each behavior. For each minute a participant was using Rippleville, six minutes had passed for the avatar.

Constant Monitoring: The simulation of the human physiology and the monitoring of physical activity and alimentation lasted for as long as the participant was logged in, even when the avatar was not doing a quest. Therefore, if the participant chose not to do any quests, the avatar would still dehydrate and need nutrition. This was an important aspect for Rippleville's learning objectives: participants should think about their nutrition and hydration even when not exercising. The avatar's health would return to default level if the participant was logged out more than 12 h.

4.3 Food & Alimentation

Rippleville offered more than 350 consumable items modeled in 3D as an individual item (e.g. an apple) or a meal (e.g. hamburger and fries). The WAVE project's nutritionists created the food list and menus. These food items were representative of the many options normally available to our participants. The participants could buy virtual food from a convenience store, a grocery store, a mid-range restaurant, a pizzeria, an Asian-fusion fast food, a Mexican fast food, or a burger fast food. Finally, they could also get a home cooked dinner at one of the soccer coach's houses. The placement of food items was based on realism (e.g. candies in the convenience store, fresh fruits in the grocery store etc.). The placement of catering buildings was also based on a need for realism (e.g. it was easier to go to the convenience store than the grocery store). We defined the easiness as the distance between the participant's *Club House* (Sect. 5) and any other point. Finally, the product's brands were invented but gave a visual nod to existing brands that were familiar to the participants (Fig. 2(a)). This was essential for the transferability of knowledge.

Convenience & Grocery Store: The WAVE study's face-to-face intervention included how to read nutritional food labels required to appear on food items in the USA. Each food item in those locations was equipped with its corresponding food label sourced from the USDA food database.

Restaurants & Fast Foods: These food items did not have food labels, but instead have a score for *Diet Quality*, represented by a tricolor system: green (good), yellow (average), and red (bad) (Fig. 5(a)). When the participants selected one or several items in the menu, a traffic light lit up with green, yellow, or red. We used a weighted average to determine the diet quality of a collection of food items.

Food Booth: A Food Booth (Fig. 5(b)) helped the participant create a meal based on a themed (i.e. breakfast or snack). It presented several random selections of food items, which would appear in the larger plate above, as they were chosen. A tricolor traffic light indicates the average *Diet Quality* of a plate.

Food Consumption: Lastly, the participants consumed the food bought at their leisure. At purchase, the food items go into the participant's inventory. Eating any food or drinks would affect the *RippleTracker* immediately.

(a) Tricolor System (b) Food Booth

Fig. 5. Elements of Rippleville (Color figure online)

4.4 Learning Strategies Summary

The WAVE study and its immersive part, Rippleville, had ambitious learning objectives. We developed strategies to incentivize learning using gamification, familiarity, and non-standard ways of presenting educational contents. Our learning strategies are summarized as follow:

1. Use a narrative to entice participant into immersive physical activity.
2. Provide physiologically accurate real-time feedback using uniform signage.
3. Provide familiarity, realism, variety, and heterogeneous choices (i.e. food, catering) to facilitate transferability of knowledge to the physical world.

5 Engagement Strategies

In this section, we present our engagement strategies. The engagement of the participants in Rippleville's activities was crucial for the WAVE study. Firstly, their engagement exposed them to the decision-making process of nutrition and physical activity. Secondly, valuable data was collected to evaluate Rippleville's efficiency. Nevertheless, engaging high school students to use a new platform outside of class time is a challenge itself. Our piloting of Rippleville led us toward various strategies to facilitate and increase engagement. The main challenge with engagement was the technical barrier imposed by the OpenSimulator (OS). We mitigated this problem by adding an additional level to our mixed-reality model called "Rippleville LIVE". In the rest of this section, we also describe strategies for self-identification, self-regulation, socializing, narratives, and creating content.

Overcoming the Technological Barrier: The OS platform required some training to control the avatar, in addition to the functionalities we created for the project. Therefore, we implemented an orientation program consisting of a hedge maze with challenges to make what could be mundane interface learning more interesting and help participants understand how to navigate the environment. However, the initial piloting

(a) Orientation Maze (b) Reporting Station & Signage

Fig. 6. Elements of Rippleville

of this hedge maze (Fig. 6(a)) revealed that it was very difficult for the participants to figure out the controls and options by themselves. Consequently, we created "Rippleville LIVE", a mixed-reality synchronous intervention that took place in both physical and immersive world. This approach aimed at minimizing frustration and dropout rate, using physical world tutoring during the immersive experience. We physically went to the high schools and setup computers connected to Rippleville's server via Internet (using both the school's Wi-Fi, and cellular network). The immersive space of "Rippleville LIVE" was not located in Rippleville's main island, but on floating platforms in high altitude above the island. Each specific skill to be taught had a dedicated workshop (e.g. how to control the avatar, modify its appearance, and interact with Rippleville's world). We had workshops of 10 min each happening simultaneously. The participants were required to go through all the workshops, but in no particular order. The analysis of the data collected from these workshops (self-assessment of skills and emotional state, behavioral recording through video etc.) will be presented in a subsequent paper.

Self-Identification: Rippleville was a village with all the familiar elements of the daily life of our participants: visual nod to existing brands, high school, fast food, shopping centers, and natural spaces. We built dedicated Club *Houses* for each soccer team, identified by their high school's colors and mascot. This provided an identity link between the participants and their team, as well as a sense of ownership of the space. Finally, each team's accumulated score was displayed on a *Leader Board to* create a friendly competition between teams. In OS, one can alter and personalize one's avatar appearance. Several *Identity Shops* offered a selection of skins, hair, and eyes for the participants to customize their avatar appearance. Additionally, Rippleville offered a variety of clothing and accessory styles and shops to appeal to different tastes. The goal was to provide the participants with many opportunities to identify with their avatar, as well as gave them incentive to participate in the simulation: clothes cost WAVE dollars and only finishing quests provided WAVE dollars, a better performance in the quest maximized the gain, and so on.

Self-Regulation: The mixed-reality asynchronous model of Rippleville required the participants to decide by themselves what they wanted to do, and it might not be what we would have wanted them to do. It might also have been difficult for a participant evolving in a free-form non-linear narrative to figure out what was the next thing to do, and to relate that to learning. Thus, we implemented an engagement strategy based on self-regulation [4, 7, 10, 11, 15]. First, the *RippleTracker* provided verbal feedback on the current state of the avatar's health. When a gauge's indicator changed color zone, the *RippleTracker* prompted the participant with a message related to that change (e.g. "You are now 2 % dehydrated, be careful"). These messages were hints for the participants to maintain a proper level for each parameter. Second, we installed signage everywhere around Rippleville to facilitate navigation and to remind the participants of the *Activity Kiosk* (Fig. 3(c)) and various catering locations (Fig. 6(b)). During the quests, the participants were prompted hints about what to do by the *RippleTracker* as well as by Non-Playing Characters (NPC). Moreover, if the participants were to have additional problem with the simulation (i.e. technical problem, bullying etc.), they could use the reporting stations (Fig. 6(b)) to send an e-mail to the Rippleville's development team. Furthermore, the development team was clearly identifiable by wearing a blue WAVE shirt and a medallion above the avatar's head. During our experimentation, this has been very useful for helping participants to identify who could assist them instantly.

Socializing: The OS platform provided a system of profile pages and instant messaging which facilitated social interactions within Rippleville. Participants could messages each other, "friend"each other, and exchange goods. The *Club Houses* (with their mini soccer fields) as well as the *Dance Club* (with the dance floor) provided spaces to hang out and have fun. Additionally, we organized seasonal synchronous events (e.g. Halloween party, Winterfest, see Fig. 2(b)) to incentivize the participants to log in at the same time. We offered them limited edition objects when they joined us (e.g. Golden soccer ball).

Consistent Narrative: Each quest was built with elements linked to Rippleville's narrative. For instance, the quest "Find the Kraken" told the story of the Kraken, the mischievous mascot of Rippleville high school.

Creating Content: The OS platform allowed programming in Linden Scripting Language (LSL). Thus, we installed sandbox areas, where the participants could shape and program their own OS elements. This encouraged creative participation and personal contributions to the world (contained to these sandboxes however). We trained the participants how to build objects during one of the Rippleville LIVE workshops.

5.1 Engagement Strategies Summary

The engagement of participants with the simulation was crucial to answer our research questions. We have deployed several systems, tools, interventions, and infrastructure within Rippleville, summarized as follow:

1. Develop training and tutoring to reduce technological barriers.
2. Provide tools, infrastructures, and events to facilitate self-identification, self-regulation, and to promote social behaviors.
3. Develop coherent content, and allow participants to create their own.

6 Programming Strategies

Figure 7 summarizes our programming strategy; each avatar was wearing a *RippleTracker* (Fig. 4), which monitors the avatar's activity in terms of intensity of physical activity, which quest was active or completed, and what alimentation was taken. It computed the health information to be displayed as well as calculated the rewards. Finally, OpenSimulator was not fit to store custom data-bases, so the *RippleTracker* sent data outside of Rippleville, to our SQL database, which collected all the information about anything the avatar did while logged in. The analysis of this database will be presented in an ulterior publication.

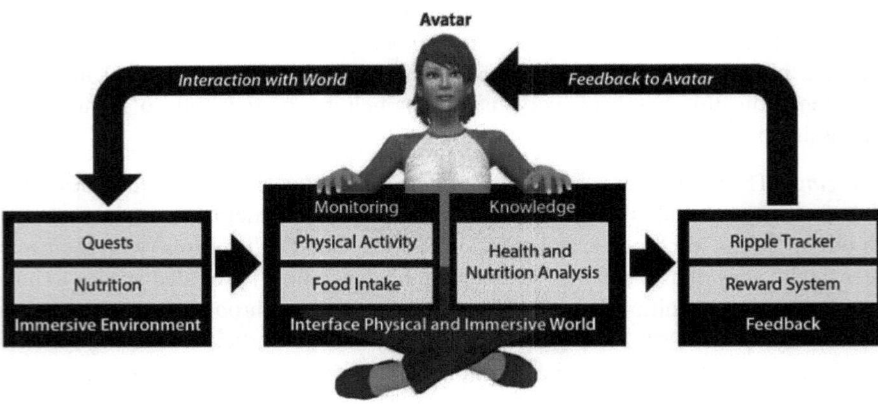

Fig. 7. The RippleTracker centralized Rippleville's programming strategy

7 Conclusion

The Oregon State University WAVE~Ripples for Change Childhood Obesity Prevention project was an interdisciplinary project examining whether health behaviors can be influenced using face-to-face instruction in the physical world paired with an IE called Rippleville. The project aimed to alleviate the negative transition behavior in adolescents by the introduction of PAN-FCS knowledge (Physical Activity, Nutrition, and Family and Consumer Sciences). Moreover, the WAVE project hypothesized that applying knowledge through an IE, such as Rippleville, could improve the learning outcomes and further influence behavioral change. The ability to answer our research question lied into the engagement of these adolescents in Rippleville. Firstly, their engagement exposed them to the decision-making process of nutrition and physical activity. Secondly, valuable data was collected to evaluate Rippleville's efficiency. In this paper, we described the strategies we implemented to achieve sufficient engagement from the participants. These strategies cover the immersive model, learning strategies, engagement strategies such as self-identification and self-regulation, and our programming strategy.

Acknowledgments. The WAVE project is sponsored by NIFA AFRI Award No. 2013-67001-20418. We also would like to acknowledge our team at Technology Across the Curriculum at Oregon State University: Sherif Abdelwahab, Michael Bonyad, Justin Bruntmyer, Britany Buttacavolli, Adrian Clement, Jianqing Cui, Jacob Day, Mark Dinsmore, Gabby Fecteau, Darcie Gardner, Mark Hammersmith, Tyler Hasenoehrl, Jake Jeffreys, Madeline Luecht, Andi McFarland, Michael Nevins, Rob Rogers, Nan Shi, Ingrid Skoog, and Chris Tucker.

References

1. Bordnick, P.S., Traylor, A., Copp, H.L., Graap, K.M., Carter, B., Ferrer, M., Walton, P.: Assessing reactivity to virtual reality alcohol based cues. Addict. Behav. **33**(6), 743–756 (2008)
2. Dean, E., Cook, S., Keating, M., Murphy, J.: Does this avatar make me look fat? Obesity and interviewing in second life. J. Virtual Worlds Res. **2**(2) (2009)
3. Garcia-Rodriguez, O., Weidberg, S., Gutierrez-Maldonado, J., Secades-Villa, R.: Smoking a virtual cigarette increases craving among smokers. Addict. Behav. **38**(10), 2551–2554 (2013)
4. Hattie, J., Timperley, H.: Selft-regulated learning in virtual worlds - an exploratory study in OpenSim. Rev. Educ. Res. **77**(1), 81–112 (2007)
5. Krebs, P., Burkhalter, J., Lewis, S., Hendrickson, T., Chiu, O., Fearn, P., Perchick, W., Ostroff, J.: Development of a virtual reality coping skills game to prevent post-hospitalization smoking relapse in tobacco dependent cancer patients. J. Virtual Worlds Res. **2**(2), 4–12 (2009)
6. Napolitano, M.A., Hayes, S., Russo, G., Muresu, D., Giordano, A., Foster, G.D.: Using avatars to model weight loss behaviors: participant attitudes and technology development. J. Diabetes Sci. Technol. **7**(4), 1057–1065 (2013)
7. Pintrich, P.R.: A motivational science perspective on the role of student motivation in learning and teaching contexts. J. Educ. Psychol. **95**(4), 667 (2003)
8. Rosenberg, R.S., Baughman, S.L., Bailenson, J.N.: Virtual superheroes: using superpowers in virtual reality to encourage prosocial behavior. PLoS ONE **8**(1), e55003 (2013)
9. Rothbaum, B., Hodges, L., Watson, B., Kessler, G., Opdyke, D.: Virtual reality exposure therapy in the treatment of fear of flying: a case report. Behav. Res. Ther. **34**(5), 477–481 (1996)
10. Schunk, D.H.: Commentary on self-regulation in school contexts. Learn. Instr. **15**(2), 173–177 (2005)
11. Shea, P., Bidjerano, T.: Learning presence: towards a theory of self- efficacy, self-regulation, and the development of a communities of inquiry in online and blended learning environments. Comput. Educ. **55**(4), 1721–1731 (2010)
12. Sullivan, D.K., Goetz, J.R., Gibson, C.A., Washburn, R.A., Smith, B.K., Lee, J., Gerald, S., Fincham, T., Donnelly, J.E.: Improving weight maintenance using virtual reality (second life). J. Nutr. Educ. Behav. **45**(3), 264–268 (2013)

13. Warburton, D., Bredin, S., Horita, L., Zbogar, D., Scott, J., Esch, B., Rhodes, R.: The health benefits of interactive video game exercise. Appl. Physiol. Nutr. Metab. **32**(4), 655–663 (2007)
14. Wengreen, H., Moncur, C., et al.: Change in diet, physical activity, and body weight among young-adults during the transition from high school to college. Nutr. J. **8**(1), 32–39 (2009)
15. Wn, J., Reddy, M.: The self-regulated community of learning within 3D virtual learning environments. In: VIWO 2009 WORKSHOP (2009)

Virtual Worlds and the 3D Web – Time for Convergence?

Hussein Bakri(✉), Colin Allison, Alan Miller, and Iain Oliver

School of Computer Science, University of St Andrews, St Andrews, UK
{hb, ca, alan.miller, iao}@st-andrews.ac.uk

Abstract. Multi-User Virtual Worlds (MUVW) such as Open Wonderland and OpenSim have proved to be fruitful platforms for innovative educational practice. However, when compared with the way educational activities have flourished through the use of the constantly evolving WWW, MUVW learning environments remain a relatively obscure niche. Since the advent and promise of Second Life, there has been no critical mass reached and no movement towards standardisation. Concomitantly, the 3D Web has emerged as a recognisable if loosely defined concept. With the advent of technologies such as WebGL and a plethora of plug-in 3D viewers for web browsers, the question arises: will MUVWs converge with the 3D Web? If so, can existing educational content be migrated to the 3D Web for mass dissemination? The paper contributes a survey of 3D Web and MUVW terms, concepts, technologies and projects, illustrating their similarities, their value for education and discusses the likelihood of convergence. The survey is complemented by a cultural heritage case study of Unity 3D support for the deployment of virtual worlds in web browsers using two different approaches.

Keywords: 3D web · Web-Based Virtual World · Multi-User Virtual World · HTTP/2 · VRML · X3D · X3DOM · Webgl · HTML-5 · O3D · Oak3d · Unity 3D

1 Introduction

Multi-User Virtual Worlds (MUVW) such as Second Life [1], OpenSim [2] and Open Wonderland [3] are sophisticated client-server systems which have been used extensively for immersive learning activities [4, 5, 6]. These MUVW systems have their own schemes for communications, programming, graphics, rendering and control. By comparison the standard web consists of universally agreed standards and protocols such as HTTP, HTML and JavaScript, thereby creating a platform for interactive educational resources that can readily be made globally accessible. So although OpenSim notably describes itself as a "prototype 3D Web" - aiming to create a web of Virtual World Grids connected through portals allowing avatars to navigate seamlessly between virtual worlds that exist in different administrative domains – participation is confined to OpenSim-based sites which are connected to the OpenSim *hypergrid*. With the advent of the "3D Web" conceived of as a direct evolution of the standard web, what is the likelihood that the rich immersive experience of educational MUVWs can be deployed

C. Allison et al. (Eds.): iLRN 2016, CCIS 621, pp. 29–42, 2016.
DOI: 10.1007/978-3-319-41769-1_3

across the standard web, delivered via standard browsers? This research seeks to identify and qualify signs of convergence between MUVWs and the 3D Web. In addition, a cultural heritage case study of the performance of a virtual world originally created in OpenSim but now capable of being run in standard browsers is included to provide performance insights into using a web browser as a virtual world viewer.

The paper is structured as follows: Sect. 2 provides background on well-known 3D Web technologies. Section 3 is divided into three parts. The first part lists some Web-Based Viewers for existing well-known MUVWs and the second part discusses some projects aiming to create Web-Based Virtual Worlds. This section then discusses how both categories of environments can be used in education. Section 4 analyses how HTTP/2, the newest version of the web network protocol, is useful for supporting virtual world traffic for the 3D Web; Sect. 5 compares the performance of WebGL and Unity Web Player versions of a virtual world and Sect. 6 concludes.

2 3D Web Technologies

In this section we provide a brief review of the most commonly used 3D Web tools and languages.

2.1 VRLM, X3D and X3DOM

Virtual Reality Modelling Language (VRML) [7] was the first technology for building and delivering 3D Web content. The language incorporates 2D and 3D graphics, multimedia and animation combined with powerful scripting and multiuser networking capabilities.

eXtensible 3D (X3D) [8] is a royalty-free standard which succeeded VRML. X3D advances include techniques such as programmable shaders, geo-location, multi-texturing and humanoid animations. Its XML encoding makes it easy to incorporate into web services leading to improved data compression and faster downloads over the web.

The X3DOM model [9] is X3D in the DOM tree. With this model, X3D can be fully integrated into any webpage in the same way as SVG (Scalable Vector Graphics) can. Nodes of X3D can be declared inside basic XHTML elements and scenes of X3D can be modified using JavaScript. The current implementation of X3DOM is based on WebGL. With the majority of browsers now supporting WebGL, X3DOM code can be embedded and manipulated without any plugin.

2.2 WebGL

WebGL (Web Graphics Library) [10] is a standard introduced by Khronos for web browsers. It consists of JavaScript Libraries accessing OpenGL ES (OpenGL Embedded System) a subset of OpenGL [11]. WebGL is rendered in the HTML-5 canvas element of a page. WebGL allows browsers to render 3D content without plug-ins.

Chrome Experiments [12] aim to prove and show the power of WebGL. They include sophisticated 3D navigation, physics engine and collision projects. Many WebGL projects demonstrate sophisticated hardware accelerated 3D Web graphics rendered in real-time using WebGL, HTML5 and CSS3-3D. In addition, Mozilla Experiments using WebGL [13] show impressive game engine performance. This shows how the web is becoming suitable for 3D games and therefore, in principle, for web-based virtual worlds.

2.3 HTML-5 and the CSS3 3D Features

In HTML-5 [14] the "canvas" element is the only facility for browsers to render bitmap images of 3D content without a plug-in. Solutions that don't require plug-ins are mainly implemented through models and languages like X3DOM and WebGL [15]. There are Canvas3D HTML plug-ins for Firefox and Opera. The Firefox plug-in works the same way WebGL does by allowing the programmer to access the OpenGL ES library through JavaScript. 3D rendering can be hardware accelerated in the Firefox Canvas 3D HTML element. Opera developed their own 3D programming API as a wrapper over the powerful and stable graphics libraries of Open GL and DirectX [16]. HTML-5 browsers include features such as multi-threaded programming which can better support immersive virtual world graphics.

CSS3 3D transformations and animations are a way to enrich CSS rules with 3D capabilities. A web programmer has the ability to scale, rotate, skew, and change the perspective of almost any DOM element creating a complete 3D space using only CSS and HTML [17].

2.4 3D Markup Language for the Web (3DMLW)

3D Markup Language for the Web (3DMLW) is an open source XML-based language for presenting 2D and 3D dynamic and interactive content on the web. By using the Lua scripting language [18], programmers can animate complex 3D scenes. Plug-ins are available for different browsers together with several authoring tools [16].

2.5 Java 3D and Java OpenGL (JOGL)

Java3D is a runtime scene graph 3D API wrapper around OpenGL and DirectX, incorporating VRML/X3D. Sun stopped supporting the development of Java3D in mid-2003 and it became a community source project. In 2012, Java3D became Java OpenGL (JOGL) a low level interface providing binding to OpenGL libraries [16].

2.6 O3D and Oak3D

O3D [16, 19] is a Google open source project originally requiring a plug-in. It works by using a JavaScript API for creating 3D dynamic and interactive content in a web browser. It exploits hardware accelerated graphics to support advanced rendering effects, detailed texturing, shadows and reflections, particle systems and physics engines in a web browser. O3D code can be edited in real time. Recent implementations [19] are built on top of WebGL and thus do not require plug-ins where a browser supports WebGL.

Oak3D [20] is an open source JavaScript library for creating interactive 3D content. It is implemented on top of HTML-5 and WebGL and like the recent version of O3D does not require a plug-in.

2.7 Web-Generated Builds from Game Engines

Unity 3D and Unreal are two of the most popular general purpose game engines. They can generate web builds for games and 3D worlds which can then be accessed through a plug-in or through HTML-5 and WebGL. Other games engines such as ImpactJS [21] and CreateJS [22] are tailored specifically for games on the web.

Unity 3D. Unity3D [23] supports the development of 3D games and complex 3D environments on a variety of platforms and devices including web browsers either through a plug-in or as WebGL. The engine has a highly optimized graphics pipeline for OpenGL and DirectX and supports many features including advanced meshes, advanced lighting and shadows, particle systems and the Ageia PhysX physics engine. Section 5 reports on the relative performance characteristics of a virtual world originally hosted in OpenSim, then transformed into Unity, then generated in two formats suitable for web browsers.

Unreal Engine. Unreal Engine [24] is developed by Epic Games. It is written in C++ which is also used as the main game programming language. The Blueprint visual scripting language with debugging capabilities can also be used. Unreal engine also supports generating a WebGL format of a game for HTML-5 browsers.

2.8 The 3D Web and E-Learning

In medical education, Birr et al. [25] developed a real-time Web surgical teaching tool derived from patient specific image data. The tool was developed using X3D and WebGL. Landro et al. [26] developed a web portal containing 3D objects simulating highly interactive virtual laboratories. In Entomology (the study of insects), X3D models are created to represent high quality natural-colour detailed 3D models of various insects [27]. 3D Web virtual labs in engineering are quite numerous. Violante and Vezzetti [28] designed web-based interactive 3D concept maps for an engineering drawing course and showed that this helped students with deficits in spatial abilities to better represent the content to be learned. SAFAS (Structure And Form Analysis System) [29], is a 3D Web design tool for architects and structural engineers. It simulates real forces, loads, displacements and deformations of 3D complex structures of steel nodes and members. In Mathematics, Hennig et al. [30] developed a blended learning scenario based on abundant use of 3D visualizations of mathematical concepts using WebGL. Raman et al. [31] Implemented a 3D convex glass lens experiment in Olab Physics using WebGL and Dynamic cube mapping. In cultural heritage education, Wang et al. [32] developed a game-based virtual environment for learning cultural heritage. The environment is built using the O3D API.

3 Web-Based Viewers and Web-Based Virtual Worlds

In this section, we present a brief overview of some of Web-Based Virtual Worlds (WBVWs) that are complete 3D spaces on the web and survey Web-Based Viewers (WBV) for existing MUVWs. WBVs offer several benefits over standalone MUVW clients in educational settings. These include:

- WBV function better in educational organizations because they use standard web protocols such as HTTP thus avoiding the problem of MUVW firewall blocking discussed in Sect. 5.
- No need for stand-alone client installation thus making these environments easily accessed in education due to the fact that many institutions have strictly controlled computer laboratories.
- Unanimity of quality through web browsers and the suitability of these environments for regular web users with no technical expertise.
- WBVs present a means of access from mobile devices with limited resources (only a browser is needed) thus promoting pervasiveness and ubiquity.

3.1 Web-Based Viewers for MUVWs

Web-Based Viewers are alternatives to the traditional stand-alone MUVW viewers. A small selection is described below.

Unity3D Based Virtual Viewer. Katz et al. [33] developed a Unity3D plug-in Virtual Viewer that connects to MUVWs and renders Second Life and OpenSim scenes.

Project Skylight - Second Life Web-Based Viewer. Project Skylight[34] was a beta testing web viewer for Second Life that was launched in November 2010. A trial offered selected visitors 60 min to explore Second Life inside their web browsers (no need to download the viewer at all). Second Life has also used the Cloud-based rendering and streaming game service Gaikai [35] in *Skylight*. Linden Labs wanted to use this tool to evaluate whether Second Life should invest in a Web-Based Viewer.

TipoDean Web Viewer. TipoDean [36] offers a conversion tool that transforms content developed in OpenSim and Second Life into Unity3D. Spatial VOIP is also supported.

3DXplorer Viewer. 3DXplorer [37] is an interactive 3D viewer created and maintained by Altadyn that allows users to design 3D immersive virtual worlds in web browsers both on desktop and mobile devices requiring no plug-in but requires the presence of a Java Virtual Machine.

Cube3. Cube3 [38] is a Unity3D based tool that allows access and usage of a set of modular/customized virtual worlds builds and environments specifically designed for educational and collaborative use. These virtual spaces are integrated with Second Life and OpenSim prim based systems. The environments contain buildings and furniture customizable under the demand of the user. These environments are accessed from any web browser and from mobile devices like iPhones.

Pixie Viewer. Pixie Viewer[39] is a browser based viewer for 3D virtual worlds. It runs on any modern HTML-5/WebGL browser including Safari, Chrome, Firefox, Opera and others. The viewer can be either connected to a standalone backbone or to OpenSim grids although this requires a special module to be available in OpenSim. Pixie Viewer has a set of building and texturing tools for users. It also has a 3D printing facility from the viewer itself for objects.

3.2 Web-Based Virtual Worlds

This section provides some examples of projects building virtual worlds on the web. Web-Based Virtual Worlds appear to be completely integrated into the web from the perspective of the user. All the user has to do is to navigate the environment from any web browser.

KataSpace. Kataspace [40, 41] is an open source project which runs on top of WebGL and HTML5. KataSpace is built using the Sirikata [42] multiuser platform for games and virtual worlds.

Virtual World Framework. Virtual World Framework (VWF) [43] is a means to connect virtual worlds and 3D entities and content via web browsers. It is an open source platform that allows anyone to build collaborative 3D applications on the web. It also extends and interfaces with existing client-server virtual worlds like OpenSim making it possible for these environments to be delivered in a lightweight manner via web browsers. VWF uses WebSockets and WebGL.

Sandbox [44] is a Virtual World Framework (VWF) authoring and delivery platform for creating 3D Environments on the web. Users can create complex and beautiful virtual worlds on the web at no cost. The tool uses WebGL and does not need a plugin.

ReactionGrid Jibe Platform Based on Unity3D. ReactionGrid Inc. [45] is company specialising in the creation of 3D Multi-User Virtual Environments on the web and on mobile devices. ReactionGrid Inc. uses Jibe, a platform based on a Unity3D plugin in web browsers. Jibe enables users to create and manage their own complex virtual environments incorporated and accessible through the web. Jibe is also integrated into Facebook through an application and can run on Android and iOS systems.

Cloud Party - A Virtual 3D Space in Browsers. Cloud Party [46] is a 3D virtual world that runs in Firefox and Chrome. The company behind it, Cloud Party Inc, has been acquired by Yahoo. The environment is integrated into Facebook and enables creating, editing and uploading of 3D objects. Users can customize avatars, land and sky, and can script objects for certain effects [47].

Altadyn Web-Based Virtual World Projects. Altadyn's products [48] allow users to access 3D spaces on the web for collaborative purposes thus bridging the gap between 3D virtual worlds and web conferencing. It works on browsers including Safari, Firefox and Internet Explorer without a plug-in but a Java Virtual Machine is needed. The 3D virtual products and services are based on JOGL and Lightweight Java Game Library (LWJGL) technologies for providing real time rendering. Environments like Business Hangouts, 3d-virtualevents, 3d-virtualembassy are examples of complex collaborative virtual worlds on the web. Altadyn WBVWs are convenient for virtual lectures to a large audience of students.

Avaya web.alive. Avaya web.alive [49, 50] is based on the Unreal Engine and 3D Web technologies. It provides a virtual environment used for collaboration, product presentations and business meetings which can be accessed from any web browser. It allows users to present documents in common formats (PPT, PDF), to stream videos, to share files, to share desktops and to use live webcams with HD audio. Avatars can be customized to suit the needs of users. Avaya has a 3D content development toolkit for editing the environment and creating content. It allows for importing models created in Autodesk product and Blender.

RealXTend Tundra [51, 52] is an open source project that allows users to create 3D virtual worlds and video games. It has an open source client called Naali. The client can also connect to Second Life and OpenSim platforms. RealXTend is implemented using the Tundra SDK and has an add-on for OpenSim. The viewer Naali and RealXTend Tundra server use HTTP and XMPP (Extensible Messaging and Presence Protocol).

Meshmoon [53], created by Adminotech Ltd., is a virtual world platform based on realXtend Tundra. It also has a 3D application hosting service which uses cloud storage and is designed to allow users to share 3D virtual worlds online. The worlds can be populated by 3D meshes imported from 3D software packages like Blender, 3DS Max, Maya among others. It is also possible to import content from PDF, web pages, pictures, media players and presentation tools into frames in the 3D Scene. Developers can use scripting to give different functionalities to 3D models. The service promises scalability and accessibility to users. Meshmoon provides communications through both VOIP chat via WebRTC [54] and text chat. Meshmoon is accessible through a web-based viewer called Web Rocket which uses WebGL and WebSockets and through a standalone application called the Rocket Client.

Open Virtual World Web Projects. Unity3D version 5 delivers WebGL content directly to a browser, obviating the need for a plug-in. Preliminary research by the Open Virtual Worlds group [55] has shown that it is possible to capture OpenSim texture packets and convert them to Unity 3D which can then be delivered to Firefox or Chrome via WebGL. Educational projects originally hosted in OpenSim/Second Life such as the Laconia Acropolis Virtual Archaeology (LAVA) [56] and Timespan

Longhouse [57] have been transformed into Unity 3D. A performance study of two web versions of the Timespan Longhouse in Chrome is presented in Sect. 5.

4 HTTP/2 and QUIC for Virtual Worlds and the 3D Web

HTTP/2 [58] and QUIC [59] protocols could be used for MUVWs and the 3D Web [60]. In most educational settings firewall port blocking inhibits the use of Second Life/OpenSim as they require a range of "unusual" UDP ports to be opened for effective client-server communication [61]. At the same time, MUVW traffic has soft real time requirements and is sensitive to delay, jitter and bandwidth constraints – hence the original Second Life communication model which has a complex set of UDP-based *circuits* and *channels*. HTTP/2 has the potential to offer the same functionality through two TCP ports, 80 & 443, which are normally open. QUIC [59] can be used in place of HTTP/2 but runs over UDP instead of TCP. QUIC uses port 80 for HTTP and port 443 for HTTPS and uses the same "HTTP" and "HTTPS" URI schemes. See [60] for further information how they could be used in virtual worlds. Features of value that are not present in HTTP 1.1 include:

- **Request and Response Multiplexing:** OpenSim traffic is divided into channels for Assets, Textures, Task, Wind [62]. Multiplexing of streams in HTTP/2 or QUIC could be used to multiplex these channels.
- **Streams can be Interleaved and Prioritized:** Studies [62, 63] show that certain type of virtual world traffic needs to have some precedence e.g. avatar control information. This leads to a better user Quality of Experience (QoE). Prioritization of HTTP/2 or QUIC streams could be used to solve this problem.
- **Server Push:** This allows a virtual world server to anticipate what a client needs and send data that might be needed later without waiting for the client to ask for it e.g. neighbouring region information.

5 Case Study: Unity 3D Builds for Web Browsers

The Timespan Longhouse (TL) [57], is part of a larger virtual world hosted originally in OpenSim and then transformed into Unity 3D by the Open Virtual Worlds group [55]. Unity can generate two types of build suitable for browsers: Unity Web Player (UWP) and WebGL (U-WebGL). The crucial difference is that UWP requires a plug-in to be installed whereas U-WebGL can be run directly in any browser that supports WebGL, such as Firefox or Chrome. A U-WebGL view of the TL displayed in Chrome is shown in Fig. 1. We focus on two key QoE metrics for comparison: frames per second (FPS) and initial download time (IDT) - a 3D Web equivalent of the widely used Page Load Time (PLT) metric in the 2D Web. FPS and Frame Time are important for the user experience in real time immersive environments. In an OpenSim viewer each frame should complete in approximately 18.18 ms (55 frames per second). "If total frame time is greater than this then simulator performance will be degraded" [64]. Similarly, in Unity3D web applications, 60 FPS is recommended.

Fig. 1. The WebGL build of the Timespan Longhouse

Figure 2 summarises results from experiments where two mobility models were used:

- Standing: Avatar remains standing still with continuous yawing for 2 min (Yaw is the change in avatar orientation or the change in the "look at" view).
- Random Walking: Avatar randomly walks for 3 min in different directions (from non-dense to dense areas) and with a constant speed.

Figure 2 shows that the UWP build performed better (i.e. higher FPS) than the U-WebGL build, especially when the avatar is walking.

Table 1 shows that a user visiting the TL for the first time while using Chrome or Firefox would have to wait 20 s for the WebGL virtual world to download compared with 4 s for the UWP version. Neither is an impressive figure compared with 2D Web expectations, where a Page Load Time of more than 1 s is considered poor. Further details about this study can be found in [65].

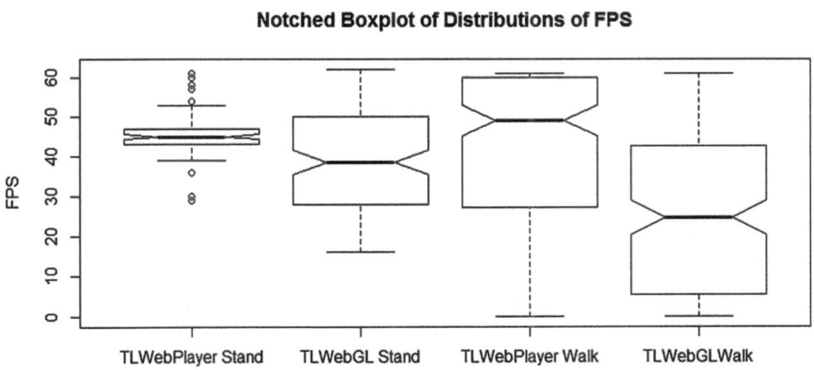

Fig. 2. Frames per Second (FPS) in the two versions

Table 1. Initial download times of Timespan Longhouse to Chrome

Timespan Longhouse	Average	Standard deviation
UWP	3934.33 ms	91.26
U-WebGL	20191.67 ms	581.46

The experiments were performed on Chrome 44 which supported Unity Web player through NPAPI (Netscape Plugin Application Programming Interface). However, in early 2016 Chrome dropped support for NPAPI based plug-ins in version 45 and onwards [66]. Other plug-ins were also affected by this strategic decision to start moving towards a plugin-less browser. The Unity plug-in version is still supported at time of writing by browsers that still support NPAPI including Firefox, Opera and Internet Explorer but this is likely to change in the future e.g. Mozilla intends to remove support for NPAPI plug-ins. In the latest Unity beta version (5.4) the UWP build option has been removed implying that Unity is moving towards a WebGL only solution. The results of our experiments showed that UWP versions perform significantly better than WebGL versions, and it will be interesting to see if Unity can produce more efficient WebGL to address this problem, whose causes are partly explained in the following section.

Unity WebGL Limitations: WebGL is supported by the majority of web browsers to some degrees (e.g. cursor locking and full screen are not supported in Safari yet). There are some limitations in WebGL itself. JavaScript does not support multithreading or direct access to IP sockets of browsers for security concerns. WebGL supports only baked Global Illumination and not real-time ones. In addition, it does not support procedural materials or linear color rendering. It supports basic Web audio API which has many limiting audio features compared to other platforms (ex: no microphone class). The initial download time of a Unity WebGL world is a lot bigger than that of its plugin counterpart of the same world due to build sizes being a lot bigger. Another concern is the memory used by Unity WebGL builds. First the heap memory which Unity uses to store loaded assets and scenes needs to be at a convenient size to fit all data required to play the content in browser. Tweaking the WebGL heap memory size avoids many out-of-memory problems encountered normally in big WebGL builds. Another issue related to memory in WebGL is the memory used by the JavaScript engines for parsing and optimizing WebGL codes in browsers. Compression and optimization techniques of Unity WebGL builds minimize the emitted JavaScript code and thus result in smaller download times and lesser memory consumption [67]. WebGL 2.0 (based on OpenGL ES 3.0) mitigates some of the limitations of WebGL 1.0 but is still experimental and is not yet supported in the majority of browsers [67].

6 Conclusion

Figure 3 shows key markers in Virtual World and 3D Web developments that have been discussed in this paper. We have shown that many 3D Web technologies and tools - especially WebGL – can now host virtual worlds similar to those built in OpenSim and Open Wonderland, and that traditional web browsers can even act as

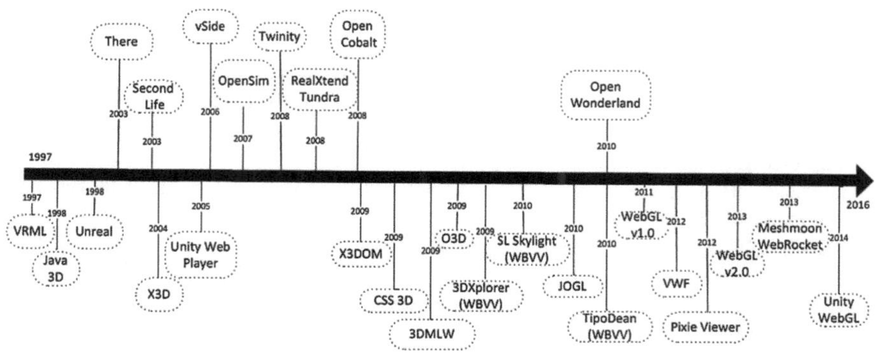

Fig. 3. Markers in the development of virtual worlds and the 3D Web

viewers for some of the existing MUVWs. Following this trend of developments it is possible that there will be a point in the future where we will see fully fledged virtual worlds on the web that have all the features currently present in MUVWs.

From the educational perspective we see that web-based learning environments are increasingly accommodating multi-user interactive 3D formats with the help of 3D Web technologies. This convergence also allows for some of the existing MUVW immersive educational content to migrate to the 3D Web where it is much more accessible.

We have posited that the most recent web network protocols, HTTP/2 and QUIC, could be useful in supporting real-time 3D traffic for both MUVWs and WBVWs, and avoid the problems encountered with restrictive campus firewalls and the use of non-standard protocols.

A small case study, taken from a larger set of experiments, has shown that the UWP version of the Timespan Longhouse, an educational cultural heritage project, performed significantly better than the WebGL version. However, with the move evidenced in Chrome and Mozilla towards plugin-less browsers Unity is dropping UWP in favour of WebGL which may result in better optimized output.

In summary there are many signs of convergence but it is still not possible to state categorically that direct support for immersive environments in the standard web will increase user demand which in turn will spur further and faster innovation in web-based immersive education.

References

1. Second Life Main Website. http://secondlife.com/. Accessed 28 Mar 2015
2. OpenSim Official Website. http://opensimulator.org/wiki/Main_Page. Accessed 02 Apr 2015
3. Open Wonderland Official Website. http://openwonderland.org/. Accessed 01 Apr 2015
4. Perera, I., Allison, C., Nicoll, J.R., Sturgeon, T.: Towards successful 3D virtual learning - a case study on teaching human computer interaction. In: 2009 International Conference on Internet Technology and Secured Transactions (2009)

5. Sturgeon, T., Allison, C., Miller, A.: 802.11 wireless experiments in a virtual world. ACM SIGCSE Bull. **41**(3), 85 (2009)
6. Mccaffery, J., Miller, A., Allison, C.: Extending the use of virtual worlds as an educational platform - network island: an advanced learning environment for teaching internet routing algorithms. In: CSEDU 2011: Proceedings of the 3rd International Conference on Computer Supported Education, pp. 279–284 (2011)
7. Carey, R., Bell, G.: The Annotated VRML 2.0 Reference Manual. Addison-Wesley Longman Ltd., Essex (1997)
8. What is X3D. http://www.web3d.org/x3d/what-x3d. Accessed 16 Feb 2016
9. X3DOM. http://www.x3dom.org/. Accessed 22 Feb 2016
10. WebGL - OpenGL ES 2.0 for the Web. https://www.khronos.org/webgl/. Accessed 16 Feb 2016
11. OpenGL. https://www.opengl.org/
12. Google Chrome Experiments using WebGL. https://www.chromeexperiments.com/webgl. Accessed 22 Feb 2016
13. Mozilla - Demos of open web technologies. https://developer.mozilla.org/en-US/docs/Web/Demos_of_open_web_technologies. Accessed 21 Feb 2016
14. Pilgrim, M.: HTML5: Up and Running. O'Reilly Media, Inc., Sebastopol (2010)
15. Yang, J., Jie, Z.: Towards HTML 5 and interactive 3D graphics. In: ICEIT 2010 - 2010 International Conference on Educational and Information Technology Proceedings, vol. 1, no. ICEIT, pp. 522–527 (2010)
16. Paulis, P.: 3D Webpages, Študentská Ved. Konf. FMFI UK, Bratislava, pp. 316–327 (2010)
17. Frain, B.: Responsive Web Design with HTML5 and CSS3. Packt Publishing Ltd., Birmingham (2012)
18. Lua programming language main website. http://www.lua.org/
19. O3D main page on Google Code. https://code.google.com/p/o3d/. Accessed 22 Feb 2016
20. Oak3D. http://www.effecthub.com/t/oak3d. Accessed 16 Feb 2016
21. Impact JavaScript Game engine. http://impactjs.com/. Accessed 22 Feb 2016
22. CreateJS. http://createjs.com/. Accessed 22 Feb 2016
23. Unity3D game engine. http://unity3d.com/
24. Unreal Engine 4. https://www.unrealengine.com/what-is-unreal-engine-4. Accessed 22 Feb 2016
25. Birr, S., Jeanette, M., Sommerfeld, D., Preim, B.: A novel real-time Web3D surgical teaching tool based on WebGL. In: Bild. für die Medizin 2011 (2011)
26. Landro, D., De Gasperis, G., Macchiarelli, M.D.G.: A collaborative distance learning portal integrating 3D virtual labs in biomedicine. In: Mascio, T.D., Gennari, R., Vitorini, P., Vicari, R., de la Prieta, F. (eds.) Methodologies and Intelligent Systems for Technology Enhanced Learning. AISC, vol. 292, pp. 149–156. Springer, Heidelberg (2015)
27. Adcock, M., Nguyen, C., Lovell, D., La Salle, J.: Accelerating entomology with Web3D insects, p. 4503 (2014)
28. Violante, M.G., Vezzetti, E.: Design of web-based interactive 3D concept maps: a preliminary study for an engineering drawing course. Comput. Appl. Eng. Educ. **23**(3), 403–411 (2015)
29. Polys, N., Bacim, F., Setareh, M., Jones, B.: Building novel Web3D user interfaces: a case study from architecture and structural engineering. In: Proceedings of 18th International Conference on 3D Web Technology, pp. 135–138 (2013)
30. Hennig, M., Gaspers, D., Mertsching, B.: Interactive WebGL-based 3D visualizations for situated mathematics teaching. In: 2013 12th International Conference on Information Technology Based Higher Education and Training, ITHET 2013, pp. 1–6 (2013)

31. Raman, R., Unnikrishnan, K.V., Rekha, S.V., Nedungadi, P.: Using WebGL to implement a glass lens in Online Labs. In: 2014 7th International Conference on Contemporary Computing IC3 2014, pp. 50–55 (2014)
32. Wang, L., Guo, J.-w., Yang, C.-l., Zhao, H.-s., Meng, X.-x.: O3D-based game learning environments for cultural heritage online education. In: Zhang, X., Zhong, S., Pan, Z., Wong, K., Yun, R. (eds.) Edutainment 2010. LNCS, vol. 6249, pp. 417–428. Springer, Heidelberg (2010)
33. Katz, N., Cook, T., Smart, R.: Extending web browsers with a unity 3D-based virtual worlds viewer. IEEE Internet Comput. **15**(5), 15–21 (2011)
34. Beta Testing of Project Skylight Web Viewer for Second Life. http://ambrosiadanceclub.com/news/beta-testing-of-skylight-webviewer. Accessed 21 Feb 2016
35. Gaikai. https://www.gaikai.com/. Accessed 21 Feb 2016
36. TipoDean Main Website. http://www.tipodean.com/. Accessed 21 Feb 2016
37. 3DXplorer. https://3dxplorer.wordpress.com/. Accessed 21 Feb 2016
38. Cube3 Main Website. http://www.cube3.com/. Accessed 21 Feb 2016
39. Pixie Viewer for OpenSim. http://pixieviewer.com/. Accessed 01 Apr 2015
40. KataSpace Application Built on Sirikata. http://www.sirikata.com/blog/2010/kataspace-application-built-on-sirikata/. Accessed 22 Feb 2016
41. Github Kataspace Repository. https://github.com/sirikata/kataspace. Accessed 22 Feb 2016
42. Sirikata. http://www.sirikata.com/. Accessed 21 Feb 2016
43. Virtual World Framework Main Website. https://virtual.wf/documentation.html. Accessed 01 Apr 2015
44. The Virtual World Framework Sandbox. https://sandbox.adlnet.gov/110/adl/sandbox/. Accessed 21 Feb 2016
45. ReactionGrid Main Website. http://reactiongrid.com/. Accessed 03 Apr 2015
46. Cloud Party Main Website. http://www.cloudparty.com/
47. Aydın, İ.G.: Comparison of two Virtual Worlds based on their pedagogical affordances and constraints as interactive learning environments, no. 2008 (2013)
48. ALTADYN Corp. https://business-hangouts.com/. Accessed 20 Feb 2016
49. AvayaLive Engage Web Site. https://engage.avayalive.com/Engage/. Accessed 22 Feb 2016
50. Benchmark of 3D Virtual Environments. https://blogs.aalto.fi/allthingsvirtual/files/2011/06/Benchmark_Report1.pdf
51. Alatalo, T.: An entity-component model for extensible virtual worlds. IEEE Internet Comput. **15**(5), 30–37 (2011)
52. Tundra. https://github.com/realXtend/tundra/wiki. Accessed 26 Feb 2016
53. Meshmoon Documentation. http://doc.meshmoon.com/index.html. Accessed 26 Feb 2016
54. WebRTC. https://webrtc.org/
55. Open Virtual Worlds. http://www.openvirtualworlds.org/
56. Getchell, K., Miller, A., Nicoll, J.R., Sweetman, R.J., Allison, C.: Games methodologies and immersive environments for virtual fieldwork. IEEE Trans. Learn. Technol. **3**(4), 281–293 (2010)
57. McCaffery, J., Miller, A., Kennedy, S., Dawson, T., Allison, C., Vermehren, A., Lefley, C., Strickland, K.: Exploring heritage through time and space supporting community reflection on the highland clearances. In: 2013 Digital Heritage International Congress, vol. 1, pp. 371–378 (2013)
58. Belshe, M., Peon, R., Thomson, M.: RFC 7540: hypertext transfer protocol version 2 (HTTP/2). Technical report, May 2015. https://tools.ietf.org/html/rfc7540
59. QUIC Protocol Official Website. https://www.chromium.org/quic. Accessed 03 Apr 2015
60. Bakri, H., Allison, C., Miller, A., Oliver, I.: HTTP/2 and QUIC for virtual worlds and the 3D web? Procedia Comput. Sci. **56**(Fnc), 242–251 (2015)

61. Allison, C., Campbell, A., Davies, C.J., Dow, L., Kennedy, S., McCaffery, J.P., Miller, A.H. D., Oliver, I.A., Perera, G.I.U.S.: Growing the use of virtual worlds in education: an OpenSim perspective. In: EiED 2012 Proceedings of 2nd European Immersive Education Summit, pp. 1–13 (2012)
62. Oliver, I.A., Miller, A.H.D., Allison, C.: Virtual worlds, real traffic. In: Proceedings of First Annual ACM SIGMM Conference on Multimedia Systems - MMSys 2010, p. 305 (2010)
63. Oliver, I., Miller, A., Allison, C.: Mongoose: throughput redistributing virtual world. In: 2012 21st International Conference on Computer Communications and Networks, ICCCN 2012 - Proceedings (2012)
64. OpenSim Client Side Monitoring. http://opensimulator.org/wiki/Client_side_monitoring. Accessed 05 Feb 2016
65. Bakri, H., Allison, C.: Measuring QoS in web-based virtual worlds: an evaluation of unity 3D web builds. In: MMSys 2016 Multimedia Systems Conference 2016 Klagenfurt am Wörthersee, Austria — 10–13 May 2016, ACM Press - Association for Computing Machinery (2016)
66. Unity Web Player Roadmap. http://blogs.unity3d.com/2015/10/08/unity-web-player-roadmap/. Accessed 03 May 2016
67. Unity Documentation. http://docs.unity3d.com/Manual/index.html. Accessed 01 Sept 2015

Virtual Reality

Towards Measuring User Experience, Activation and Task Performance in Immersive Virtual Learning Environments for Students

Daniela Janßen(✉), Christian Tummel, Anja Richert, and Ingrid Isenhardt

Institute Cluster IMA/ZLW & IfU of RWTH Aachen University, Aachen, Germany
{daniela.janssen, christian.tummel, anja.richert, ingrid.isenhardt}@ima-zlw-ifu.rwth-aachen.de

Abstract. The technological progress in the field of Virtual Reality (VR) facilitates the availability and applicability in learning scenarios. Applying VR technologies in a virtual environment (VE) can further intensify the students' learning experience to a more immersive and engaging involvement in the learning process. In order to use immersive virtual learning environments (VLE) in high school and higher education as a teaching and learning tool, first it has to be assessed which individual-related variables influence the VLE experience and in which way the user experience (UX) affects task performance in VLEs. The paper describes the concept of a specific VLE using Minecraft as a setup for a research study. Furthermore, the research design is outlined. The paper describes the conducted pretest of the study and presents preliminary results of the pretest.

Keywords: Immersive learning · User experience · Virtual reality · Higher education · Virtual learning environment · Immersion · Presence · Minecraft

1 Introduction

Due to the technological development within society and industry driven by the Industry 4.0, new demands and competences are required of employees nowadays. The term Industry 4.0 has emerged in Germany within the high-tech strategy of the German government in order to demonstrate the potential of the fourth industrial revolution [1]. Herman et al. [2, p. 8] stated "that Industry 4.0 is 'a collective term for technologies and concepts of value chain organization' with the four key components of Cyber Physical Systems, Internet of Things, Internet of Services and Smart Factory." The term is spreading out to other fields, even in the field of Education 4.0 or Teaching and

IMA – Institute of Information Management in Mechanical Engineering; ZLW – Center for Learning and Knowledge Management; IfU – Associated Institute for Management Cybernetics e.V.

C. Allison et al. (Eds.): iLRN 2016, CCIS 621, pp. 45–58, 2016.
DOI: 10.1007/978-3-319-41769-1_4

Learning 4.0. In context of education, future employees have to be prepared for the changes in working environment [3], which ideally start in school or high school. Highly individualized and specific processes as well as a more extensive Human-Computer-Interaction (HCI) shape the future working environments.

Currently, practical experiences and the relevance of theoretical knowledge is often an underrepresented field in education [4]. Therefore, real-world experiences are one major requirement in the context of education in order to prepare students for their future working life. In some courses, practical experiences are acquired in laboratories [5]. However, they are not available for all students at any times. Due to high costs, complexity or their dangerous nature, some areas of studies are not feasible in real laboratories. Virtual environments (VE) thus provide a chance by enabling all students to gather these experiences. Advances in 3D virtual environments and VR technology facilitate a more natural experience in a VE and provide new opportunities for teaching and learning. VR is a future technology, which gains an increasing importance in research and industry. The progress in this area is driven by the rapid growth of hardware and technology, like new interaction tools and tracking systems [6]. Thus, VEs have recently become a popular trend in education. Researchers, e.g. [7–10] have lately investigated the potential of VLEs for education and have shown that VLEs increase students' learning motivation and activation in learning activities. Moreover, VEs provide a hazard-free, explorative learning and a visualization of complex and abstract processes and real-phenomena for students [11]. The technological advances and the growing availability of VR technology, like head-mounted displays (HMD), facilitate the access to universities because of their easier use and the decreasing costs of HMDs. Applying VR technologies in education can further increase the students' learning experience to a more immersive and engaging involvement in learning processes [12]. The immersion into a virtual world offers students the potential to experience virtual objects and to interact with the environment. Thereby, a constructivist perspective of the learning process can be encouraged, in which students learn in an active, self-controlled way in situational, problem-oriented contexts. Beyond higher education, immersive VR has already been used comprehensively in other training and learning fields, like medicine, e.g. [13] or military training, e.g. [14]. Moreover, it is effectively used in contexts of Virtual Reality Exposure Therapy (VRET), like Phobias or anxiety [12].

VEs provide a setting, which facilitates a more personalized learning process matching students' requirements and offering higher learning autonomy [7]. In the context of immersive VLEs, one central assumption is that VR technology leads to greater immersion in the VE and in turn higher immersion leads to better learning outcomes [15]. In order to fulfill the students learning requirements, the interaction between immersive hardware and students have to be improved. Therefore, individual-related factors, which influence the students learning process in a VLE, have to be identified. With the aim of using immersive VLE in high school and higher education as a teaching and learning tool, first it has to be assessed which individual-related variables influences the VLE experience and in which way user experience (UX) affect task performance in VLEs. The central question here is: For which user profiles are immersive virtual learning environments applicable? First, the theoretical background of learning in an immersive VLE is outlined, and then the study design with its set of variables is described in detail. Finally, the paper presents the already conducted pretest of the main study and the preliminary results of this pretest with regard to future work in this field.

2 Theoretical Framework: Learning in an Immersive Virtual Environment

2.1 Virtual Reality Technology

VR is characterized by the following factors: technology aspects (3D content), new ways of HCI and mental or psychological experience of VR. In particular, VR is adjudged by its capability of immersion. Immersion is the central feature of VR, which distinguished VR from other Human-Computer interfaces [6]. There are two existing perspectives to understand immersion: a technical and a user or mental perspective. Issing and Klimsa [16] stated that the technology capability of immersion of a VR system means that the user is surrounded by the VR so that barriers between the virtual world and the user have been removed. This leads to a greater level of users' attention and focusing [16]. The users' mental experiences in a VR environment are generally summarized by the term 'user experience' (UX), which can further be subdivided into certain theoretical constructs: immersion, presence and flow, which are described in detail.

2.2 User Experience: Immersion, Presence and Flow

The term UX is particularly used in the research field of HCI. UX is an umbrella term for qualitative experiences of a user during media reception or interaction with technology [17]. This includes subjective expectations, perception, emotions as well as psychological and physiological reactions bevor, during or after media use [18]. To measure UX, different concepts from various academic disciplines are being applied, mainly immersion, presence and flow [19, 20] as concepts of a qualitative UX.

Immersion. Awidespread definition of immersion is from Murray [21], who defines it as a state, in which a user is surrounded by another reality claiming his full attention. Witmer and Singer [15] outlined immersion as a "psychological state" and stated that the "degree to which they feel immersed in the VE [will increase]" by effectively isolating users from the real world. Furthermore, they assumed that a "VE that produces a greater sense of immersion will produce higher levels of presence" [15, p. 227]. Wirth and Hofer [22] even share this view. In contrast to this psychological perspective, Slater and Wilbur [23] defined immersion as a technical characteristic of a VR system and understood presence as a consequence of an immersive technology. This paper follows the psychological understanding of Witmer and Singer [15] and Wirth and Hofer [22]. "Presence" and "flow" are two of the numerous variations of immersion and immersive experience [24].

Presence. Presence is defined "as the subjective experience of being in one place or environment, even when one is physically situated in another" [15, p. 225]. In context of VE, presence means the experience of the VE rather than the physical [15]. Presence is the most influenced and researched concept in the field of VE. In contrast to immersion, presence is commonly understood as a user variable and not a technological characteristic.

Wirth and Hofer [22] developed a two-level model for the occurrence of spatial presence experience, which comprehends presence experience as a spatial perceptual phenomenon. The model includes two dimensions: self-localization and possible actions. The user considers himself in the VE, recognizes and practices possible actions in the VE [22]. Beside media factory influencing presence, also individual-related variables, like personality traits and demographic factors influence spatial presence [25]. Increased time spent in the VE is another impact factor, which can both raise presence because of adjustment and knowing as well as reduce presence due to negative effects intensify over time [26]. The examination of the relationship between presence and performance is mostly based on correlation studies. Therefore, possible factors affecting presence and performance have to be experimentally controlled in further research studies [26].

Flow. Flow is defined as a reflection-free merging in smooth ongoing activities that have been under control despite high strain [27]. Flow is the most general concept of all three kinds of experience, because the experiences are not limited to media use, but to a series of activities [28]. The concept has its origin in happiness research and was originally used in daily activities [27]. Research studies have shown that the state of flow has an influence on information processing, cognitive load and physiological processes [29].

In conclusion, the three concepts presented characterize several dimensions of UX. A higher level of immersion and presence leads to better learning outcomes [15]. Therefore, it is assumed that immersion, presence and flow are requirements for a successful learning process in VE [30]. To confirm this assumption further empirical evidence is necessary, especially if immersive VLE should be an appropriate tool for education. Therefore, the presented study design focuses on the following questions:

1. What influence do individual-related variables have on UX, activation and task performance in immersive VLEs?
2. What influence do immersive VLEs have on UX, activation and task performance?
3. For which user profiles are immersive virtual learning environments are suitable?
4. How do UX, activation and task performance relate to each other?

In order to answer those questions, a VLE is developed and a research design is set up, which is presented in the following.

3 Development of a Virtual Learning Environment

For the research study a VLE based on the open-world sandbox game Minecraft is designed. Minecraft was chosen as the VLE because of the several reasons (Fig. 1). Numerous researchers, e.g. [31, 32] have already applied Minecraft in learning contexts.

Minecraft can be used in different academic disciplines, like biology, mathematics and engineering as well as for teaching and learning soft skills, such as problem solving, teamwork and creativity [33]. It offers opportunities to explore a VE in a free and experimental way and build new objects. Programming capabilities from students or teachers are not required, which eases the use in education due to cost, time and personal resources. In order to setup Minecraft as a VLE, the conception is related to the game design steps according to [34, 35]. These steps are: define learning outcomes of the game, define the target group, define the game and shape the game idea, elaborate the details (storyline) and the (technical) implementation of the game [34, 35].

The target group of the developed VLE constitutes university as well as high school students. University students are chosen because they are currently in university and already use digital media or digital games in university. High school students are added because they are the next university students and have to be prepared early for university in order to get familiar with new teaching and learning tools and methods. Moreover, in education problem solving skills are even more required with regard to future working life. Therefore, in the experimental setting, the task includes a logistical problem-solving process, which addresses both student groups. The task is embedded in a storyline in an industrial factory setting where students are employees of a company, which produces soft drinks, especially lemonade. In order to transport the ingredients for the lemonade, a driverless transportation route on rails has to be built on the industrial area, where certain requirements have to be fulfilled. For a transparent learning process, the definition of learning outcomes is crucial for students. This enables them to evaluate their actions and personal benefit. The designed VLE has the following learning outcomes accordingly to the required steps of the students to solve the task:

1. Spatial orientation: at first students have to get an overview of the industrial area, where they have to build the driverless transportation route on rails.
2. Decision Making: after getting an overview of the area and the various possibilities to build the transportation route, they have to make a decision in terms of the requirements on the task, like efficiency and rapidity.
3. Problem solving: there are certain barriers in the industrial area, like silos or cars, which have to be considered by choosing and building the transportation route.
4. Psychomotoric skills: Students have to use the hardware appropriate and have to navigate through the virtual environment.

Fig. 1. Screenshots of the implemented VLE in Minecraft

4 Study Design

4.1 Experimental Setup

To understand which user characteristics and user interface factors influence UX, activation and task performance within the developed VLE in Minecraft a controlled experiment is carried out (Fig. 2).

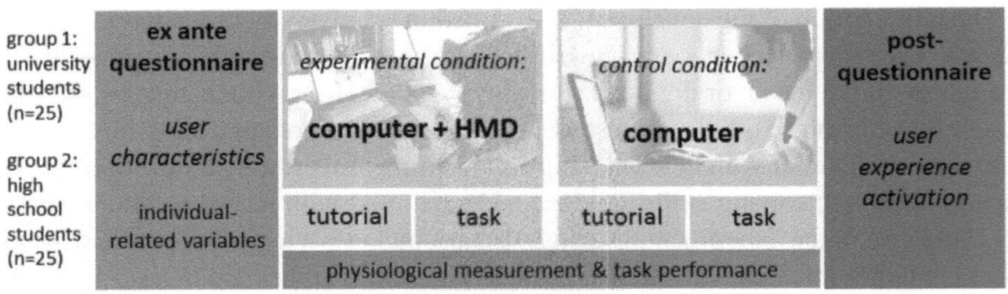

Fig. 2. Research design

The controlled experiment is set up as an experimental research design with two experimental hardware conditions: immersive and non-immersive. The immersive condition includes the HMD, (in this study, the Oculus Rift DK 2 was used), whereas the non-immersive condition is a computer version without HMD. Participants are randomly assigned to experimental condition (HMD) and control condition (computer). The physiological measurement of the participants is conducted three times during the experiment. To run a baseline measurement of each participants without engaging in any task, first a one-minute baseline is recorded in advance, which serves as a reference value to the physiological measurement during the task. After the task, a third measurement is carried out.

4.2 Experimental Task

The experimental task is designed accordingly to meet the requirements and knowledge from high school and university students. Apart from the professional competence imparting in university, even soft skills such as method, media and social competences are conveyed in university and are required in future career. Complex and constantly changing environments in education and in working life required the ability to cope with these circumstances. Therefore, problem-solving ability gains more and more importance in education. Problem-solving tasks require a self-employed, active way of finding solutions. In this study, a problem-solving task is designed in which participants have to solve a logistical problem task in a VLE. Their task is to build a driverless transportation route on rails in order to transport freight from a warehouse to a factory. As requirements to solve the task, participants have to construct the transportation route on rails in an efficient, resource saving and rapid way. Before starting the task, the participants have the opportunity to enter a tutorial so that they get to know the VE and the control system. Furthermore, they can learn the basics of using Minecraft, especially how to lay and remove the rail tracks and how to move in the VE.

The students that are in the experimental group can additionally use the tutorial to familiarize with the HMD and the immersive effect. To measure the task performance, a specifically programmed tool records the following performance parameters: time, number of used rails, errors in form of the number of removed rails and traveled distance of each participant. In addition to that, a screen capturing software is recording the student's movement within the VLE while solving the task. During the task, the physiology of the participants is measured by means of biofeedback sensors.

4.3 Measurement and Variables

A set of independent and dependent variables is defined to investigate the effects of user characteristics (individual-related variables) and the user interface (immersive capacity of the user interface) on UX, activation and task performance (Fig. 3).

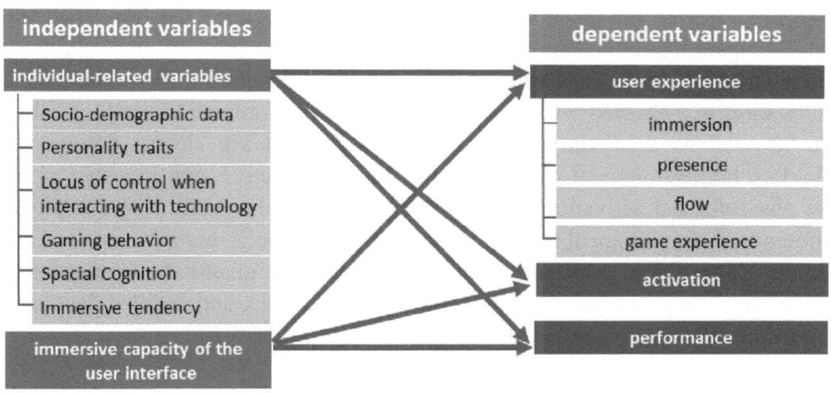

Fig. 3. Set of independent and dependent variables

Independent Variables. The individual-related variables are operationalized with the following sub-scales. As sub measures we examined socio-demographic data, like age and gender (contrasting a high school group and a higher education group) as typical "carrier variables", which need to be detailed regarding other individual moderator variables. Furthermore, user characteristics, like the actual gaming behavior and the frequency of using games, serves as further independent variables, which are collected via self-report in form of a questionnaire. To measure personality traits, the scale 10 Item Big Five Inventory is used. The tendency of a person to be involved in VE is measured via the Immersive Tendency Questionnaire (ITQ), which is based on self-report information [15]. Within the HCI, the technology- and individual-related traits can influence the assessment and use of VE. With the scale locus of control when interaction with technology (LOC) [36] the individual locus of control in a technological context is measured. Moreover, spatial orientation is a crucial characteristic of VE. Some empirical studies have shown that there are great inter-individual differences in spatial learning- and orientation performances [24]. Self-evaluation report can predict the actually spatial orientation and learning performance [37]. The Questionnaire Spatial Strategies (QSS) [37] provides a reliable and valid self-report measurement for the use of spatial strategies for orientation. To sum up, all of these measuring instruments are elected in order to set up comprehensive user profiles of each participants by using an immersive VLE.

Dependent Variables. As dependent variables, the construct UX, activation and task performances are assessed. UX is operationalized with the constructs immersion, presence, flow and game experiences. For these constructs already existing reliable and valid instruments are used which are based on subjective reports as a common method to measure UX [26]. Witmer and Singer [15] measure presence via the widely used Presence Questionnaire (PQ). They [15] have shown that the PQ was positively related to measure task performances in VE. To measure flow, the Flow Short Scala (FKS) [38] is used, which is a reliable and valid, frequently used questionnaire. Game experiences is measured via the Game Experience Questionnaire (GEQ) from Ijsselstein et al. [39], which is chosen because of different subscales like challenge, competence, positive and negative affect and tension/annoyance. Thereby, a wide range of the participant's emotions are retrieved. All items of the pre- and post-questionnaire were answered on a six-scale, ranging from 1 = total disagree to 6 = total agree.

Activation is measured with two instruments: a questionnaire based on subjective reports as well as a psychophysiological measurement via electro dermal activity (EDA). Psychophysiological measurements offer an objective, non-invasive method to collect physiological activation during the experiences of a VLE [40]. Mandryk [41] has shown that physiological indications serves as an objectively indicator of UX with computer games. The various methods (self-report, quantitative questionnaires, objective physiological measurements) constitute a complex and detailed description of the conscious and subconscious UX of the students in the VLE.

4.4 Preliminary Results of the Pretest

In the conducted pretest, the complete organizational, technical and content-related procedure as well as the abovementioned research design with the measuring instruments was tested for improvements. The participants are randomly assigned to the experimental and control group. The sample of the pretest contains 10 students from university at an average age of 24,9 years. The majority of the participants are playing digital games to an average game time of 3.75 h per week. Furthermore, 70 % of the participants have already used a VR technology and 50 % have already played Minecraft. In the following means, standard derivations as well as the minima and maxima of the independent and dependent variables are reported.

In the Big Five Inventory, participants showed a mean score of 4.2 for Extraversion (SD = 1.42), 3.9 for Agreeableness (SD = 0.81), 4.4 for Conscientiousness (SD = 0.91), 3.3 for Neuroticism (SD = 1.1), and 4.6 for Openness to Experience. The mean

Locus of Control when Interaction with Technology was 3.9 (SD = 0.93). The Immersive Tendency Questionnaire had a mean score of 4.4 for Focus (SD = 0.67), 3.24 for Involvement (SD = 0.69), and 2.25 for Game (SD = 1.28). The Spatial Strategies of the participants were more pronounced in Global Strategies (M = 3.35, SD = 1.29) and Strategies Based on Overview (M = 3.47, SD = 1.14) than in strategies based on Cardinal Directions (M = 1.2, SD = 0.63).

The average high values of the subscales extraversion, conscientiousness and openness to experience of the Big Five indicate that the participants of the pretest are more extrovert individuals. Extrovert people tend to be action-oriented individuals who have a higher social engagement and like interacting with people. People with a higher value of conscientiousness tend to be more self-discipline and aim for achievements. High values indicate a preference for planned behavior. People with a higher value in openness to experience are more willing to try new things, they tend to be more creative and aware of their feeling. The average value of the ITQ shows higher values in the subscale focus which in turns means that people with a higher ITQ tend to be more involved or immersed in a VLE [15] (Fig. 4).

Scale	Subscale	*M*	*SD*	*Min*	*Max*
Big Five	Extraversion	4.20	1.42	1.50	5.00
	Agreeableness	3.90	0.81	3.00	5.50
	Conscientiousness	4.40	0.91	3.00	6.00
	Neuroticism	3.30	1.10	2.00	5.50
	Openness to Experience	4.60	1.37	1.50	6.00
Locus of Control when Interaction with Technology	-	3.90	0.93	2.14	4.88
Immersive Tendency	Focus	4.40	0.67	3.00	5.17
	Involvment	3.24	0.69	1.86	4.29
	Game	2.25	1.28	1.00	4.00
Spatial Strategies	Global	3.35	1.29	1.50	5.50
	Cardinal Directions	1.20	0.63	1.00	3.00
	Strategies Based on Overview	3.47	1.14	1.67	5.00

Fig. 4. Means, standard derivations, minima, and maxima of the independent variables (n = 10)

The user experience varied considerably across participants (see Fig. 5). The questionnaire data of the participants show that they did experience Flow (M = 4.46, SD = 0.71), Presence (Total Score: M = 4.4, SD = 0.53; Involvement/Control: M = 4.67, SD = 0.65; Natural: M = 3.87, SD = 1.02; Haptic: M = 4.75, SD = 0.82; Resolution: M = 5.1, SD = 0.97; Interface Quality: M = 4.5, SD = 1.36), and Immersion (M = 3.93, SD = 0.45). When asked about their Game Experience, they indicated to have had low Tension and Annoyance (M = 1.27, SD = 0.56) and Negative Affect (M = 1.73, SD = 0.61). Participants overall experienced a rather high Positive Affect (M = 4.96, SD = 0.78) reporting a feeling of Flow (M = 3.88, SD = 0.75), Competence (M = 4.42, SD = 0.93), and Sensory and Imaginative

Scale	Subscale	*M*	*SD*	*Min*	*Max*
Flow	-	4.46	0.71	3.00	5.50
Presence	Involvment/Control	4.67	0.65	3.18	5.55
	Natural	3.87	1.02	2.33	5.00
	Haptic	4.75	0.82	3.50	6.00
	Resolution	5.10	0.97	3.00	6.00
	Interface Quality	4.50	1.36	1.00	5.67
	Presence (Total Score)	4.30	0.53	3.12	4.93
Immersion	-	3.93	0.45	3.14	4.64
Game Experience	Tension/Annoyance	1.27	0.56	1.00	2.33
	Negative Affenct	1.73	0.61	1.00	2.75
	Positive Affect	4.96	0.78	3.75	6.00
	Flow	3.88	0.75	3.00	5.40
	Competence	4.42	0.93	2.60	5.60
	Sensory and Imaginative Immersion	3.62	0.78	2.67	4.67
	Challenge	2.38	0.99	1.25	4.25

Fig. 5. Means, standard derivations, minima, and maxima of the dependent variables (n = 10)

Immersion (M = 3.62, SD = 0.78). Most participants felt that the task did not pose too much of a Challenge (M = 2.38, SD = 0.99).

The descriptive statistics of the dependent variables display a wider range in the scores than the independent variables. In particular, the value of the interface quality varies the most. At this point, the different user interfaces respectively the two conditions in the study (immersive/non immersive) have an effect on the user experience. When it comes to the experience of the VLE the mean experience flow have a higher value on an average which means that the participants immerse in the VLE and therefore have the feeling of being in the VLE.

Complementary, we run a correlation between independent and dependent variables. Taking into account that the pretest was with a very small sample, why any significant correlations have a low statistical power. Some interesting correlation with a special view to user traits are presented. Participants with a higher Neuroticism (Big Five) have a lower flow experience ($r = -.68$, $p < .05$), a lower value in the subscale positive affect ($r = -.69$, $p < .05$), competence ($r = -.75$, $p < .05$) and sensory and imaginative Immersion ($r = -.68$, $p < .05$) of the GEQ. Participants with a higher openness for experiences (Big Five) have a higher value in the subscale focus of the ITQ ($r = .72$, $p < .05$). Participants with a higher locus of control when interacting with technology have a lower value in the subscale negative affect of the GEQ ($r = -.74$, $p < .05$).

Concerning correlations between dependent variables, participants with a higher flow experience have higher values in the subscale positive affect ($r = .89$, $p < .01$), competence ($r = .89$, $p < .01$) and sensory and imaginative immersion ($r = .69$, $p < .05$) of the GEQ. Participants with a higher value in the subscale negative affect (GEQ) have a lower immersion experience (IEQ) ($r = -.87$, $p < .01$) and a higher value in the subscale tension/annoyance ($r = .67$, $p < .05$) (GEQ). Participants with a higher value in the subscale Flow (GEQ) have a higher immersion experience (IEQ) ($r = .65$, $p < .05$) and a higher value in the subscale challenge ($r = .67$, $p < .05$) (GEQ).

To sum up, the statistical correlations show that there are relations between the students' individuality and personality and their experiences of the VLE. Regarding the individual-related variables, the initial results point out that students with more anxious, reserved characteristics have a more negative experience in the VLE. Whereas more open-minded and social students are convinced to handle technological problems in general and in the VLE. Furthermore, they have a more positive experience of the VLE. Moreover, they adjudged themselves a higher competence in solving tasks. Students, which have a more negative experience in the VLE, had at the same time a lower experience of immersion and felt more strained. The correlations indicate that flow experience and a positive game experience are interconnected with each other.

Finally, it has to be taken into account that it is a small sample; therefore these correlations cannot explain the cause-effect relationship between independent and dependent variables. Hence, these correlations have to be investigated with a larger sample in order to validate these preliminary findings.

With regard to the task performance, the quantitative analysis of the task performance has shown that the students take from 3:30 min up to 8 min to solve the task. On an average, the task is solved in 4:30 min. The average usage of rails lay by 130 rails. In the number of used rails, there are no significant differences between the two conditions. As it has already been approved participants, who are familiar with Minecraft and the VR technologies, solve the task more quickly and made less mistakes in terms of removing rails. Further analysis is required to get a deeper insight how the task performance is related with the user experience.

These results might be an initial indication that UX in VLE depend on individual traits, which in turns influence how strongly a user immerse in a VLE. Concerning the effects of user traits on UX in immersive VLE, the initial results have shown that there exists an impact. Thus, it can be assumed that they have an effect on the task performance and thereby on the learning process in education. The 10 Item Big Five Inventory Questionnaire constitutes a reference model to measure personality [28]. Personality describes a specific set of psychological characteristics, which influences the individuals' thinking models, actions, behavior and experiences in the real world and in a VE. Mandryk [41] have demonstrated that the personality traits have an influence on presence in VLEs. Personality traits therefore provide an explanatory approach how users perceive, process, evaluate and experience media [28].

Furthermore, the immersive tendency of a user to be involved in the VE has an effect of the user experience, like flow, immersion and presence. Witmer and Singer [15, p. 237] assumed that "If high ITQ scores reflect a greater tendency to become involved or immersed, then individuals who score high on the ITQ should report more presence on the [Presence Questionnaire] PQ when exposed to a particular VE." With the ITQ, the students that probably have the most advantages from a VLE could be recognized [15]. At this point, further research is needed in order to investigate which user traits have a central role in the user experience of immersive VLEs.

5 Summary and Outlook

The conducted pretest of the follow-up study has given a first insight into the influencing individual-related variables on the students' experience in the VLE. The results of the pretest have shown that individual traits and characteristics influence the experience of a user in a VLE. Therefore, it can be expected that for some users learning in a VLE has a greater benefit than for others. In the follow-up study, it has to be investigated which user traits have an impact and to what extent when using immersive VLE in education. Furthermore, immersion is hypothesized as the key construct for better learning [21]. These hypotheses will be analyzed and answered in the follow-up study. The relation between user traits and the UX in an immersive VLE has to be assessed in detail with a link to the task performance in learning settings. The following main study with a larger sample aims to set up user profiles in terms of immersive VLE, especially for whom immersive VLE brings a benefit in the learning process. This helps to get deeper insight into the specific preferences of students in education.

In further research studies the aspect of technology acceptance has taken into consideration [42]. The application of new technologies for educational purpose in school and higher education is associated with certain challenges and requirements. One specific challenge in this context lies in the technological acceptance as well as in potential usage barriers. Technological acceptance has become a key concept for a successful application of technology, even in the field of teaching and learning. A lack of knowledge about the benefits and disadvantages as well as a lack of usage experiences with new technologies and the (un)-certainty of potential risks in this context play a crucial role for the willingness to use technology. Furthermore, the usage context as well as individual-related variables like age, gender or self-confidence when dealing with technology are factors which influences the usage and the effectiveness of technology use in education. In order to fully understand the conditions of the acceptance of VR technologies in formal and higher education, other stakeholders next to the students have to be considered, such as teachers, educational institutions, and, in case of high school student, parents.

Overall, an important contribution for using immersive VLEs in learning scenarios in school and universities with a special view to digitalization in education can be made.

References

1. Guo, Q.: Learning in a mixed realty system in the context of 'Industrie 4.0'. J. Tech. Educ. **3** (2) (2015)
2. Hermann, M., Pentek, T.; Otto, B.: Design principles for Industrie 4.0 scenarios: a literature review. Audi Stiftungslehrstuhl Supply Net Order Management. TU, Dortmund (2015)
3. Schuster, K., Groß, K., Vossen, R., Richert, A., Jeschke, S.: Preparing for Industry 4.0 - collaborative virtual learning environments in engineering education. In: Proceedings of the International Conference on E-learning in the Workplace (ICELW) (2015)
4. Janßen, D., Schilberg, D., Richert, A., Jeschke, S.: Pump it up! - an online game in the lecture computer science in mechanical engineering. In: Proceedings of the 8th European Conference on Games Based Learning, pp. 805–808 (2014)

5. Schröder, S., Janßen, D., Leisten, I., Vossen, R., Isenhardt, I.: On-professional competence in engineering education for XL-classes. In: Proceedings of the IEEE Frontiers in Education Conference (FIE 2013), pp. 29–34. IEEE (2013)
6. Dörner, R., Broll, W., Grimm, P., Jung, B.: Virtual and Augmented Reality (VR/AR). Grundlagen und Methoden der Virtuellen und Augmentierten Realität. Springer, Berlin (2013)
7. Chau, M., Wong, A., Wang, M., Lai, S., Chan, K.W.Y., Li, T.M., et al.: Using 3D virtual environments to facilitate students in constructivist learning. Decis. Support Syst. **56**, 115–121 (2013)
8. Li, T.M.H., Chau, M., Wong, P.W.C., Lai, E.S.Y., Yip, P.S.F.: Evaluation of a web-based social network electronic game in enhancing mental health literacy for young people. J. Med. Internet Res. **15**, e80 (2013)
9. Asgari, M., Kaufman, D.: Relationships among computer games, fantasy and learning. In: Proceedings of Educating Imaginative Minds: 2nd Annual Conference on Imagination and Education, Vancouver, BC (2004)
10. Tüzun, H., Özdinc, F.: The effects of 3D multi-user virtual environments on freshmen university students' conceptual and spatial learning and presence in departmental orientation. Comput. Educ. **94**, 228–240 (2016)
11. Dalgarno, B.; Hedberg, J.: 3D learning environments in tertiary education. In: Ascilite 2001: Meeting the Crossroads, pp. 33–36 (2001)
12. Chittaro, L., Buttussi, F.: Assessing knowledge retention of an immersive serious games vs. a traditional education method in aviation safety. IEEE Trans. Vis. Comput. Graph. **21**, 529–538 (2015)
13. Silverstein, J.C., Dech, F., Edison, M., Jurek, P., Helton, W.S., Espat, N.J.: Virtual reality: immersive hepatic surgery educational environment. Surgery **132**, 274–277 (2002)
14. Cruz-Neira, C., Reiners, D., Springer, J.P., Neumann, C., Odom, C.N.S., Kehring, K.: An integrated immersive simulator for the dismounted soldier. In: The Interservice/Industry Training, Simulation and Education Conference (2011)
15. Witmer, B., Singer, M.: Measuring presence in virtual environments: a presence questionnaire. Presence: Teleoper. Virtual Environ. **7**, 225–240 (1998)
16. Issing, L.J., Klimsa, P. (Hg.): Information und Lernen mit Multimedia und Internet. Lehrbuch für Studium und Praxis. Beltz PVU, Weinheim (2002)
17. Hassenzahl, M., Eckoldt, K., Thielsch, M.T.: User experience und experience design – Konzepte und Herausforderungen. In: Brau, H., Diefenbach, S., Hassenzahl, M., Kohler, K., Koller, F., Peissner, M., Petrovic, K., Thielsch, M., Ullrich, D., Zimmermann, D. (eds.) Tagungsband UP09, pp. 233–237. Fraunhofer Verlag, Stuttgart (2009)
18. ISO 9241-210
19. IJsselsteijn, W., De Kort, Y.A.W., Poels, K., Jurgelionis, A., Bellotti, F.: Characterising and measuring user experiences in digital games. In: International Conference on Advances in Computer Entertainment Technology, vol. 2, p. 27, Salzburg, AU (2007)
20. Jennett, C., Cox, A.L., Cairns, P., Dhoparee, S., Epps, A., Tijs, T., Walton, A.: Measuring and defining the experience of immersion in games. Int. J. Hum. Comput. Stud. **66**, 641–661 (2008)
21. Murray, J.: Hamlet on the Holodeck: The Future of Narrative in Cyberspace, pp. 98–99. MIT Press, Cambridge (1997)
22. Wirth, W., Hofer, M.: Präsenzerleben - eine Einführung aus Medienpsychologischer Perspektive. Montage AV **17**, 159–175 (2009)
23. Slater, M., Wilbur, S.: A framework for immersive virtual environments (five): speculations on the role of presence in virtual environments. Presence: Teleoper. Virtual Environ. **6**, 603–616 (1997). MIT Press

24. Malinoswki, J.C., Gillespie, W.T.: Individual differences in performance on a large-scale, real-world wayfinding task. J. Environ. Psychol. **21**, 73–82 (2001)
25. Mögerle, U., Böcking, S., Wirth, W., Schramm, H.: Unterhaltungserleben in virtuellen Medien. Die Rolle von Medien und Rezipienteneigenschaften beim Entstehen von Spatial Presence. In: Schramm, H., Wirth, W., Bilandzic, H. (eds.) Empirische Unterhaltungs forschung: Studien zu Rezeption und Wirkung von medialer Unterhaltung, pp. 87–106. Nomos, Glashütte (2006)
26. Nash, E.B., Edwards, G.W., Thompson, J.A., Barfield, W.: A review of presence and performance in virtual environments. Int. J. Hum. Comput. Interact. **12**, 1–41 (2000)
27. Csikszentmihalyi, M.: Flow: The Psychology of Optimal Experience. Harper and Row, New York (1990)
28. Wünsch, C., Schramm, H., Gehrau, V., Bilandzic, H. (eds.): Handbuch Medienrezeption. Nomos, Baden-Baden (2014)
29. Keller, J., Landhäußer, A.: Im Flow sein. Experimentelle Analysen des Zustands optimaler Beanspruchung. Psychologische Rundschau **62**, 213–220 (2011)
30. Schuster, K.: Einfluss natürlicher Benutzerschnittstellen zur Steuerung des Sichtfeldes und der Fortbewegung auf Rezeptionsprozesse in virtuellen Lernumgebungen. Tectum Verlag, Marburg (2015)
31. Schifter, C.; Cipollone, M.: Minecraft as a teaching tool: one case study. In: McBride, R.; Searson, M. (Eds.): Proceedings of Society for Information and Technology and Teacher Education International Conference 2013, pp. 2951–2955. AACE, Chesapeake, VA (2013)
32. Reem, A., Bana, J., Knight, I., Benson, E., Afolabi, O., Kerr, A., Blanchfield, P., Hopkins, G.: Design of a math learning game using a Minecraft mod. In: Proceedings of the European Conference on Games Based Learning (2014)
33. Short, D.: Teaching scientific concepts using a virtual world - Minecraft. J. Aust. Sci. Teach. Assoc. **58**, 55–58 (2012)
34. Pivec, M., Moretti, M.: Game-Based Learning: Discover the Pleasure of Learning. Pabst Science Publishers, Lengerich (2008)
35. Morsi, R., Jackson, E.: Playing and learning? Educational gaming for engineering education. In: Frontiers in Education Conference – Global Engineering: Knowledge Without Borders, Opportunities Without Passports, pp. F2H-1–F2H-6. IEEE (2007)
36. Beier, G.: Kontrollüberzeugungen im Umgang mit Technik. Rep. Psychologie **24**, 684–694 (1993)
37. Münzer, S., Hölscher, C.: Entwicklung und Validierung eines Fragebogens zu räumlichen Strategien. Diagnostica **57**, 111–125 (2011)
38. Rheinberg, F., Vollmeyer, R., Engeser, S.: Die Erfassung des Flow-Erlebens. In: Stiensmeier, J., Rheinberg, F. (eds.) Diagnostik von Motivation und Selbstkonzept, pp. 261–279. Hogrefe, Göttingen (2003)
39. IJsselsteijn, W.A., de Kort, Y.A.W.; Poels, K.: The game experience questionnaire: development of a self-report measure to assess the psychological impact of digital games (in preparation)
40. Kivikangas, J.M., Chanel, G., Cowley, B., Ekman, I., Salminen, M., Järvelä, S., Ravaja, N.: A review of the use of psychophysiological methods in game research. J. Gaming Virtual Worlds **3**, 181–199 (2011)
41. Mandryk, R.: Physiological measures for game evaluation. In: Isbister, K., Schaffer, N. (eds.) Game Usability: Advancing the Player Experience. Morgan Kaufmann, Burlington (2008)
42. Ziefle, M.: Ungewissheit und Unsicherheit bei der Einführung neuer Technologien. Nutzungsbarrieren am Beispiel von Medizintechnologien im häuslichen Umfeld. In: Jeschke, S., Jakobs, E.-M., Dröge, A. (eds.) Exploring Uncertainty, pp. 84–104. Springer Fachmedien, Wiesbaden (2013)

Virtual Reality for Early Education: A Study

Adeola Fabola(✉) and Alan Miller

School of Computer Science, University of St Andrews, St Andrews, Fife, UK
{aef6, alan.miller}@st-andrews.ac.uk
http://www.cs.st-andrews.ac.uk/

Abstract. This paper investigates the use of Virtual Reality (VR) as a tool for cultural heritage learning, using St Andrews Cathedral as the subject matter. As part of a module focused on local history, first year secondary school pupils in a school in the town of St Andrews took part in virtual tours of the Cathedral as it stood in the 14th Century using the Samsung Gear VR, Google Cardboard, Oculus Rift, computer screen and Xbox controller, and answered questions aimed to elicit their experiences with the various systems. The system design and implementation is presented and the findings, observations and lessons learnt from the study are discussed.

Keywords: Virtual reality · Google Cardboard · Samsung Gear VR · Cultural heritage

1 Introduction: Heritage Interpretation in St Andrews

St Andrews Cathedral is one of the most iconic monuments in Scottish history, as it was the center of religious activities and domicile of eminent figures in its heyday. Owing to its importance, the Open Virtual Worlds Group at the University of St Andrews embarked on a reconstruction of the Cathedral as it stood in 1318 (See Figs. 1 and 2), and this reconstruction has been a valuable resource in exploring and teaching cultural heritage through deploying it in schools, museum installations and over the Internet [1].

St Andrews Cathedral reconstruction has served as the basis upon which other resources have been built. Pertinent to this paper, is the development of a mobile tour of St Andrews Cathedral which works with the Google Cardboard [2] and the Samsung Gear VR. These systems have been deployed in a school in the town of St Andrews in Scotland and used as the basis for learning local history as part of a module.

A study carried out to investigate the efficacy of such technology for learning history is discussed in this paper. Section 1.1 summarises some work done on using virtual reality for learning and hones in on cultural heritage, Sect. 2 discusses the study and provides an overview of the system implementation and features, Sect. 3 discusses the data analyses and results, and Sect. 4 provides a conclusion and summary of lessons learnt.

C. Allison et al. (Eds.): iLRN 2016, CCIS 621, pp. 59–72, 2016.
DOI: 10.1007/978-3-319-41769-1_5

Fig. 1. St Andrews Cathedral West Door: 1318 (left) and today (right)

1.1 Related Work: Virtual and Augmented Reality for Learning

It is important to define what we mean by the concepts of Virtual Reality (VR) and Augmented Reality (AR) and situate them in the context of this work. VR refers to systems characterised by environments which are comprised solely of artificial elements courtesy of computer-generated imagery, and represent one extreme in the Reality-Virtuality Continuum proposed in [3], with the other extreme representing the real environment which is the world governed by the laws of physics e.g. gravity, time, space and so on. Between the Virtual Environment and Real Environment exists the concept of Mixed Reality (MR), which represents systems made up of real and virtual environments [3]. Augmented Reality (AR) refers to a class of Mixed Reality systems where a real environment is annotated with virtual (or synthetic) elements, in order to add information and context, or otherwise improve the real environment. This work focuses on VR because it facilitates the distinct exploration of two realities (the virtual and the real) in parallel, whereas AR merges both realities into one.

Virtual reality environments are equipped with certain features – such as the ability to facilitate shared experiences, encourage natural user interaction and enable unique learning experiences to meet individuals' needs – that make them suitable for learning [4]. Three challenges to the adoption of virtual reality for education are identified in [4]: *cost*, *usability* and *fears* of the technology. These challenges posed significant drawbacks to the adoption of virtual reality in the early 90's (and before). However, reductions in cost, and increases in the power of microprocessors and improved user interfaces have led to new paradigms that enhance usability and accessibility of VR systems.

The growing popularity of virtual reality for learning is investigated and confirmed by [5], which present a review of empirical studies conducted on the application of virtual reality for learning from 1999 to 2009. It is evident from this work that in the last decade, virtual reality has been leveraged for learning in a broad range of disciplines from the sciences to the social sciences, and that virtual reality is appropriate for teaching and learning, as well as for training and entertainment purposes [6]. The use of virtual reality as a tool for learning has been investigated by several scholars. Studies conducted by [7] suggest that virtual reality technologies can serve not only as an invaluable resource but also as an effective tool for learning and teaching. A virtual reality system for teaching routing algorithms by leveraging the graphical capabilities of an open source virtual reality platform to visualise network packets on a routing island is introduced in [8], [9] presents a case study for teaching a university module using a shared, 3D virtual environment, and [1] discusses the deployment of the 3D model in several scenarios such as museum exhibitions, science centres, schools and festivals.

Collaborative learning systems have also been developed using virtual reality technology. [10] recognizes the importance of social connectedness amongst learners and thus facilitates collaboration through features such as dedicated meeting spaces (such as coffee areas) that mimic real-world environments. The authors conducted an initial study to ascertain the acceptance of the system as a collaborative learning tool and the results suggest that with a few exceptions, users are receptive to the use of such systems for learning. On-site exploration of heritage sites using mobile technology has also been largely discussed in the public domain. A Virtual Time Window (VTW) which facilitates on-site exploration of heritage sites using an open source virtual reality server and a mobile (tablet) client viewer is introduced in [11], [12] introduces a location-aware, Augmented Reality (AR) mobile application for exploration of a historical street, [13] discusses the use of a "serious game" for heritage learning during museum visits, and the use of Google Cardboard [18] to facilitate an on-site comparison of the past and present states of St Andrews Cathedral, armed with location-awareness and audio narratives was discussed in [2].

The concept of experiential learning has also been facilitated by virtual reality systems, for instance, [15] leverage immersive, game-based virtual reality systems to simulate the experience of archaeological excavations so as to foster a better understanding of the process, and the application of game-like methodologies to the learning process in this system is presented in [14]. The application of virtual reality for learning has also been investigated from a pedagogical standpoint. [16] investigate learners' attitudes towards virtual reality learning environments. The authors conclude that appropriate teaching practices should be taken into consideration in the development of virtual reality learning environments, and suggest that the effectiveness of using virtual reality for learning should be further explored. This is the motivation for this study.

Fig. 2. St Andrews Cathedral Cloister: 1318 (left) and today (right)

2 Study: A Comparative Analysis of VR Systems

The systems used for the study were built using several tools and frameworks. 3D modelling software was used in the reconstruction of St Andrews Cathedral, while game engines and open-source libraries were used to deploy it to mobile platforms and to interconnect the components. Open Simulator (OpenSim), an open-source virtual environment was used to develop the 3D model of St Andrews Cathedral [1]. For the game engines, a few alternatives were explored. Unity3D (versions 4 and 5) [20] and Unreal Engine 4 [21] were chosen and both engines were used to develop two versions of the mobile system. The system built using the Unity 3D (version 4) was ultimately chosen for the study owing to better performance on the mobile platforms.

The system architecture employed for the mobile platforms is shown in Fig. 3. The system takes advantage of inbuilt features of commodity smartphones. The multimedia resources (images, audio and video) are stored on the device's storage, the gyroscope is used for head-tracking to provide a 360° view of the environment, the GPS is used for location-awareness and the screen provides touch input into and visual output from the system. Four system set-ups were implemented: Samsung Gear VR (SG, Fig. 4b), Google Cardboard (GC, Fig. 4a), Oculus Rift and Xbox controller (OX) as well as screen, mouse and keyboard with Xbox controller (SX).

The Samsung Gear VR and Google Cardboard facilitated discrete exploration of the Cathedral from distinct viewpoints. These systems featured ten locations, obtained from the 3D reconstruction of St Andrews Cathedral (see [1]), linked together to form a trail. The locations were made out of spherical panoramas (Fig. 5a, b), as described

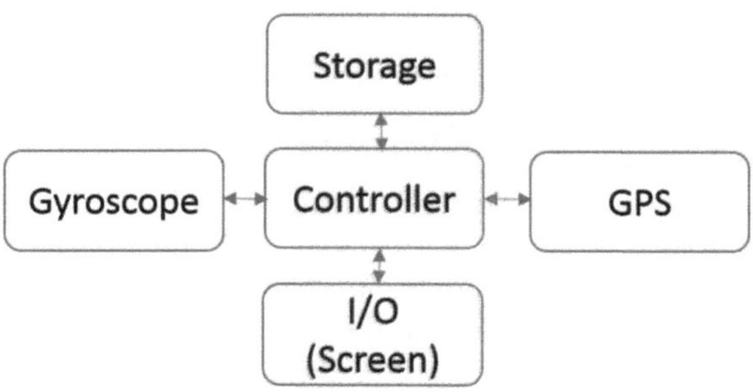

Fig. 3. System architecture

Fig. 4. Mobile VR Headsets: Google Cardboard [18] & Samsung Gear VR [19]

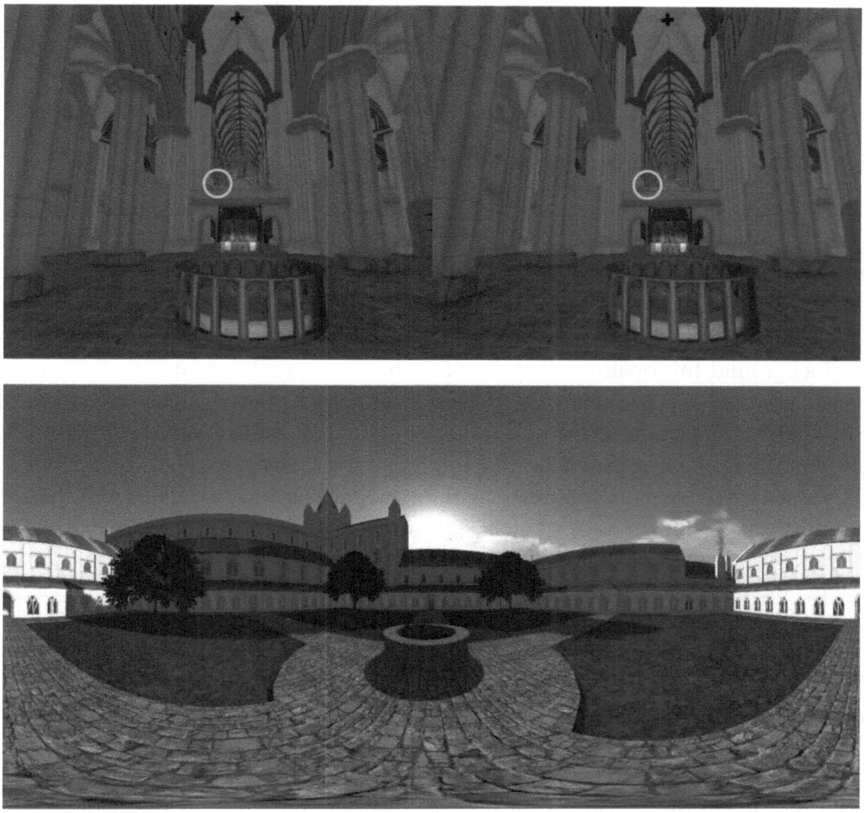

Fig. 5. Reconstruction of the Nave and projection of Cloister

in [2]. Audio narratives were associated with each location to serve as tour guides and additional content for the user. A significant difference between the Samsung Gear VR and the Google Cardboard systems was the navigation technique, i.e. the mechanism for moving from one location to another. On the Google Cardboard, navigation was hands-free by means of hotspots which are triggered when they overlap with a central crosshair for a few seconds. On the Samsung Gear VR, navigation took the form of a hands-on approach facilitated by a touch-pad on the side of the headset.

In contrast, the use of the Xbox controller with the Oculus Rift and the computer screen facilitated continuous exploration of the Cathedral. With these systems, the subjects had the freedom to explore the 3D model with an avatar that can walk, run and fly around the 3D space. Subjects had the option to see the Cathedral from different perspectives and viewpoints, as they could toggle between a first-person view and a third-person view. It is important to note that although the mobile systems restricted subjects' exploration to distinct viewpoints, their mobile nature allowed for on-site exploration, such that subjects could walk around the (remains of the) actual site of the Cathedral while viewing the virtual reconstruction from equivalent vantage points. This would not have been possible with the screen and/or Oculus Rift tethered to a computer, as the size and power requirements confine its usage to specific (usually indoor) locations. The distinction between the different set-ups made for an interesting comparison of the benefits and limitations of each, as discussed in the sections that follow.

2.1 Method: Data Collection and Feedback

The four systems were set up in the library of a local school for a week, and cohorts of first year pupils were invited to explore St Andrews Cathedral using the systems. Each cohort comprised of up to 30 pupils and they were further divided into groups of 5, each of which took turns in exploring the four systems. Data collection was by means of questionnaires and observation, with both quantitative and qualitative data collected.

"Background Information" (See Table 1) for each pupil was recorded. Each pupil then had up to 10 min to explore the cathedral using each system, after which they filled the "Experience" section of the questionnaire shown in Table 2 on a five-point Likert scale describing their experiences enabling qualitative analysis. The averages of subjects' responses to each questionnaire item for each set-up was calculated and charted in order to observe a holistic view of the responses. For each questionnaire item, a one-way Analysis of Variance (ANOVA) was conducted across the four set-ups to determine whether there was a statistically-significant difference in the means. A statistically-significant difference would suggest that the subjects felt differently about the set-ups for a particular questionnaire item, while the absence of a statistically-significant difference would suggest otherwise. For cases where a statistically-significant difference was observed, a t-Test (Two-Sample assuming unequal variances) was conducted with set-up pairs (i.e. SG and GC, SG and SX, GC and SX, and so on) to determine which pairs have means with statistically-significant differences. In order to determine the impact that the systems had on the subjects, correlation was conducted between the subjects' responses to some of the User Experience Items and Background Information; the rationale for this is explained further in Sects. 2.2 and 3.

The questionnaire also provided spaces for the pupils to provide three words describing their experience and to suggest what aspects of the experience could be improved on. In addition to these, the pertinent actions and spoken words of participants as observed by the researchers were noted. These data were collected for qualitative analyses (see Sect. 3). Specifically, the three words requested from each of the participants were used to form a tag cloud and a frequency analysis was conducted to observe the most occurring words in the sequence, which would provide a holistic representation of the user experience. Similarly, the pupils' responses to what aspects of the experiences could be improved on, in conjunction with their actions and spoken words while using the system, were analysed to observe recurring patterns. These are discussed in Sect. 3.

2.2 Hypotheses: Statistical Tests and Inferences

The following hypotheses were proposed for the study:

H_0: *The headset-based set-up will stimulate more interest in learning history than the screen-based set-up*. This will be verified by analysing the means of subjects' responses to Item 4 across the Samsung Gear VR, Google Cardboard (headset-based set-ups) and the Screen and Xbox Controller. A One-way Analysis of Variance (ANOVA) will be conducted to determine whether there are statistically-significant differences between the means of the set-ups and if there are, a t-Test (Two-Sample assuming unequal variances) on pairs of the means of SG and SX, and GC and SX will be conducted. A statistically-significant difference between the means would suggest a difference in the levels of stimulation provided by the set-ups and in such a case, a comparison of the means would reveal which set-ups stimulate more interest in the subjects.

H_1: *The headset-based set-up will provide more immersion than the screen-based set-up*. This will be verified by analysing the means of subjects' responses to Item 5 across the Samsung Gear VR, Google Cardboard (headset-based set-ups) and the Screen and Xbox Controller. A One-way ANOVA will be conducted to determine whether there are statistically-significant differences between the means of the set-ups and if there are, a t-Test (Two-Sample assuming unequal variances) on pairs of the means of SG and SX, and GC and SX will be conducted. A statistically-significant difference between the means would suggest a difference in the level of immersion provided by the set-ups and in such a case, a comparison of the means would reveal which set-ups provide more immersion than others.

H_2: *Virtual Reality is easy to use regardless of prior experience*. This will be verified by correlating subjects' previous experience with Virtual Reality (Background Item 4) with subjects' perceived ease of use of the system (Item 1). The absence of a strong positive correlation between Background Item 4 and Item 1 will suggest that there is no relationship between subjects' prior experience with virtual reality and subjects' perceived ease of use. This, coupled with high mean scores for subjects' responses to Item 1 would suggest that virtual reality is easy to use regardless of prior experience.

Table 1. Subject Background Information (ranked on a three-point Likert scale)

Background Information 1 - How good are your English skills?
Background Information 2 - How good are your IT skills?
Background Information 3 - How interested are you in History?
Background Information 4 - Do you have previous experience with Virtual Reality (VR)?
Background Information 5 - Do you have previous experience with VR Headsets?

Table 2. User Experience Items (ranked on a five-point Likert scale)

Item 1 (Easy to use) - I think that this system is easy to use
Item 2 (Would recommend) - I would recommend this system for learning history
Item 3 (Changed perception) - This system has changed how I think about the Cathedral
Item 4 (Stimulated interest) - I am now more interested in learning about local history
Item 5 (Immersion) - I felt like I was there in the virtual environment

3 Analyses, Results and Discussions

The data collected was analysed using a combination of qualitative and quantitative techniques. Qualitative techniques took the form of a word analysis on the subjects' feedback and observations of their actions while statistical techniques such as a One-way Analysis of Variance (ANOVA), t-tests and correlation were used to analyse the quantitative data.

Qualitative Data Analysis. A tag cloud was created to visualise the most common words used by the pupils to describe their experiences. A frequency analysis of the tag cloud (shown in Fig. 6) revealed that the top twelve (12) words were "fun", "interesting", "cool", "amazing", "good", "realistic", "awesome", "exciting", "educational", "real", "weird" and "different". Each word was placed in one of three categories depending on whether the experience described by the word was positive, negative or neutral. Negative words (such as weird, scary, uncontrollable) and neutral words (such as different, tricky) combined accounted for ≈ 6 % of the total words while ≈ 94 % of the words were positive. Table 3 shows the result of a frequency analysis carried out on the words the subjects used to describe their experience. The observations made during the study are described in the following section.

Fig. 6. Tag cloud visualising words participants used to describe their experiences

Table 3. Frequency analysis of subjects' descriptive words

Position	Word	Frequency	Percentage	Category
1	Fun	44	10.45	Positive
2	Interesting	38	9.03	Positive
3	Cool	33	7.84	Positive
4	Amazing	23	5.46	Positive
5	Good	17	4.04	Positive
6	Realistic	13	3.09	Positive
7	Awesome	10	2.38	Positive
7	Exciting	10	2.38	Positive
9	Educational	9	2.14	Positive
10	Real	8	1.90	Positive
10	Weird	8	1.90	Negative
10	Different	8	1.90	Neutral

Observations. The shape, size and physical features of VR headsets can contribute to and/or inhibit user experience. For instance, the Samsung Gear VR is designed to shut off the display and audio when there is no proximity sensor reading i.e. when the headset is not being worn. As the study subjects were pre-teen children, the size of the Gear VR meant that it was too big for the heads of some of them (even after fastening the strap as tight as possible) and this caused the headset to lose contact with their faces and by extension lose contact with the proximity sensor, often resulting in a break in transmission.

Cues (such as eye level) in the virtual environment play a part in the user experience. It was observed that the eye levels in the virtual scenes did not align with the eye levels of the subjects. This is because the virtual scenes were taken at the eye level of an average male, which is higher than the eye level of the pre-teen subjects. Some of the subjects expressed perceived dissonance as a result of this, while others did not report any such symptoms. A subject also reported the strange feeling of being "there [in the virtual world] but not there", as they felt like they were in the virtual environment but knew that they were seated in a chair in the real world.

In addition to visual cues, audio cues can play a big role in the user experience. During the study a subject was observed trying to put the headset (Google Cardboard) close to their ear, and by implication taking the headset away from their face, perhaps to hear the audio narrative. This could suggest that the subject wished for louder audio and needed the narrative to bolster the experience. In attempting to improve the audible experience (by hearing louder audio), the subjects inadvertently broke the visual experience. This may not have been the case if the audio was loud enough for them, but as it wasn't, they were willing to sacrifice the visual experience for the audible one. This could suggest that the audio is just as (or perhaps more) important than the visuals in virtual reality.

It was observed that the subjects expressed themselves more when they used the device with other subjects present; and they were quieter when they used the device alone. Subjects were also observed asking each other where they were on the tour, as if to suggest that they wanted to be at the same places at the same time. This could affirm the case for social exploration of heritage sites [17].

The interaction paradigm plays a role in the user experience. A subject was observed trying to lean forward and backward to zoom in and out respectively. This suggests that the immersive experience provided by the system caused the subject to assume that by leaning forward in real-life, their view in the virtual environment would become closer. For this reason, a "lean-to-zoom" feature (where a user leans forward or backward to zoom in or out respectively) could be valuable (and intuitive) in the use of virtual reality headset systems. Such a feature is currently being developed for use in a future release of the system with a view to investigate the level of usefulness and intuitiveness. Also, it was observed that swivel chairs facilitate better exploration of 360° environments while seated, because they provide the ability to completely rotate around a fixed axis as compared to non-swivel chairs. This is not an issue while exploring 360° environments while standing; however, standing poses an increased risk of injury (by falling or bumping into walls or objects for example).

Virtual reality can be a valuable tool for learning (as proven by H_0 in Sect. 3), but this may not always be the case. It was observed that for some subjects, the fun factor of the system detracted from the learning objective. This could suggest that there may be some conditions – configurations, content, scenarios and so on – under which a virtual reality system could be an effective learning tool, and others under which it would not be ideal for learning. This warrants further investigation.

User inclinations and preferences can determine the nature of the experience. For instance, it was observed a few subjects refrained from properly fastening the headset strap over their heads. The experiences of said subjects were limited, as their hands were occupied with holding up the device on their faces, and this occasionally resulted in shaky movements that led to a loss of contact with the proximity sensor which resulted in a break in transmission. This suggests that users' inclinations (such as vanity, timidity, fear and so on) can get in the way of effective device usage and consequently inhibit the experience.

Some statements uttered by the subjects while interacting with the system are highlighted below: *"Like a big, massive cinema screen" "Nice shadows"* – referring to the realistic nature of the digital model viewed in the display *"I hear people but I don't see them" "I like this world better than the world we are in" "It's weird and really sickening" "Don't look at this if you're scared of heights"* – referring to scenes with significantly raised eye levels *"It's a shame you can't walk about yourself" "Ooh... scary"* – said with excitement *"This virtual life is really confusing"*.

Quantitative Data Analysis. The mean scores and a one-way ANOVA test were carried out on the data. A snapshot of the data collected is shown in Fig. 7. The feedback to each questionnaire item was ranked on a five-point Likert scale, where 1 (strongly disagree) and 2 (probably disagree) represent negative feedback, 3 (neither agree nor disagree) represents neutral feedback, and 4 (probably agree) and 5 (strongly agree) represent positive feedback. As shown in Fig. 7, the means of all four set-ups for Item 1 are positive (i.e. above neutral or greater than 3). However, a One-way (ANOVA) of subjects' responses to Item 1 for the four set-ups revealed that there is no

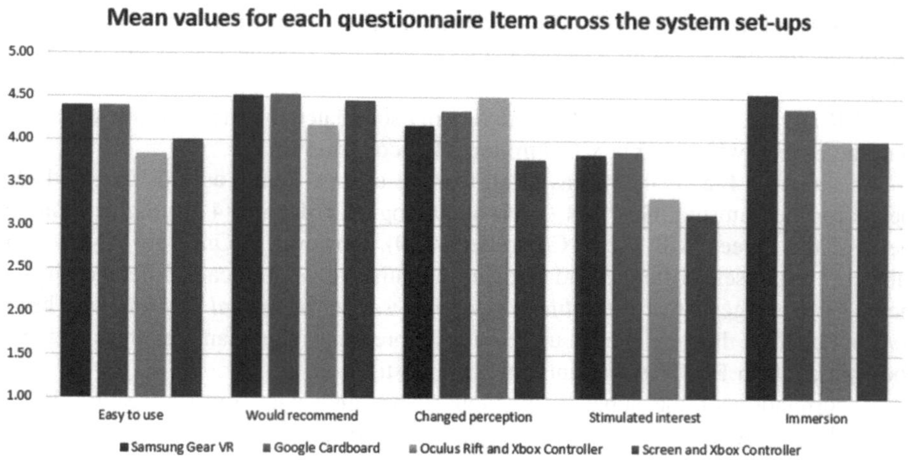

Fig. 7. Mean values for each questionnaire Item across the system set-ups

statistically-significant difference in the means. This suggests that subjects felt that the four *virtual reality systems are easy to use*, but no one set-up is significantly easier to use than others.

As shown in Fig. 7, the means of all four set-ups for Item 2 are positive. However, a One-way ANOVA of subjects' responses to Item 2 revealed that there is no statistically-significant difference in the means. This suggests that the *subjects would recommend virtual reality as a tool for learning history;* this is in line with previous work [7, 12, 13] and for learning in general [8, 9]. However, the lack of a statistically-significant difference in the means suggests that the subjects would not necessarily recommend one type of the four virtual reality set-ups over another for learning history.

As shown in Fig. 7, the means of all four set-ups for Item 3 are positive. However, a One-way ANOVA of subjects' responses to Item 3 revealed that there is no statistically-significant difference in the means. This suggests that the *subjects' views about St Andrews Cathedral were changed by the virtual reality systems*, but no one set-up influenced the subjects views of St Andrews Cathedral more than the others. This demonstrates the impact that virtual reality systems can have on users when deployed in a learning context.

For Item 4, it was observed that the means for all four set-ups are positive, which suggests that the *subjects' interests in learning history were stimulated by the systems.* A One-way ANOVA of subjects' responses revealed that there is a statistically-significant difference in the means, which suggests that some set-ups stimulated the subjects interests more than the others. Further tests to determine which means are different were conducted. A t-Test (Two-Sample assuming unequal variances) on pairs of the means revealed that there is a statistically-significant difference between the Samsung Gear VR and the Screen with Xbox Controller, and also between the Google

Cardboard and the Screen with Xbox Controller. This, coupled with the higher mean responses for the Samsung Gear VR (3.83) and the Google Cardboard (3.88) as compared to the Screen with Xbox Controller (3.14), suggests that the Samsung Gear VR and the Google Cardboard individually stimulated the subjects' interests more than the Screen with the Xbox Controller. This confirms H_0.

As shown in Fig. 7, the means of all four set-ups for Item 5 are positive, with the means for the Samsung Gear VR (4.54) and Google Cardboard (4.38) higher than the mean of the Screen with Xbox Controller (4.00). However, a One-way ANOVA of subjects' responses to Item 5 did not find a statistically-significant difference in the means. This suggests that the *subjects felt immersed in the virtual environment*, but it does not confirm that any one set-up provided more immersion than the others and thus does not confirm H_1. This warrants further investigation.

A correlation of the subjects' previous experience with Virtual Reality (Background Item 4) with subjects' perceived ease of use of the system (responses to Item 1 for all the set-ups) revealed a weak, positive correlation of 0.01. The weak correlation suggests that there is little relationship between prior experience with virtual reality and perceived ease of use of the system, hence the positive mean scores (4.40, 4.39, 3.83, and 4.00 on a 5-point scale for SG, GC, OX and SX respectively) recorded by the subjects for ease of use suggests that the system is easy to use regardless of prior experience and thus proves H_2.

4 Conclusion

The efficacy of virtual reality as a tool for learning history has been demonstrated in this work. Virtual reality has the potential to stimulate interest in a subject matter and present information in engaging and interactive ways. The findings of this study suggest that several factors can contribute to (or otherwise inhibit) the user experience. Visual and audio cues can enhance the experience, and other factors such as the device shape, size and interaction mechanism determine the nature of the user experience. Overall, given the appropriate conditions, virtual reality systems can be a suitable tool for learning history in early education. This study investigates three hypotheses – H_0, H_1 and H_2. The method used was a combination of quantitative and qualitative techniques (see Sect. 2.1) and the results (see Sect. 3) confirmed H_0, that *headset-based virtual reality systems stimulate young pupils' interest in learning history more than screen-based virtual reality systems*, and H_2, that *young children find virtual reality systems easy to use for learning regardless of prior experience*. Interestingly, the results did not confirm H_1, as although subjects reported higher levels of immersion with the Google Cardboard and Samsung Gear VR than with the screen and Xbox Controller (see Fig. 7), the ANOVA test did not find a statistically-significant difference in the means. One possible explanation for the similar levels of immersion provided is the nature of the exploration facilitated by the systems. The headset-based systems facilitated exploration of the Cathedral from pre-defined points of interest hence the subjects were confined to interacting with contents from distinct viewpoints, whereas the screen-based system provided more freedom to explore the grounds beneath (by walking around) and skies above (by flying over) the cathedral. Ideally, the

3D model of the Cathedral should have been deployed to the mobile headset-based systems for exploration, but this posed a technical challenge owing to the insufficient memory and processing power of the mobile phones used in the headset-based systems as compared to the PC used in the screen-based system. That said, there is a case to be made for the use of mobile devices in heritage learning, as they enable users to perform on-site exploration of heritage sites as compared to computer systems that restrict users to indoor (off-site) usage due to their size and power requirements. An informal expedition in which university students took part in an on-site tour of the Cathedral using the Google Cardboard yielded positive feedback, and this use case will be further explored in a future study. It is arguable that if the mobile headsets were equipped with the full 3D model of the Cathedral and the ability to explore the space in a continuous fashion, subjects would have reported significantly-higher levels of immersion in the virtual environment.

Acknowledgment. Special thanks to Madras College, Fife, UK.

References

1. Kennedy, S., Fawcett, R., Miller, A., Dow, L., Sweetman, R., Field, A., Campbell, A., Oliver, I., McCaffery, J., Allison, C.: Exploring canons and cathedrals with Open Virtual Worlds: The recreation of St Andrews Cathedral, St Andrews day, 1318. In: 2013 Digital Heritage International Congress, pp. 273–280, October 2013
2. Fabola, A., Miller, A., Fawcett, R.: Exploring the past with Google Cardboard. In: 2015 Digital Heritage International Congress (2015)
3. Milgram, P., Takemura, H., Utsumi, A.: Kishino, F: Mixed reality (MR) reality-virtuality (RV) continuum. Syst. Res. **2351**, 282–292 (1994). Telemanipulator and Telepresence Technologies
4. Bricken, M.: Virtual reality learning environments: potentials and challenges. ACM SIGGRAPH Comput. Graph. **25**(3), 178–184 (1991)
5. Mikropoulos, T.A., Natsis, A.: Educational virtual environments: a ten-year review of empirical research (1999–2009). Comput. Educ. **56**(3), 769–780 (2011)
6. Pan, Z., et al.: Virtual reality and mixed reality for virtual learning environments. Comput. Graph. **30**(1), 20–28 (2006)
7. Jacobson, J.: Ancient architecture in virtual reality; does visual immersion really aid learning? Ph.D. dissertation, University of Pittsburgh (2008)
8. McCaffery, J., Miller, A., Allison, C.: Extending the use of virtual worlds as an educational platform - network Island: an advanced learning environment for teaching internet routing algorithms. In: CSEDU, vol. 1, pp. 279–284 (2011)
9. Perera, I. et al.: Towards successful 3D virtual learning - a case study on teaching human computer interaction. In: International Conference for Internet Technology and Secured Transaction (ICITST), pp. 1–6 (2009)
10. Monahan, T., McArdle, G., Bertolotto, M.: Virtual reality for collaborative e-learning. Comput. Educ. **50**(4), 1339–1353 (2008)
11. Davies, C., Miller, A., Allison, C.: Mobile cross reality for cultural heritage. In: Digital Heritage International Congress (DigitalHeritage 2013), vol. 1, pp. 331–338 (2013)

12. Haugstvedt, A.C., Krogstie, J.: Mobile augmented reality for cultural heritage: a technology acceptance study. In: IEEE International Symposium on Mixed and Augmented Reality (ISMAR), pp. 247–255 (2012)
13. Coenen, T., Mostmans, L., and Naessens, K.: MuseUs: case study of a pervasive cultural heritage serious game. J. Comput. Cult. Heritage (JOCCH), **6**(2), 8:1–8:19 (2013)
14. Getchell, K., Oliver, I., Miller, A., Allison, C.: Metaverses as a platform for game based learning. In: Proceedings on the International Conference on Advanced Information Networking and Applications AINA, pp. 1195–1202 (2010)
15. Getchell, K., Miller, A., Nicoll, J.R., Sweetman, R.J., Allison, C.: Games methodologies and immersive environments for virtual fieldwork. IEEE Trans. Learn. Technol. **3**(4), 281–293 (2010)
16. Huang, H.M., Rauch, U., Liaw, S.S.: Investigating learners' attitudes toward virtual reality learning environments: based on a constructivist approach. Comput. Educ. **55**(3), 1171–1182 (2010)
17. Suh, Y., Shin, C., Woo, W.: A mobile phone guide: spatial, personal, and social experience for cultural heritage. IEEE Trans. Consum. Electron. **55**(4), 2356–2364 (2009)
18. Google: Google Cardboard. https://www.google.com/get/cardboard/. Accessed 14 Mar 2016
19. Samsung: Gear VR. http://www.samsung.com/global/galaxy/wearables/gear-vr/. Accessed 14 Mar 2016
20. Unity3D. https://unity3d.com/. Accessed 14 Mar 2016
21. Unreal Engine. https://www.unrealengine.com/. Accessed 14 Mar 2016

REVRLaw: An Immersive Way for Teaching Criminal Law Using Virtual Reality

Markos Mentzelopoulos[1(✉)], James Parrish[1], Paresh Kathrani[2], and Daphne Economou[1]

[1] Faculty of Science and Technology, University of Westminster, London, UK
{mentzem, j.parrish, d.economoul}@westminster.ac.uk
[2] Department of Law, University of Westminster, London, UK
p.kathrani@westminster.ac.uk

Abstract. Computer games have now been around for over three decades and the term serious games has been attributed to the use of computer games that are thought to have educational value. Game-based learning (GBL) has been applied in a number of different fields such as medicine, languages and software engineering. Furthermore, serious games can be a very effective as an instructional tool and can assist learning by providing an alternative way of presenting instructions and content on a supplementary level, and can promote student motivation and interest in subject matter resulting in enhanced learning effectiveness. REVRLaw (REal and Virtual Reality Law) is a research project that the departments of Law and Computer Science of Westminster University have proposed as a new framework in which law students can explore a real case scenario using Virtual Reality (VR) technology to discover important pieces of evidence from a real-given scenario and make up their mind over the crime case if this is a murder or not. REVRLaw integrates the immersion into VR as the perception of being physically present in a non-physical world. The paper presents the prototype game and the mechanics used to make students focus on the crime case and make the best use of this immersive learning approach.

Keywords: Educational games · Cognition · Interactive learning environments · Virtual environment · Head Up Display (H.U.D.)

1 Introduction

Although the name and the concept of virtual reality sound familiar, coming up with a precise answer is surprisingly hard, as even the casual inquiry into the matter opens a whole series of additional questions. However Craig et al. [6] rightly defines VR as *"a medium composed of interactive computer simulations…giving the feeling of being immersed…"*, while Zhuang and P. Wang expressed it better and finely as a high end Human-Machine Interface, that combine various technologies such as computer graphics, image processing, pattern recognition, artificial intelligence, networking, sound systems and others to produce computer simulation and interaction, which gives the feeling of being present through multiple synthetic feedback sent to sensorial channels like virtual, aural, haptic and others [7].

C. Allison et al. (Eds.): iLRN 2016, CCIS 621, pp. 73–84, 2016.
DOI: 10.1007/978-3-319-41769-1_6

Most educators agree that the interactive nature of e-learning and mobile technologies increase the teacher and student communication. But to date, learning on social media and other e-learning platforms has been a poor substitute for classroom learning. To address this issue a number of academic institutions have introduced *blended* [8] and *flipped* [9] learning strategies. In the former classroom strategy, students learn through a "blended" model of in-person (with a teacher) and technology-based instruction with some student control over time, place path and/or pace of the curriculum. In a flipped classroom model, students gain the necessary knowledge before class, typically through the use of educational technology such as online videos, and during class time they explore that knowledge in greater depth through various methods including discussions, project-based learning and laboratory experiments guided by a teacher.

In an effort to motivate and engage students in these new "hybrid" environments, instructors have recently started introducing game-based learning experiences as part of the learning process in the classroom as well as part of the online instructional materials. The incorporation of game elements in non-game contexts is widely referred to as "gamification" [4]. Gamification is being increasingly recognized as the process/technique of extracting motivating and engaging elements found in games and applying them to real-world productive or educational activities [1]. The successful incorporation of gamification particularly in educational context is challenging. One of the trivial aspects behind virtual learning environments is to establish what motivates users, optimizes their feelings and engage them in the actual scenario. This process is what is called User-Cantered Design (UCD) [4].

Virtual reality can be used to support gamification learning purpose as it tries to alter a person's perception of reality by tricking the senses and providing artificial computer-generated stimuli [2]. The ultimate goal of VR is to create a perfect illusion, an artificial experience so realistic that it is practically indistinguishable of the real thing. It is, however, a somewhat utopian endeavor. On the other hand, tricking human senses is much harder than tricking the mind. Human's mind is good at abstract thinking and ready to accept some degree of inconsistences. It is capable of *"filling in the Blanks"* left by the missing or malformed information. As human senses, however, are attuned to distinguishing minute differences a complete illusion is not even necessary. An easier, more achievable goal is creating a believable experience by providing the sort of artificial stimuli that are just good enough to prompt the mind to complete his own illusion. *This can be achieved by* multimodality interactivity.

Multimodality implies the usage of more than one mode of behavior or action. In the case of immersion in a virtual environment, this means engaging more than one human sense. Our perception of reality and sense of presence is always multimodal. Our senses do not operate independently. A multimodal approach can enhance the feeling of immersion as various artificial stimuli can serve to complement each other.

However, despite the increased number of systems featuring intelligent agents, in various learning domains, and despite the immersiveness of interactive technologies there are limited developments that have incorporate VR as part of teaching [3]. In this paper the game presented is a simulation of a tutorial that teaches the 'Law of murder' modified form the original book-learning approach into a VR interactive game. Students are presented with a case, they are asked to apply the law and decide if this is a murder or not. During the game the main principle of 'learning by doing' is applied. One of the objectives of the game is to make students to focus on the topic and make the best use of the 'learning momentum' using appropriate set of evidence.

The selection of a law-establish VR game is because of the interactivity in a murder case scenario, the atmospheric view and the multimodal interactivity with Intelligent Agents (also known as NPC's – Non Playable Characters) which adds some high complexity in the game scenario. Previous games that tried to use crime investigation as part of their theme were quite successful. *"Criminel"* is an IOS game for iPads by 4PM, a small indie company [16]. The similarity with the proposed project is that the player needs to be observant to notice all the key information and be able to put them together to come to a conclusion as to what really happened. *"Murdered: Soul Suspect"* [17], a 3rd person game requires to place together evidence to find out who their own murder is. One of the interesting points is the way hints are displayed to direct the player to the evidence due to the floating text. On the other hand, *"L.A. Noire"* [18] is a story driven open world detective game which mostly revolves around interrogating suspects and following up on leads. The dialog conversation with an intelligent agent is one of the strongest points for the game as the player needs to establish the validity of peoples statements before making a decision on what they believe happened as well as the examining of evidence via close up inspection.

In Sect. 2 of this paper we present the REVRLaw game design scenario. Section 3 includes key-game mechanic elements based on heuristic research that are essential for this VR game scenario. In Sect. 4 there is an evaluation of the prototype focusing on the user interface and gamified elements following by the conclusion with directions for further extension to address user experience feedback form the law students, as well as directions for further development of the framework.

2 Game Design

REVRLaw game has been designed following a UCD process, aiming to address specific educational requirements in Higher Education for Westminster Law School at the University of Westminster, who will use the simulation as teaching and learning tool. The project is based on a VR multimodal interaction, which includes collectable items and interaction with NPC's to obtain verbal information.

In Law school instructors give students either a problem question to gauge their ability to apply the law to a fictitious case to advise a client; or an essay question to look at their critical reasoning skills. The above is a typical problem question. Students have to read the facts/information to spot the relevant offence (in this case murder). They then have to research the source, definition and elements of that offence, with a view to applying it to the facts and concluding by advising a client. It generally resonates with the following Criminal Law module aims as validated:

- Identify the theories and concepts that underpin the theoretical framework of Criminal Law and stress competing perspectives
- Develop the ability to identify issues in terms of policy and place the Criminal Law in its wider context

- Increase understanding of the nature of judicial reasoning and legal argument
- Enable students to analyze fundamental offences and defenses that form the core of Criminal Law and appreciate the wider contextual dimension of the subject
- Enable students to apply a wide range of research skills, particularly of sources of law and academic materials, and develop effective writing skills with limited supervision.

Murder is a core offence on the Criminal Law module that is taught in the first semester. As part of a tutorial, they answer a problem and/or essay question on it with a view to putting into practice the above aims. Traditionally, for problem questions, they present them with a set of written facts similar to the above and they have to advise a client. This is one place where Oculus Rift CSI will fit in: in supplementing the traditional, written problem questions as a means of analyzing information and the law to advise a client.

Players have to adopt the standpoint of a police officer who has been called out to the office complex upon hearing someone who has been killed. The actor will arrive in the crime scene (Fig. 1) and see the victim laying in a pool of blood. The player will then have to research/know the law of murder and take a walk around the scenario and identify items that are collectable and valuable to the case in order to obtain information, like the life insurance, letters etc. – and also speak to other NPC 's– in order to put together an evidential picture. Once they have this, then they can analyze it to assess to what limit Robert (the accused Avatar) has the *"Actus Reus of murder"* (AR) and the internal state of *"Mind Element"* (MR) of murder – and decide whether to charge him for murder. That is what the student must analyze/fine out. The extents to which all the clues/evidence that have been built in to the scenario show that Robert has the AR and MR of murder. Figure 2 is a Use-Case diagram for the player-avatar with all possible multimodal interactions and the sequence of events that need to follow to release specific hidden codex's to obtain further vital information.

Fig. 1. A screenshot from the game scenario. On the left the crime building and on the right the victim. For supporting player, we use collectible appearance.

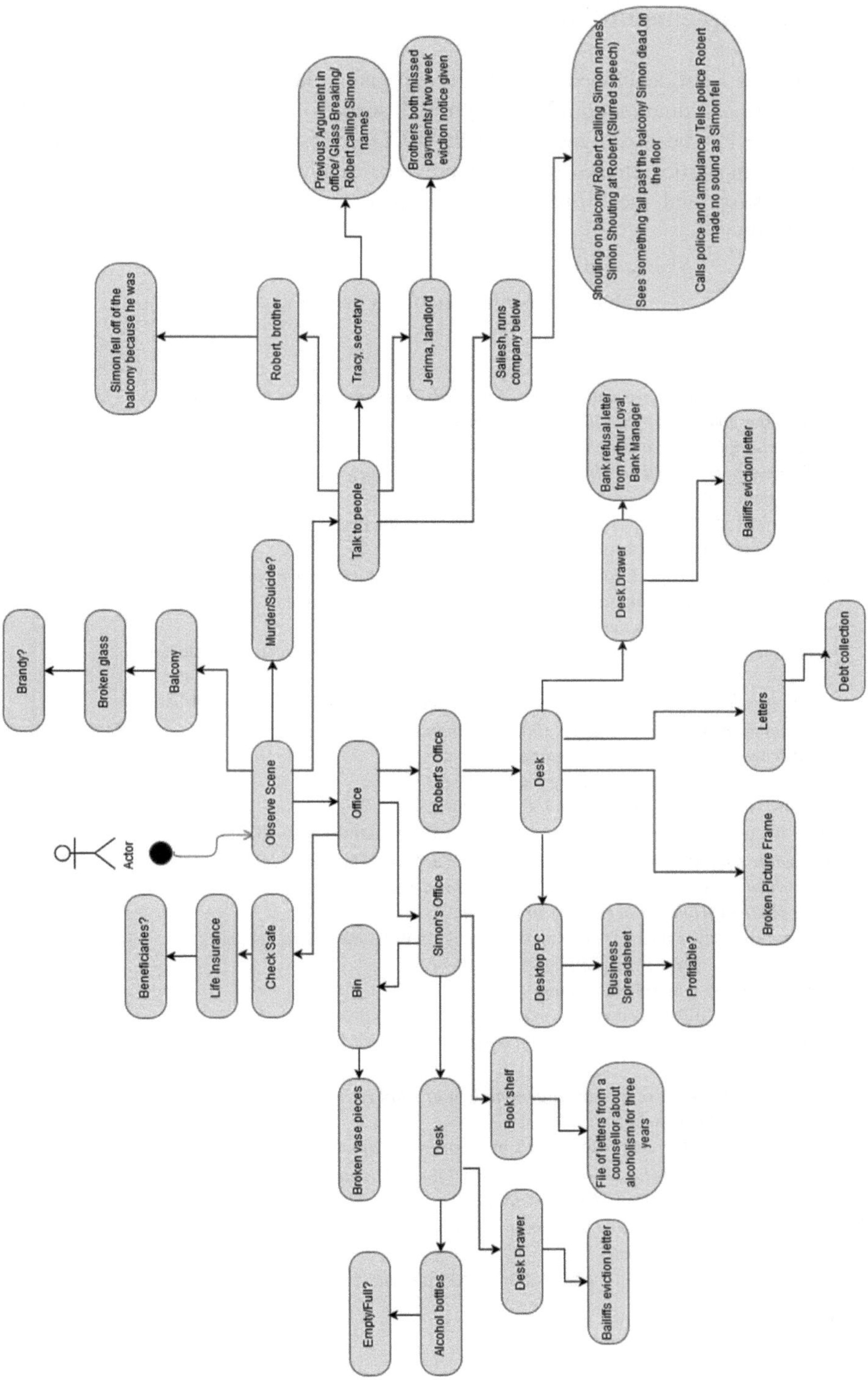

Fig. 2. User activity diagram – event sequence and codex release

3 Level Implementation

The game has been developed using Unity 3D game platform coupled with 3DSMax and ICT Virtual Human toolkits to design both scenario elements and Virtual Agents. As the game has been designed using the UCD philosophy we tried to incorporate video game heuristics chosen based on previous qualitative reviews [5], concerning game/play story and the virtual interface. Some key-heuristics are summarized in Table 1 below:

Table 1. Heuristics summary for REVLAW

No	Heuristic	Reference source
1	***The player should be presented with "clear goals" early enough or be able to create her own goals and "should be able to understand and identify them". There can be "multiple goals on each level", so that there are more strategies to win. Furthermore, the player should know how to reach the goal without getting stuck.*** – The game will start with a briefing by a police officer. – Hints will appear near certain objects to show what the player should be thinking e.g. "I wonder what is in that safe".	[11–14]
2	***The player should "feel that they have control over the character" and that they have "impact over the game world". They should also be able to "respond to threats and opportunities".*** – The player can choose what evidence to rely on and which to discard as irrelevant – Fig. 4 – The player will be able to choose their own approach to gathering the information.	[10–12, 14]
3	***The storyline should be "meaningful" and support the game play and be "discovered" throughout the game.*** – The scenario will be devised by the End User – There will be a lot going on and a lot to uncover. – As the player uncovers elements the player will see flashback to what happened.	[12, 14]
4	***The game should be responsive to the player's actions. There should be consistency between the game elements, settings and story. It should "suspend disbelief" and be planned from the beginning to the end.*** – When the player interacts with an object there will be immediate feedback. – The scenario will be realistic. – There will be atmospheric sounds. – The dialog will be planned and mapped out. – Once the player has marked a certain number of evidence as key they will be invited to make a decision	[10, 12, 14]
5	***The player should have a clear understanding of what is going on and be given the room to make mistakes.*** – The player has the choice to make a piece of evidence key or not – Fig. 4	[11]
6	***There should be varying degrees of difficulty" for a "greater challenge". The game should be "easy to learn but hard to master.*** – Once the player has started uncovering evidence it will become harder and harder to find all the last little bits. – It is not essential to find them all, they need only find enough	[10, 12, 13]

(*Continued*)

Table 1. (*Continued*)

No	Heuristic	Reference source
7	***The artificial intelligence should be reasonable" and "visible to the player, consistent with the player's expectations" while remaining unpredictable.*** – NPC's will have a set routine and will act mainly as background characters – Fig. 3 – During the dialog, NPCs will have different reactions based on what you say forming a basic level of AI using if statements and some randomization – Fig. 3.	[10, 12, 13, 15]
8	***The player should be able to identify game elements such as avatars, enemies, obstacles, power-ups, threats or opportunities.*** – As the player approaches an avatar they will be prompted to talk to them – Fig. 3 – When the player looks at an item they will be prompted to interact with it – Fig. 1	[10, 11, 14]
9	***The interface should be as non-intrusive as possible. It should be consistent in control, color, and typography and dialog design.*** – There will be no HUD – A 3D interface will appear in the form of a hologram when the player accesses their inventory.	[11–13]
10	***The player should be rewarded with positive feedback to get the game moving without any delay in understanding.*** – The police officers in the game will be positive in their responses to your findings. – The player will reward themselves through discoveries and understanding.	[12]
11	***Input methods should have the appropriate level of sensitivity and responsiveness*** – The Oculus Rift and Controller will be balanced together to get the right range of motion as the player turns.	[10–12]

Fig. 3. Interaction with NPC in the game – server room.

Fig. 4. Interaction with collectible items. As part of storing data through the investigation and re-examine them we use an iteration mode. The focused (middle) reminds to the user the information obtains. At the same moment the user can transverse using the pad left and right option to release previous collectible information for re-investigation based on new retrieved facts.

4 Experiment and Data

The above described game was developed for the "Criminal Law" module, at the Unversity of Westminster, that is attended by over 300 students. A proper testing will be designed for these students and is expected to take place in September-October 2016. Up to spring 2015, an evaluation has been completed from computer games students prior to the release to the law department, to ensure that main development mechanical issues can be identified and addressed before the end-user evaluation experience from the law department.

4.1 Evaluation Procedure and Apparatus

The pilot evaluation of the platform was carried out with 16 subjects (10 undergraduate students and 6 member of staff) with only 50 % having previous experience using Oculus Rift. The study took place at the University of Westminster, London premises and each participant was tested individually. Each session lasted for approximately 20 to 30 min. The participants had to use each system for 10 min and then answer a short questionnaire. The questionnaire consisted of 20 questions in total. All the questions were multiple choices on a Likert scale of one to five (one being the least favourable answer and the five the most favourable answer). The evaluation focused on usability issues, system capabilities and system learning. All participants used the same apparatus (Fig. 5).

Fig. 5. 3rd person screenshot from the primary investigation scene

4.2 Results

Seven questions were targeted in assessing the general usability of the UIs and scenario playability and to identify potential bugs issues. The results revealed a very positive assessment regarding the usability of the UIs (Table 2 questions 1–7). Participants found that using the VR system generally was easy to use, not very complex and they considered that they did not need to learn many things before starting to use it and adapt to its atmospheric world view. They found it consistent and not cumbersome and that they did not need any technical assistance. Additionally they felt very confident in using the UI and they were willing to use it frequently. Overall they had a pleasant experience using VR with the Xbox pad.

The next part of the evaluation focused on the systems' capabilities (Table 2, questions 8–11). The aim was to test the systems' speed and reliability along with other technical characteristics a VR is a very expensive tool to process in real time and needs high specification PC's and good quality graphic cards. The results were again very positive along the scale regarding the speed and the reliability with a small discrepancy over the user feedback on the click-events as part of collision-noise due to precision – for the project we used the standard bounding box and sphere functions that Unity engine has rather than creating more systematic approach, but with the possibility of speed cost.

The last part of the evaluation focused on aspects related to learning the UIs learning capability (Table 2, questions 12 & 13). Participants felt that they could easily explore the environment and therefore get to know more the rooms and possible do more object interactivity, and become familiarize with the VR concept. A very

Table 2. User interface (UI) usability, capability & learning scale results based on likert scale obtain from 16 users.

System/UI usability	Average likert scale	UI capabilities	Average likert scale
(1) I found the UI unnecessarily complex	1.3	(8) UI Speed	4.4
(2) I thought the UI was easy to use	4.2	(9) UI reliability	4.1
(3) I think that I would need the support of a technical person to be able to use this UI	1.8	(10) UI tends to be noisy	3.6
(4) I found the various functions in the UI well integrated	4.8	(11) Designed for all level of users	4.1
(5) I would imagine that most people would learn to use this UI very quickly	4.1		
(6) I felt very confident using the UI	3.4	**UI learning**	**Average likert scale**
(7) I need to learn a lot of things before I could get going with this UI	3.4	(12) Exploring new features by trial and error	4.2
		(13) Messages on the screen	4.8

interesting aspect of the testing was the messages on the screen. The participants felt that they were extremely helpful as well as their presentation style.

5 Conclusions

In this paper we presented the initial step over the development of a serious game simulating platform based on a real crime scenario to support educational purposes for the law department of Westminster University using Virtual Reality - REVRLaw. We analyzed the game using a number of evaluators targeting in first stage the usability of the game features, both form mechanics and hardware perspective. The usability evaluation of the UIs revealed some very positive results. Participants in general found the system very easy to use, not complicated and they thought they were consistent and did not require a lot of effort to be learned. However, the majority of the participants had prior experience of such UIs and that had also affected their perceptions. Furthermore, they found the technical capabilities of the UIs very acceptable and the demands for learning the system very easy.

The experimental process indicated that future work should be focusing on three main steps. Firstly, the system performance will be evaluated from the law students to obtain an end-user experience based on the quality of information they will be able to understand and use, as well as compare it with their current learning curve of using standard books to evaluate the crime case. This will help us identify potential logical errors/missing to match the teaching criteria and update the game. The second step will be to integrate latest human computer interaction hardware like PrioVR, STEM or Kinect 2 to provide greater accessibility to the player and then to evaluate the effectiveness of the varieties of these immersive environments with the new control systems against traditional GUI interface and other PUI interfaces. The final stage will be to expand the game into a proper framework by creating further hypothetical scenarios for different level of law scenarios.

References

1. Hoover, L.: The 2011 Horizon report: challenges and innovation in classroom: conference report. J. Electron. Resour. Librarianship **24**(1), 55–57 (2011)
2. Zyda, M.: From visual simulation to virtual reality to games. IEEE Comput. **38**, 25–32 (2005)
3. Bogdanovych, A., Ijaz, K., Simoff, S.: The city of Uruk: teaching ancient history in a virtual world. In: Nakano, Y., Neff, M., Paiva, A., Walker, M. (eds.) IVA 2012. LNCS, vol. 7502, pp. 28–35. Springer, Heidelberg (2012)
4. Economou, D., Doumanis, I., Bouki, V., Pedersen, F., Kathrani, P., Mentzelopoulos, M., Georgalas, N.: A dynamic role-playing platform for simulations in legal and political education. In: Proceedings of the IMCL 2014 International Conference on Interactive Mobile Communication Technologies and Learning, 13–14 November 2014, pp. 232–236. IEEE, Thessaloniki (2014)
5. Koeffel, C., Hochleitner, W., Leitner, J., Haller, M., Geven, A., Tscheligi, M.: Using heuristics to evaluate the overall user experience of video games and advanced interaction games. In: Bernhaupt, R. (ed.) Evaluating User Experience in Games. Human-Computer Interaction Series, pp. 233–256. Springer, Heidelberg (2010)
6. Craig, A.B., William, R.S., Jeffrey, D.W.: Developing Virtual Reality Applications: Foundations of Effective Design. Morgan Kaufmann Publishers, Burlington (2009)
7. Zhuang, C.H., Wang, P.: Virtual Reality Technology and Applications. Publishing House of Electronics Industry Beijing, Beijing (2010). (in Chinese)
8. Staker, H., Horn, B.M.: Classifying K-12 Blended Learning (2012). http://goo.gl/PqExzZ. Accessed 12 May 2015
9. Bilton, J., Esher High School: Motivation and cognitive load in the flipped classroom: definition, rationale and a call for research. High. Educ. Res. Dev. ahead-of-print **34,** 1–14 (2014)
10. Pinelle, D., Wong, N., Stach, T.: Heuristic evaluation for games: usability principles for videogame design. In: Proceeding of the Twenty-Sixth Annual SIGCHI Conference on Human Factors in Computing Systems, CHI 2008, Florence, Italy, 05–10 April 2008, pp. 1453–1462. ACM, New York (2008)
11. Schaffer, N.: Heuristics for usability in games. Technical report, Rensselaer Polytechnic Institute (2007). http://friendlymedia.sbrl.rpi.edu/heuristics.pdf. Accessed 07 Dec 2008
12. Desurvire, H., Caplan, M., Toth, J.A.: Using heuristics to evaluate the playability of games. In: CHI 2004 Extended Abstracts on Human Factors in Computing Systems, CHI 2004, Vienna, Austria, 24–29 April 2004, pp. 1509–1512. ACM, New York (2004)
13. Federoff, M.A.: Heuristics and usability guidelines for the creation and evaluation of fun in videogames. Master's thesis, Department of Telecommunications, Indiana University (2002)
14. Koivisto, E.M.I., Korhonen, H.: Mobile game playability heuristics. Forum Nokia (2006). http://www.forum.nokia.com/. Accessed 07 Dec 2008

15. Röcker, C., Haar, M.: Exploring the usability of videogame heuristics for pervasive game development in smart home environments. In: Magerkurth, C., Chalmers, M., Björk, S., Schäfer, L. (eds.) Proceedings of the Third International Workshop on Pervasive Gaming Applications – PerGames 2006, pp. 199–206. Springer, Heidelberg (2006)
16. 4PM, Criminel (2015). http://www.pocketgamer.co.uk/r/iPad/Criminel/review.asp?c=64212. Accessed 14 May 2016
17. Square Enix, Murdered: Soul Suspect (2014). http://store.steampowered.com/agecheck/app/233290/. Accessed 14 May 2016
18. Team Bondi, Rockstar Games (2011). http://uk.ign.com/games/la-noire/ps3-760495. Accessed 14 May 2016

Customized Games, Off the Shelf Modifications

Self-regulated Learning in Computer Programming: Strategies Students Adopted During an Assignment

Daniela Pedrosa[1,2(✉)], José Cravino[1,2], Leonel Morgado[3,4], and Carlos Barreira[5]

[1] Universidade de Trás-os-Montes e Alto Douro (UTAD), Vila Real, Portugal
{dpedrosa, jcravino}@utad.pt
[2] Research Centre "Didactics and Technology in Education of Trainers", Aveiro, Portugal
[3] Universidade Aberta, Coimbra, Portugal
leonel.morgado@uab.pt
[4] INESC TEC, Porto, Portugal
[5] Faculdade de Psicologia e Ciências da Educação da Universidade de Coimbra, Coimbra, Portugal
cabarreira@fpce.uc.pt

Abstract. The SimProgramming teaching approach has the goal to help students overcome their learning difficulties in the transition from entry-level to advanced computer programming and prepare them for real-world labour environments, adopting learning strategies. It immerses learners in a business-like learning environment, where students develop a problem-based learning activity with a specific set of tasks, one of which is filling weekly individual forms.

We conducted thematic analysis of 401 weekly forms, to identify the students' strategies for self-regulation of learning during assignment. The students are adopting different strategies in each phase of the approach. The early phases are devoted to organization and planning, later phases focus on applying theoretical knowledge and hands-on programming. Based on the results, we recommend the development of educational practices to help students conduct self-reflection of their performance during tasks.

Keywords: Self-regulation learning · Computer programming · Self-regulated learning strategies

1 Introduction

In higher education, high rates of academic failure and students' difficulty in learning to program are common in computer programming courses [1], particularly in the transition from entry-level programming to advanced programming. Reasons include the teaching approach and the attitudes/strategies used by students in computer programming [2], and lack of motivation and involvement in study [3, 4]. After graduation,

C. Allison et al. (Eds.): iLRN 2016, CCIS 621, pp. 87–101, 2016.
DOI: 10.1007/978-3-319-41769-1_7

most students come to the job market lacking necessary skills to meet the expectations of employers [5], such as: teamwork and cooperation skills [6].

In advanced programming courses the level of complexity is much greater than entry-level programming courses. For instance, students have difficulties learning in situations involving large code sizes, where the team dimension hinders communication or regular changes to existing code become necessary. When applying architectural styles such as Model–View–Controller (MVC) [7], students have difficulties grasping the rationale of architectural styles and other software engineering concepts [8]. Further, students need to develop complex programming skills [9] and social skills [6].

In higher education, one key element is self-regulated learning (SRL), which allows students to be proactive and manage their learning and development of life skills [10]. The application of SRL strategies typically predicts high academic achievement [11]. SRL processes can be improved with appropriate interventions [12], and it is typically recommended that teachers contribute and promote students' development of metacognitive knowledge about academic work and task-specific strategies [13].

In computer science, students that apply SRL and metacognitive strategies exhibit good performance [14]. Often students are not aware of SRL and metacognitive strategies that can be used, so instilling them is important [15].

We developed the SimProgramming approach [16], and applied it in the academic year 2012/2013 to the Programming Methods 3 (PM3) course, part of the second year of the bachelor programmes in Informatics Engineering (IE) and Information & Communication Technologies (ICT) at the University of Trás-os-Montes e Alto Douro (UTAD), Portugal. In the SimProgramming approach, students develop a problem-based learning (PBL) activity within the syllabus of the course, with a specific set of tasks based on the conceptual foundations of SimProgramming. One of these tasks is the filling of weekly forms, which are handed in by each student with a self-reflection on performance of the weekly development of the course assignment. We conducted thematic analysis of the 401 weekly forms to identify the SRL strategies mentioned by students during the development of the assignment.

2 Background

SRL is seen as the students' proactive and intentional monitoring of their actions, adapting and regulating cognition, behavior, emotions, and motivation using personal strategies to enhance learning processes and achieve personal goals [17–20].

Zimmerman proposes a cyclical model of SRL based on social cognitive theory. This model has three phases for self-regulation: (1) forethought, which is the goal setting and planning before the assignment/study; (2) performance, which is when the students use various strategies, monitoring and controlling their learning; and (3) self-reflection, reflecting about the learning process after assignment/study [20, 21, 17].

Self-regulated learners are active participants in their learning and develop academic skills [22], adopting various learning strategies [21] during an academic assignment. SRL allows students to get acquainted with effective practices/strategies for their study, such as: time management; resource management; environmental management; incorporating feedback; and management of learning objectives and results [22, 23]. Students construct their own meanings, goals, and strategies from the information available in the external environment and in their own minds [19].

SRL strategies (SRLS) are specific skills that are part of the SRL process, and can be taught for students to apply in real contexts [20, 21], such as: strategies for goal setting and planning, organizing and transforming, seeking information, rehearsing and memorizing, environmental strategies/structuring, seeking social assistance, self-consequences, records and monitoring, reviewing records, and self-evaluation [21].

The adoption of SRLs helps students obtain and retain knowledge about the adoption of a methodological approach and structured their learning, affecting the results of student learning [11]. According to [24], the application of SRLS are usually predictors of a good academic performance.

When students make effective self-reflection, they analyze how they learned, understood the objectives of the learning process and what is necessary to create conditions for success [18]. Also, they manage their learning and their commitment to meet challenges [18]. The interaction between the compromise, self-control, autonomy and students' self-discipline allows regulating their actions to achieve their learning goals [25].

The pedagogical context contributed for the learners engagement and resolve to achieve learning outcomes [26]. According to Wang et al. [17], in higher education it is important prepare students for the challenges of real work, and also to provide students with opportunities to develop their self-regulation and co-regulation skills, through activities that improve collaborative and active learning.

In engineering education, learning approaches are typically not aligned with the requirements of the labor market [27, 28], not giving priority to skills aligned with professional realities, such as active learning or integrating knowledge [29].

Students are immersed in business-like tasks mediated by structured and semi structured social interactions. Pedagogical techniques such as role playing stimulate students to learn about similar real-world situations, with problem-solving, active learning, providing opportunities to learn by doing and feedback for building new knowledge [30]. They also help develop professional identities [31].

3 The SimProgramming Approach: Immersive Features that Stimulate Self-regulated Learning

Pedrosa et al., including the authors of this paper, developed a teaching approach to help students learn computer programming in the transition from entry-level to advanced computer programming: the SimProgramming approach [16]. This approach is based on four conceptual foundations (ibid.): (1) business-like learning environment, (2) SRL; (3) co-regulation learning, and (4) formative assessment. Through these conceptual foundations, teaching strategies are adopted to stimulate SRLS by students with specific environment, roles, tasks, and deadlines during a course-long assignment.

The first conceptual foundation, *Business-like learning environment,* stipulates the simulation of a business-like environment, in order for students to have contact with aspects of their professional reality and teamwork expectations. Each participant plays a role and becomes immersed in the skills they have to develop during the assignment.

Problem-Based Learning (PBL) is used to promote collaborative discovery for the resolution of the problem [32].

The course lecturer plays the role of general manager, taking responsibility for the course content and monitoring. Course tutors or teaching assistants play the role of project managers, doing close monitoring, mentoring, and providing feedback, based on the Scrum method for project management and agile software development [33]. Students play different roles as members of development teams.

Each team of students divides the work according to the role played by each member. For example: one student acts as team leader and the remaining students handle subsets of work (work packages). The team leader facilitates the integration of information and guides the group [6], making sure that team members keep a global view of the project context and status, integrating knowledge. Others students have each a specific role in the team, having to master their individual packages and cooperate with the team leader.

In the *conceptual foundation 2: SRL,* also detailed in [16], the goal is to promote students' SRLS through active participation and engagement in meaningful activities before, during, and after completion of academic work [25].

In SimProgramming, students are expected to be immersed: team members should focus the development of their role-specific skills, on research and exploration tasks for development of assigned problem/packages, throughout promoting active learning and helping students improve their self-regulation skills.

Each student has to solve their individual packages and contribute to the overall perspective of the team problem. The team leader integrates research and exploration output of all members, reporting weekly at project management meetings. He/she also ensures the information flow within the team. Weekly, each student makes a self-reflection about their work, ponders on what to do the following week, and reflects upon the factors that prevented him/her from achieving the team and the individual objectives.

Other aspects of immersion are time management and procrastination. It is common, in real work environments, that programming teams have to adapt their plans and overcome difficulties to meet deadlines for tasks. So, in SimProgramming we encourage students to develop the concept of having to do their work regularly and adopt study routines, by creating a context where tasks are performed continuously, with feedback and monitoring support for self-reflection and self-regulation.

SimProgramming also encourages *co-regulated learning* (*conceptual foundation 3*). Assignments include team tasks, namely: reports and presentations about the work.

The search for help among professional communities is also a common practice in real-world labour, so we encourage students to be involved in pre-existing online communities of professionals (outside academia) not just to seek help, but to help others, contributing to problem-solving and discussing the technologies under study or used in their future profession [3]. On this regard, during contact with tutors (in meetings, classes, and on-line), the goal is to stimulate students' initiative to search for social help (peers, teachers, tutors, etc.), not only clarify their doubts and difficulties. The tutors/assistants and the professor provide this support by advising on methods of gradual participation and involvement in communities, including suggestion of specific tasks for clarification, and development the homogenous peer-based contributions and discussion, supporting community development, informal interactions and debate, which all were promoted and monitored via a Facebook group for the course.

Finally, is it well-known that companies conduct assessments of team performance. *Conceptual foundation 4: Formative Assessment*, aims to improve formative assessment throughout management feedback (tutors/assistants and professor).

SimProgramming Phases	Phase 1	Phase 2	Phase 3	Phase 4
Assignment Goals	-Searching for information on the technologies under study; -Interaction in online communities; -Group work: Initiate problem-solving.	- Integration of technologies; - Group work hands-on examples.	- Improving the assignment; - Final presentation with problem-solving	- Final improvement of the assignment.
Specifics Tasks	Weekly forms (individual) Weekly meetings between team leaders and tutors Report interaction in community of practice (team) Report about learning progress (team) Presentation of the team work	Weekly forms (individual) Weekly meetings between team leaders and tutors Report interaction in community of practice (team) Report about learning progress (team) Presentation of the team work	Weekly forms (individual) Weekly meetings between team leaders and tutors Report about learning progress (team) Presentation of the team work	Weekly forms (individual) Weekly meetings between team leaders and tutors Report about learning progress (team) Final Report (team) Grids about self-assessment of individual students and hetero-assessment by team members (of individuals) Extra task for extra credit or replacement credit (individuals or team)
Duration of the Phases	3 weeks	3 weeks	2 weeks	2 weeks

Fig. 1. SimProgramming phases: goals, specifics tasks and duration.

The Professor and assistants/tutors employ face-to-face and online contact to provide monitoring, meetings, and social media interactions, including motivational mentoring and feedback on individual package status. SimProgramming stipulates self-assessment of individual students and hetero-assessment by team members at the end.

3.1 SimProgramming Phases: Learning Assignment Process

In the SimProgramming approach [16], the learning assignment is developed along four phases and students have specific tasks in each phase (Fig. 1), based on the SimProgramming conceptual foundations presented above. During all phases, weekly meetings take place between tutors and team leaders, providing feedback for motivation, self-regulation, possible support for technical doubts, and internal team issues.

What are the individual weekly forms?

The individual weekly forms is where each student self-reflects upon his/her work, ponder on what to do the following week, and reflect upon the factors that prevented him/her or the team from achieving objectives [16]. Students need to answer 3 questions: (1) "What have you made this week for the assignment?"; (2) "What will you do next week for the assignment?"; and (3) "Any reason(s) for not completing tasks?".

4 Teaching Context and Learning Assignment

4.1 Teaching Context

Before reaching the Programming Methods 3 course (PM3, 2nd curricular year), students learned introductory programming in two previous courses, plus extra concepts in a Computational Logic course. PM3 is provided in parallel (joint lectures, but separate hands-on lessons) for students of two programmes of studies IE and ICT.

The goal in PM3 is to introduce the students to large-scale programming concepts, one of the learning objectives of the ACM/IEEE Computer Science Curricula (CSC). Specifically, students are introduced to the MVC architectural style, which divides programs among three blocks: the model (e.g., program state), the view (e.g., output), and the controller (e.g., program flow). The original MVC style proposal of Krasner and Pope [34], which handles input in the controller, is contrasted [4] with a more recent flavour proposed by Curry and Grace [7], which handles input in the view.

4.2 Learning Assignment in PM3

We combined face to face teaching techniques and technology-enhanced learning (TEL) [35] for support during the assignment. The tutors scheduled face-to-face meetings with team leaders, either individually or as a team, when they identified problems or difficulty fulfilling the tasks.

We used the Moodle LMS as the on-line environment for the professor and the tutors to track the development of the assignment, and organized the tasks into modules over several weeks. In the LMS, we provided supporting materials for development of tasks, scheduling, overall objectives of the assignment and individual objectives of each task, a forum for doubts and for contacting tutors, and other course materials (e.g. slideshows used in lectures). Also, we employed other on-line tools to support students: e-mail, instant messaging (GTalk), Facebook, and a locally-developed course management system, SIDE [36] for students to submit their completed tasks.

The learning assignment is based on PBL [32]. We assigned to each team a specific problem involving a MVC-related software architecture in order to stimulate and foster advanced programming skills in students. Students must develop a written document with a detailed explanation of the coding approaches they used to apply an MVC related architectural style to specific frameworks, libraries, and/or APIs [3, 4, 16, 37].

The SimProgramming approach was used throughout, along all the 4 phases, during 10 weeks of the academic semester, described ahead. In the 2012/2013 academic year, students formed 15 teams (Table 1). 11 teams successfully achieved the learning goals, two teams completed the requested tasks albeit falling short of achieving the goals, and two teams never actually started. Of the 97 students, 66 attained a final grade [16].

Table 1. Nr. of the students in assignment

Teams	Nr. students with a final grade	Comments
A	6/6	–
B	7/7	–
C	6/7	One student quitted the assignment
D	4/7	Of the 7 students, 3 quitted the assignment
E	6/7	One student quitted the assignment.
F	4/4	–
G	0/6	All students quitted the assignment, without even starting
H	7/7	–
I	5/6	One student quitted the assignment.
J	4/6	Two students never delivered the tasks, quitting the assignment
K	0/6	All students quitted the assignment, without even starting
L	2/7	Only 2 students delivered some of the requested tasks, performing the extra task. The remaining 5 members of the team never handed in any task (quitted at the beginning)
M	7/7	-
N	3/8	Only 3 were devoted and accomplished the tasks (the remaining 5 students quitted during the assignment)
O	4/5	One student quit the assignment
Total	66/97	

5 Methodology and Data Collection

During the 10 weeks of the assignment, each student had to submit their individual weekly form, with the exception of week 2, and week 10 (the final week). The delivery of the weekly forms changed along the SimProgramming phases (Table 2).

Table 2. Distribution of the weekly forms delivered in the SimProgramming phases

SimProgramming phases	Weeks	Nr. weekly forms delivered	Total
Phase 1	Week 1	81	150
	Week 3	69	
Phase 2	Week 4	55	168
	Week 5	65	
	Week 6	51	
Phase 3	Week 7	31	70
	Week 8	39	
Phase 4	Week 9	7	13
	Week 10 (in team)	6	
Total			401

As mentioned above, of the 97 students initially registering for the assignment, 66 completed phase 1, performing the tasks, and 31 others quit. In first week, 81 students delivered the weekly forms, but by week 3 this had decreased, and only 69 weekly forms were delivered. In Phase 2 and Phase 3 occasionally some students would miss a weekly delivery of forms. Finally, in phase 4, 7 students delivered their weekly forms on week 9, and 6 of the 15 teams delivered the team form.

As Table 2 shows, we observed stability during the initial weeks. However, on the week 7 there was a sharp decline. This was the week after Easter break, and students reported being a time when they had many mid-terms and assignment deadlines piling up:

> *"I had mid-terms and works deadlines for other courses, and I feel really tired, since we are near the end of the middle of the second semester."* (E38, Week 7, 22/03/2013)

> *"Although there are no classes during the Easter break, the work remained the same. Now, what's starting to worry me are the final assignments, mainly from courses on [Another course] and [Yet another course]."* (E13, Week 7, 29/03/2013)

> *"Lack of time was the main cause of the failures that occurred in the presentation. It is not easy to manage and bring together a group of six elements: we all have different courses and assignments, and this is sometimes also an impediment to reaching the goal of the group (...)"* (E5, Week 8, 12/04/2013)

In this paper, we analyse the 401 weekly forms using thematic analysis [38] with the goal of identifying the self-regulated learning strategies mentioned by students during the assignment. We constructed content analysis matrices based on background about the types of self-regulated learning strategies, identifying difficulties and factors that they believed influenced their motivation.

We organized content into categories, subcategories, indicators, and recording units (snippet sentences), which were restated during the process of content analysis. Then, we conducted a cyclical process of improvement, synthesis, and reflection. The steps adopted for the data analyses were as follows:

1. Construction of content analysis matrices for each team, with the SRLS reported by students (phrases/snippet sentences that students reported on the weekly forms,

explaining what they did). The content analysis matrices are composed of grid lines (each line for a strategy –the "indicators"); and columns to record in which week it was reported by students. In the cells we entered codes identifying the student reporting that strategy that week (e.g. E.3).
2. Afterwards, we developed general syntheses of each team references (students) for each of the indicators.
3. For each subcategory of the strategies (e.g. *Organizing and planning strategies*) we counted the number of students who reported each indicator (e.g. 1.1 = 113).
4. Finally, we did a general syntheses of the indicators in each of the phases.

6 Results and Discussion

6.1 Self-regulated Learning Strategies – Results of Analysis of the Weekly Forms

Regarding organizing and planning strategies for the assignment, detailed in Table 3, during the early stages (Phase 1 and Phase 2) the strategies most commonly adopted by students were information search, checking the material provided by the tutors/ professor or other courses, recording of practices in online communities and team meeting to define tasks.

Table 3. Organizing and planning strategies

Indicators	SimProgramming phases			
	Phase 1 (N = 150)	Phase 2 (N = 168)	Phase 3 (N = 70)	Phase 4 (N = 13)
3.1. Organizing – Information search	113	103	17	1
3.2. Organizing – Collected information	23	43	23	1
3.3. Planning – Work plan development	2	2	0	0
3.4. Planning - Following guidelines provided by tutors and professor	1	4	2	0
3.5. Had no planned strategy	0	3	0	0
3.6. Transforming – Drafting notes about collected information	9	3	2	0
3.7. Transforming - Application of existing knowledge about the practice	16	74	38	13
3.8. Organizing - Understand the project goals	4	0	1	0
3.9. Organizing - Checking the material provided by the teacher or other courses	16	5	0	0
3.10. Transforming - Understanding (learning) through the collected information search	53	82	22	4
3.11. Organizing - Recording practices online communities	66	15	0	0
3.12. Planning - Team meeting to define tasks	98	89	37	5
3.13. Planning - Meeting scheduling with tutors	1	2	0	0
3.14. Organizing - Meeting schedule with team colleagues	4	3	1	0
3.15. Organizing - Meeting with tutors	4	3	1	0
3.16. Planning - Defining specific tasks for next week	33	55	33	4

Table 4. Identifying of the difficulties in time management

Indicators	SimProgramming phases			
	Phase 1 (N = 150)	Phase 2 (N = 168)	Phase 3 (N = 70)	Phase 4 (N = 13)
4.1. Time management (TM) - Lack of time	2	3	1	0
4.2. TM- Lack of time due to other responsibilities	5	11	5	0
4.3. TM- Initiating the activity at the last moment (procrastination)	1	6	2	0
4.4. TM- Submitted in following week	8	10	4	0
4.5. TM - Difficulties in TM due to work in others courses or tests	49	80	30	1

Afterwards, still in phase 2, students initiate the application of existing knowledge about the practice, understanding (learning) through the collected information search, and defining specific tasks for the following week. In phase 3, the strategies remained the same as those applied in the preceding phase.

In the end (phase 4), students deepen their practical skills in teamwork (indicators 1.7 and 1.12). During assignment execution, other strategies were mentioned less often.

As shown on Table 4, the lack of time and difficulties in time management were frequently mentioned by students, due to a diversity of responsibilities but mainly because many tasks and tests that had to be performed in different courses. The most critical phases were phase 2 and phase 3.

As shown in Table 5, the difficulties students encountered while performing the assignment were at the level of theoretical content and practical implementation of the assignment. Difficulties in team work and scarce feedback obtained from on-line communities were also mentioned, mainly in phase 2. In phase 3 the most mentioned difficulties were about the implementation of the practical component.

Strategies mentioned by students to resolve their difficulties, as shown in Table 6, were varied, with a prevalence of SOA (teachers, peers, others). Only in the early phases (phase 1 and phase 2) did the students mention interaction with online communities.

Table 5. Identifying difficulties in the assignment

Indicators	SimProgramming phases			
	Phase 1 (N = 150)	Phase 2 (N = 168)	Phase 3 (N = 70)	Phase 4 (N = 13)
5.1. Difficulties – Theoretical knowledge about the technology being studied	3	16	0	0
5.2. Difficulties – The practical component implementation	2	19	14	1
5.3. Difficulties – Team work	9	15	3	1
5.4. Difficulties – Too many tasks per week	8	1	0	0
5.5. Difficulties - Scarce feedback obtained in on-line community	11	41	9	1

Table 6. Strategies for resolution of difficulties

Indicators	SimProgramming phases			
	Phase 1 (N = 150)	Phase 2 (N = 168)	Phase 3 (N = 70)	Phase 4 (N = 13)
6.1. Resolution of Difficulties (RD) - Use of practical exercises	0	6	1	0
6.2. Seeking Social Assistance (SOA) – Teachers	3	7	6	4
6.3. SOA – Team peers	2	3	0	0
6.4. SOA - Senior colleagues	4	1	1	1
6.5. SOA - Others	0	4	1	2
6.6. RD - Interactions in online communities	34	32	7	0

Also, some students expressed factors that affected their motivation during the assignment, as shown on Table 7. Most are of personal nature, for example, the need to achieve success in PM3 in order to attain completion of the programme of studies; the will to learn; interest in programming; the grade impact of the assignment. But some factors are linked to interpersonal and social dimensions, namely teamwork, being the leader with the associated responsibility, and the feedback obtained.

Table 7. Factors influencing motivation

Indicators	SimProgramming phases			
	Phase 1 (N = 150)	Phase 2 (N = 168)	Phase 3 (N = 70)	Phase 4 (N = 13)
7.1. Motivation (MT) – Completing PM3	0	3	0	0
7.2. MT - Interest in programming	1	0	0	0
7.3. MT- Comply with an obligation	0	3	0	0
7.4. MT - Grade impact of the assignment	2	2	0	0
7.5. MT - Responsibility for teamwork	1	3	0	0
7.6. MT – Found the process interesting (SimProgramming approach)	0	1	0	0
7.7. MT – Learning	3	2	0	0
7.8. Lack of motivation – Is tired (of studying)	0	0	0	1
7.9. Lack of motivation – Overall grades are not enough to complete the course	0	1	0	0
7.10. MT – Feedback obtained with tutors	0	6	0	0

Regarding self-reflection by students about their completed tasks, detailed in Table 8, few students made a thorough self-reflection with details about their performance in the required tasks and self-learning. They generically referred only on having achieved or not their goals. Only in the end phase did the students become more reflective.

Table 8. Self-reflection

Indicators	SimProgramming phases			
	Phase 1 (N = 150)	Phase 2 (N = 168)	Phase 3 (N = 70)	Phase 4 (N = 13)
8.1. Self-reflection (SR)- Achieved the goals	68	57	37	3
8.2. SR - Achieved the goals with difficulties	16	31	10	1
8.3. SR - Aware of lacking team leader skills - asked to be replaced	1	0	0	0
8.4. SR- Wants to get feedback from tutors to know if the objectives were achieved	1	0	0	0
8.5. SR - Did not reach the goals due to overload	27	44	20	6
8.6. SR - Reflection on specific tasks	9	24	13	8

7 Conclusions

Along the phases of the SimProgramming approach, the students have shown in their weekly forms that they were adopting many different strategies in each phase. In the early phases (phase 1 and phase 2), strategies were mostly about organization and planning. In the following stages (part of phase 2, but mostly phases 3 and 4) this shifted towards the application and transformation of information: application of theoretical knowledge and implementation of the hands-on component (programming). These strategies are skills necessary for the development of project teamwork in real-world labour. Students improved their competence in such skills during the SimProgramming phases and are expectably better prepared for the transition to the real-world labour.

In the weekly forms, students mentioned SRLS, especially on organizing and planning. They also mentioned strategies for resolution of difficulties, identifying difficulties in time management and difficulties in assignment, and factors influencing their motivation – strategies that had also been identified in our earlier work [37]. This highlights the difficulties students feel managing their time because of tasks and tests they need to account for in the various courses throughout the semester.

Some students mentioned in the weekly forms the adoption of transformation strategies and showed that they were aware of their specific difficulties in the tasks, aspects that were not reported so often in our previous work [37].

The students engaged in self-reflection about their learning, explaining whether or not they had reached their personal goals or the goals of the SimProgramming approach. However, only some students did a more thorough self-reflection about their performance. This confirms the need to help students become aware of the strategies that they can take to improve self-regulated learning [37]. Interestingly, as a team, the students reflected with significant detail about their performance.

We believe that the weekly forms or a similar instrument (for example, weekly meetings with students and tutors) contribute to the improvement of the adoption of self-regulated learning strategies because they raised students' awareness about important skills/strategies for real-world labour.

Acknowledgments. Pedrosa, D. wishes to thank the Fundação para a Ciência e Tecnologia (FCT), Portugal, for Ph.D. Grant SFRH/BD/87815/2012.

This work was partly financed by the ERDF – European Regional Development Fund through the Operational Programme for Competitiveness and Internationalisation - COMPETE 2020 Programme within project «POCI-01-0145-FEDER-006961», and by National Funds through the FCT – Fundação para a Ciência e a Tecnologia (Portuguese Foundation for Science and Technology) as part of project «UID/EEA/50014/2013».

We would like to thank all the students and teachers who collaborated on this research.

References

1. Lahtinen, E., Ala-Mutka, K., Järvinen, H.M.: A study of the difficulties of novice programmers. ACM SIGCSE Bull. **37**(3), 14–18 (2005)
2. Gomes, A., Mendes, A.J.: Learning to program-difficulties and solutions. In: International Conference on Engineering Education–ICEE, Coimbra, Portugal (2007)
3. Morgado, L., Fonseca, B., Martins, P., Paredes, H., Cruz, G., Maia, A.M., Nunes, R., Santos, A.: Social networks, microblogging, virtual worlds, and web 2.0 in the teaching of programing techniques for software engineering: a trial combining collaboration and social interaction beyond college. In: Global Engineering Education Conference (EDUCON), pp. 1–7. IEEE (2012)
4. Nunes, R.R., Pedrosa, D., Fonseca, B., Paredes, H., Cravino, J., Morgado, L., Martins, P.: Enhancing students' motivation to learn software engineering programming techniques: a collaborative and social interaction approach. In: Antona, M., Stephanidis, C. (eds.) UAHCI 2015. LNCS, vol. 9177, pp. 189–201. Springer, Heidelberg (2015)
5. Kumar, B.: Gamification in education-learn computer programming with fun. Int. J. Comput. Distrib. Syst. **2**(1), 46–53 (2012)
6. Sancho, P., Moreno-Ger, P., Fuentes-Fernández, R., Fernández-Manjón, B.: Adaptive role playing games: an immersive approach for problem based learning. Educ. Technol. Soc. **12** (4), 110–124 (2009)
7. Curry, E., Grace, P.: Flexible self-management using the model-view-controller pattern. IEEE Softw. **25**(3), 84–90 (2008)
8. Cagiltay, N.E.: Teaching software engineering by means of computer-game development: challenges and opportunities. BJET **38**(3), 405–415 (2007)
9. Jenkins, T.: On the difficulty of learning to program. In: Proceedings of the 3rd Annual Conference of the LTSN Centre for Information and Computer Sciences, vol. 4, pp. 53–58 (2002)
10. Fernández, E., Bernardo, A., Suárez, N., Cerezo, R., Núñez, J.C., Rosário, P.: Predicción del uso de estrategias de autorregulación en educación superior. Anales de Psicología **29**(3), 865–875 (2013)
11. Broadbent, J., Poon, W.L.: Self-regulated learning strategies & academic achievement in online higher education learning environments: a systematic review. Internet High. Educ. **27**, 1–13 (2015)
12. Zimmerman, B.J.: Investigating self-regulation and motivation: historical background, methodological developments, and future prospects. Am. Educ. Res. J. **45**(1), 166–183 (2008)
13. Cazan, A.M.: Teaching self regulated learning strategies for psychology students. Procedia-Soc. Behav. Sci. **78**, 743–747 (2013)

14. Bergin, S., Ronan R., Desmond, T.: Examining the role of self-regulated learning on introductory programming performance. In: Proceedings of the First International Workshop on Computing Education Research. ACM (2005)
15. Alharbi, A., Paul, D., Henskens, F., Hannaford, M.: An investigation into the learning styles and self-regulated learning strategies for computer science students. In: Proceedings of Ascilite (2011)
16. Pedrosa, D., Cravino, J., Morgado, L., Barreira, C., Nunes, R.R., Martins, P., Paredes, H.: Simprogramming: the development of an integrated teaching approach for computer programming in higher education. To Appear in Proceedings 10th Annual International Technology, Education and Development Conference (INTED 2016), Valencia, Spain (2016)
17. Räisänen, M., Postareff, L., Lindblom-Ylänne, S.: University students' self- and co-regulation of learning and processes of understanding: a person oriented approach. Learn. Individ. Differ. (2016). http://dx.doi.org/10.1016/j.lindif.2016.01.006
18. Hadwin, A.F., Järvelä, S., Miller, M.: Self-regulated, co-regulated, and socially shared regulation of learning. In: Zimmerman, B.J., Schunk, D.H. (eds.) Handbook of Selfregulation of Learning and Performance, pp. 65–84. Routledge, New York (2011)
19. Pintrich, P.R.: A conceptual framework for assessing motivation and self-regulated learning in college students. Educ. Psychol. Rev. **16**(4), 385–407 (2004)
20. Zimmerman, B.J., Schunk, D.H.: Self-regulated learning and performance. An introduction and an overview. In: Zimmerman, B.J., Schunk, D.H. (eds.) Handbook of Self-regulation of Learning and Performance, pp. 1–12. Routledge, New York (2011)
21. Zimmerman, B.J.: From cognitive modeling to self-regulation: a social cognitive career path. Educ. Psychol. **48**(3), 135–147 (2013)
22. Clark, I.: Formative assessment: assessment is for self-regulated learning. Educa. Psychol. Rev. **24**(2), 205–249 (2012)
23. Nicol, D.J., Macfarlane-Dick, D.: Formative assessment and self-regulated learning: a model and seven principles of good feedback practice. Stud. High. Educ. **31**(2), 199–218 (2006)
24. Wang, C.H., Shannon, D., Ross, M.: Students' characteristics, self-regulated learning, technology self-efficacy, and course outcomes in online learning. Distance Educ. **34**(3), 302–323 (2013)
25. Hattie, J., Timperley, H.: The power of feedback. Rev. Educ. Res. **77**(1), 81–112 (2007)
26. Johri, A., Olds, B.M.: Situated engineering learning: bridging engineering education research and the learning sciences. J. Eng. Educ. **100**(1), 151–185 (2011)
27. Duderstadt, J.J.: Engineering for a changing world. In: Grasso, D., Burkins, M.B. (eds.) Holistic Engineering Education, pp. 17–35. Springer, New York (2010)
28. Sheppard, S.D., Macatangay, K., Colby, A., Sullivan, W.M.: Educating Engineers: Designing for the Future of the Field, vol. 2. Jossey-Bass, San Francisco (2008)
29. Adams, R., Evangelou, D., English, L., De Figueiredo, A.D., Mousoulides, N., Pawley, A. L., Schiefellite, C., Stevens, R., Svinicki, M., Trenor, J.M., Wilson, D.M.: Multiple perspectives on engaging future engineers. J. Eng. Educ. **100**, 48–88 (2011)
30. Bransford, J., Brown, A., Cocking, R. (eds.): How People Learn: Brain, Mind, Experience, and School, Committee on Developments in the Science of Learning, Commission on Behavioral and Social Sciences and Education. NRC, National Academy Press, Washington, D.C. (2000)
31. Duarte, M.O., Oliveira, I., Félix, H., Carrilho, D., Pereira, A., Direito, I.: Active classrooms: role-playing experience in telecommunications engineering education. Int. J. Eng. Educ. **27** (3), 604–609 (2011)

32. Savery, J.R.: Overview of problem-based learning: definitions and distinctions. In: Walker, A., Leary, H., Hmelo-Silver, C., Ertmer, P. (eds).: Essential Readings in Problem-Based Learning, pp. 5–16. Purdue University Press, Indiana (2015)
33. Schwaber, K.: Agile Project Management with Scrum. Microsoft Press, Redmond (2004)
34. Krasner, G., Pope, S.: A description of the model view controller paradigm in the small-talk-80 system. J. Object Oriented Program. **1**(3), 26–49 (1988)
35. Kirkwood, A., Price, L.: Technology-enhanced learning and teaching in higher education: what is 'enhanced' and how do we know? A critical literature review. Learn. Media Technol. **39**(1), 6–36 (2014)
36. Barbosa, L., Alves, P., Barroso, J.: SIDE - teaching support information system. In: 6th Iberian Conference on Information Systems and Technologies (CISTI), pp. 1–6. IEEE (2011)
37. Pedrosa, D., Cravino, J., Morgado, L., Barreira, C.: Self-regulated learning in higher education: strategies adopted by computer programming students. To Appear in Proceedings of 8th International Symposium on Project Approaches in Engineering Education (PAEE), Guimarães, Portugal (2016b, in press)
38. Braun, V., Clarke, V.: Using thematic analysis in psychology. Qual. Res. Psychol. **3**(2), 77–101 (2006)

Mind, the Gap

Paul McCullagh(✉)

Computer Science Research Institute, Ulster University, Jordanstown, UK
pj.mccullagh@ulster.ac.uk

Abstract. Training is needed to exercise our most important organ: the brain, exploit its full potential and sustain it for our later years. Does a gap exist in our capacity for learning, a gap between what our brain could potentially achieve and what we are currently prepared to accept? The 'prototype' follows an ambitious undergraduate Computer Science student as he gets drawn into psychophysiological experiments that explore brain-training, involving image recognition, cognition, subliminal delivery, and imagined movement. Such technology has great potential for promoting and assessing learning and possibly exploring under performance or dysfunctional learning. However, as with all technology that enhances the human, there is potential for unintended use that we should be mindful of.

Keywords: Brain computer interface · Immersion · Stimulation · Brain-training · Enhancement · Subliminal learning · Brain-washing

1 Introduction

Our mind is our intellect, our ability to think and reason. In his book exploring the human mind, Professor Robert Winston [1] states, "*With the help of science we can now begin to understand the extraordinary complexity of the brain's circuits: we can see which nerve cells generate electricity as we fall in love, tell a lie or dream of a lottery win. And inside the 100 billion cells of this rubbery network is something remarkable: you.*" However, eminent neurosurgeon, Henry Marsh recently stated that we understand more about the universe than our own consciousness [2]. As scientists and educators, we need to further understand the mind and its underlying hardware, the brain. If we do not train our bodies, then such neglect is obvious by sight; quantified by metrics, such as body mass index. Labels to describe poor conditioning are in everyday use: sedentary, obese; this has led to new terms in our vocabulary such as 'diabesity'. But what happens if we neglect our brain, if we under-stimulate the mind. At the developmental stage (i.e. early years and school) will the brain ever reach its full potential? Peer judgement on intellect is less obvious but 'measures' such as Intelligent Quotient (IQ) and examination grades are widely used by society and subsequent labels can be harsh and detrimental to the individual. If a person fails to achieve a pass in an examination then there may be many contributing factors beyond intelligence: motivation, appropriate learning and teaching, even social class and proper nutrition. And what of people with special educational needs, such as Attention Deficit Syndrome (ADS) or dyslexia? Such needs often go undiagnosed leading to inappropriate teaching

C. Allison et al. (Eds.): iLRN 2016, CCIS 621, pp. 102–112, 2016.
DOI: 10.1007/978-3-319-41769-1_8

environment and support. As we mature into adulthood then surely we can achieve even more if we continue to stimulate and train our brains. How does advancing age affect our intellectual abilities: can brain-training reduce the incidence of forgetfulness, cognitive decline, even the onset of dementia? These are significant societal questions as the ageing demographic rises.

But how can we measure learning in real-time? This paper investigates the possibilities of brain computer interface (BCI) technology [3] for image identification and extrapolates this to learning[1]. It takes the viewpoint that the brain is under-utilized and would benefit from increased stimulation, in an immersive environment. However to be beneficial, we need to measure and quantify changes in brain activity. Visual Evoked Potentials (VEP) [4] and Cognitive Event-Related Potentials (ERP) [5] can be measured in neurophysiology laboratories. Could this technology be translated into mainstream learning in the future, to human enhancement? The public is equally fascinated and suspicious of emerging technology. This is particularly true of BCI devices, which are seen as clinical and invasive, the stuff of medicine or even science fiction [6]. One well-known myth of BCI is that it can be used for 'brain-washing'. *Or is it a myth?* This prototype addresses BCI for learning application in immersive education. Adoption of such technology could throw up unanticipated consequences. Technology such as Oculus Rift can provide appealing and stimulating immersive environments; eye-tracking can provide an objective measure of eye gaze on a computer screen; combined this powerful technology can be linked to user engagement. But there is a gap, how do we as teachers know that a student has *really* understood a topic? We should mind the gap.

2 Rationale for a Prototype

The fictional work is motivated by the mystical lyrics of the 1971 David Bowie song, *Quicksand* [7]. The 2016 release of the his last record *Blackstar* and accompanying videos[2], featuring a preacher and his 'blind' followers, reignited interest in Bowie's fascination with the occult (evidenced in his *Station to Station* album, 1976), magician Aleister Crowley and the Golden Dawn cult [8, 9]. The visual imagery was particularly poignant, as it provided many subliminal indicators to Bowie's imminent death, which duly occurred on 10th January 2016, 2 days after the album release. So this prototype is an investigation of BCI and learning; homage to a *guy that's been*. It weaves a make believe web, linking characters: Crowley (a persona projected onto the research Psychologist), poet W.B. Yeats and renaissance artist Michelangelo[3], all with reported interests in mysticism and cults. The prototype blurs what is currently possible with BCI technology; crossing the line from the human being in control, through to shared autonomy and to eventual brain-washing, with human subservient.

[1] This step takes us beyond the current state-of-the-art, into the realms of sci-fi prototype.

[2] Two controversial videos, "Blackstar" and "Lazarus" were recorded as Bowie contemplated his final act, whilst battling liver cancer.

[3] Yeats referred to Michael Angelo [misspelt] in his poem, *Under Ben Bulben.*

There are many gaps. The title of this paper refers to the 'gap' between what a human brain and mind can currently achieve and what maybe possible. However it could also refer to the gap that neuroscience currently has in understanding the complex brain, the scientific gap in our knowledge.

3 Fictional Story – The Golden Dawn Experiment

"Mind the gap"[4]. I'm on the subway in London waiting for a tube. "Mind the gap". I'm headed for the *Villa.* I'm not sure whether the journey will end in enlightenment or oblivion. The tube arrives. "Mind the gap".

> *"I'm closer to the Golden Dawn,*
> *Immersed in Crowley's uniform of imagery"* [7]

3.1 Cats and Dogs in the Psychophysiology Laboratory

{A few days earlier}

"This is the future of education?" I pondered as I made my way to the Psychology Department. I had replied to an intriguing email from an organisation called, 'ORMEN: Operations and Research for Mental Enhancement Network'. It sought student volunteers to take part in a pedagogy experiment called 'Golden Dawn'. I had finished my exams at last and had time on my hands. The information provided was not very specific:

> *The focus of this special track will be to explore the possible ways immersive-reality technology might change future education.*

I had achieved good grades in my Computing degree so far and I was particularly interested in research into human computer interaction, so I fulfilled the inclusion criteria. I was also interested in the fee of £10 per hour-long session, which would definitely be worth it, if I was selected for continued participation throughout the day. On arrival, I filled in some run of the mill 'consent' paperwork, which I probably should have read more closely and found myself in a laboratory with a couple of dozen others, presumably like-minded cash-poor undergraduates.

I was seated in front of a computer, with a keyboard, mouse and a set of virtual reality (VR) glasses, under starters orders. An announcement was made on the screen. "`You will see some images on the screen. All you have to do is count the number cats and dogs. Ignore the other images`". The screen flickered into life in front of me. Images were presented sequentially. Each time a dog or cat appeared, I pressed left or right mouse button as appropriate, and as fast as I could. It was easy, not much to this Psychology at all, I thought. After about thirty minutes the experiment ended and a message on the screen appeared that I could proceed; I should continue to be seated. There was the movement of chairs and some

[4] 'Mind the gap' is an audible warning provided on London's tube network and railway stations. Announcer Phil Sayer died in April 2016, aged 62.

people left the lab, presumably they had difficulty distinguishing a cat from a walrus, a dog from a duck, either this or they were happy with their tenner and were heading to the pub for lunch.

A further announcement: "`This is an immersive test. Put on the glasses. You will see some interesting images. All you have to do is count the number cats and dogs`". I was always a 'techie', so this really appealed. The glasses flickered into life and the cats, dogs and other strange creatures, some mystical, again appeared, but this time in glorious 3D. I felt a bit disorientated as bizarre lifeforms flew past me, and lingered behind, above and below. A few more targets were visible to me in the periphery of my vision, and with the VR I could *turn and face the 'strange'*; the count went up. I was dizzy and probably needed a glass of water, but somehow I felt I couldn't ask for one. At the end of this session, I was again successful. It was just like being on The Krypton Factor[5], I thought. A few sighs from around the room and the number of participants was again reduced.

A third session followed, this time in the dark, pitch black and eerie. Fainter images were interspersed with the brighter easier identified targets. They must have been there all the time, and I hadn't spotted them. There is something to this Psychology.

> *"I'm torn between the light and dark*
> *Where others see their targets in divine symmetry"* [7]

Still I was retained in the diminishing group of participants. In the next session, the speed of delivery was increased. Was that a cat? I thought I saw 10 dogs or was it 11? Maybe there were a few I missed? Now my mind was working overtime. A bit surprised this time, as I again got successful feedback. This brought us to lunchtime; a free lunch, yet another bonus.

At lunch I was directed to a table with four other 'select' participants and our tutor, a Dr. Crowley. She put us at ease straightaway, and praised us for our vision and quick reactions. We were disarmed. We discussed the motivation for volunteering. The others were definitely motivated by research, as of course was I (although in truth, I was feeling a bit out of my depth). We were asked about our interests. With the others responses were quite high-brow, art and poetry; for me it was seventies pop music and David Bowie in particular. "Interesting", posed Crowley. "That's my era, seems too dated for you". "I got into Bowie, from my mother's old vinyl collection. It keeps my memories of her alive", I said. "Interesting" was again the sparse comment. She was probably a fan, I thought. Crowley informed us that we were the top performing participants. She suggested that we could continue with this mundane pedagogy work in the afternoon or undertake some 'real' research. Of course this was like a red rag to a bull. Perhaps we had already been psychologically profiled, I pondered. Swept along by ego, I plumped for the real research. That made five of us.

---

[5] The Krypton Factor was a 'serious' game show in the UK which pitted contestants in physical and mental challenges.

3.2 A Sublime Afternoon

We were directed down a labyrinth of corridors to a smaller electrophysiology suite in the bowels of the building. The rest of the participants went back to the original lab to 'play' with the computer gadgets. Our group was then prepared for the afternoon experiments, which involved the acquisition of our 'select' brain electrical activity in response to visual stimulation. I had read articles on this type of Brain Computer Interface (BCI) experiment [10]. This was exciting work, at the forefront of Computing and it could be a real benefit to humanity. People who had peripheral neural dysfunction or 'locked-in' syndrome could benefit from it as an assistive technology. This was Psychology and Computer Science in sweet harmony. I was definitively in the right group, with the elite. Instead of pressing a button to signify a response, the researchers could study my brain patterns in real time to check my brain's response to the visual stimuli. Crowley had a couple of lab assistants. They expertly applied electrodes to our scalps. After a little bit of tweaking, a bit of scraping and a tiny bit of boring, which provided some mild discomfort, and a fair bit of hair gel, we were ready. I enquired about the paperwork for this research, but I was reassured that I had already given my consent in the morning. I couldn't recall this bit but hey, this was real research.

A familiar announcement was made. "`This is an immersive test. Put on the glasses. You will see some images. All you have to do is count the number cats and dogs. We will do the rest`". The lights went down and my anticipation rose. Then…what a let-down! The same images were presented, cats, dogs and an array of animals some real, others mystical, some bright, others faint. What was worse, for the next two hours we had to endure three more sessions, some presented faster, others slower, but an overdose of feline and canine targets. At about 4 pm it was over. The helpers took off the electrodes. My scalp stung due to the alcohol solution that dissolved the electrode gel, and my brain hurt through overuse. I was disoriented, practically seeing stars. Well that should be about £80, not bad for a day's work, I consoled myself. I assumed that we would be leaving, then but there was one more session - a test. I had overdosed on exams already.

3.3 Testing Times

We five donned the goggles again. Our instructions were familiar. "`You will see multiple choice questions. All you have to do is choose a, b, c, or d on the keyboard`". An image flashed. It was Irish Nobel laureate, William Butler Yeats. I identified him correctly, most people would. Second question: Where was Yeats born? I quickly answered, *c: Sandymount in Dublin*, although I'm pretty sure it was Sligo. Where did Yeats study? I answered, *a: Erasmus Smith High School*, completely guessing now. Oh dear!, I never really studied poetry at school. Questions continued: Complete the verse: *We rode in sorrow, with strong hounds three*. I choose option, *d: Bran, Sceolan, and Lomair*. In all I answered 20 questions, and then time was up.

We then awaited feedback from Crowley and we all hoped that the test results wouldn't influence our payment, in any way. Results from the tests; we had ALL scored either 19 or 20 out of 20. I looked around puzzled, at my colleagues. They all must be from the English department, studying poetry, I thought. I offered some explanation to my tutor. "Lucky guesses by me, I said". But Crowley retorted, "PJ, can you finish this poem?

"Proof That There's a purpose set
Before the secret working mind:...."

"...*Profane perfection of mankind;*" [11], I replied, before I could even think. I was facing the *strange* indeed, it couldn't be a guess. "You're an expert on W.B. Yeats", she said. I liked being called an expert, but I was now definitely in some surreal zone, head spinning, not really sure what was happening. Crowley continued to the group, "You will receive payment as you leave. I would like you all to come to a session tomorrow. Remuneration will again be provided. Can you make it?" My four colleagues confirmed straight away, as did I, actually before giving it any thought. But another £80 in the bank was all to the good.

On my way back to my apartment, my head was filled with the poetry of Yeats. Funny, thoughts of computing, science or old seventies tunes normally swirled through my brain. Today, I knew everything Yeats, but how? After some rest and gathering of my wits, I guessed that I was in the middle of some sort of subliminal study. I wanted to ask some probing questions about this, but I felt inhibited. And why didn't the others ask, anyway?

3.4 The Next Day: Michelangelo

The next day followed a similar a pattern. This time we five elite were looking for *daffodils* and *roses*, but I soon realized that this was totally unimportant. After a day of electrophysiological recording, we were tested again. I had developed significant expertise in the art of Michelangelo; works, many with subliminal meaning that I could readily identify during the end of day test. I was able to confirm that the depiction on the ceiling of the Sistine Chapel of *The creation of Adam* provided an anatomical illustration of the human brain in cross-section; *Separation of Light from Darkness* gave a ventral view of the brainstem [12]. Then we all received another invitation for day three.

Firstly, expertise on W.B. Yeats and then an appreciation of the works of Michelangelo: not bad for a Computing second year. I revised my television quiz aspiration upwards to *Mastermind*[6] contestant; I'll take Yeats in the first round and Michelangelo in the semi-final, I mused. This subliminal learning was powerful stuff. Should I persist or should I question it? Would I be removed from the study and relinquish the easy money? But my thirst for this easy knowledge was also growing more powerful. I could be an expert on composers, artists, potentially anything. Computing next please, I thought. Imagine, final year would be a breeze; no late nights, no popping pills to stay awake and enhance brain-power.

[6] Mastermind is the regarded as one of the more demanding television quizzes, usually for the more esoteric and intellectual.

Day three, and I didn't have to ask. When we arrived Crowley was there to brief us. "We have a new 'network' experiment, cutting edge research this time", she stated. "I guess you are all wondering what's going on". After a pause, to check our complete acquiescence with the process, she continued, but this time with much more passion and feeling. "The brain is very powerful, it takes up 20 % of the body's energy resource. It can process 11 million bits of information each second. But most people use less than 10 % of its capacity. Our research, the Golden Dawn project, is addressing this shortcoming. If we all use even 50 % of our brain-power, humanity will enter a renaissance, a golden dawn of enlightenment. We will reach a higher level of wisdom, people with less able brains can be identified, and defects rectified. We can discover the genes responsible for intelligence." After a pause, she calmed a bit. "As you may have deduced we have been stimulating your brains with images that are not readily perceptible to you. We know the response of your brain to an image you are searching for. We know that you have searched for it because we have monitored your gaze with the glasses. We know much about your interaction in the Golden Dawn experiment. If we get this same response to an image that you haven't looked at, we know that your brain has detected it, but you probably are unaware that you have seen it; the image may have been too faint or may have been too fast. All the same, because of the untapped power of the brain, you have still noticed it and can recall it."

"But why…", I thought to interrupt. Crowley pre-empted, "You haven't asked questions because in the experiments, we keep telling you not to, it's a frequent stimulus you don't perceive – we call it the *Don't Ask* stimulus! It's in the form of a white star" No need for me to finish then. "Your brain can detect an image long before you can press a button. You five have the most reliable visual perception. But sometimes, even one of you will miss a stimulus. This is unacceptable if we are to capture the knowledge". "We need volunteers for the next study. Who's in?" We all said "yes". Did we have any choice? I guessed there was probably a *Say Yes* stimulus too. I didn't ask.

3.5 Big Lou – A 'Real' Brain Neural Network

My appetite for knowledge was becoming more powerful; it was a drug. Crowley was right, think of what we could achieve, and we five were in the vanguard, we could become 'versatilists' of all knowledge. The next day, we were prepared as normal, nothing new. The experiments started again. This time I identified targets of colourful "fish" and cuddly "rabbits". But what would I learn? What would be the real test? I sought more expertise.

When I took the test, I realized that we were subconsciously straying into somewhat uncomfortable territory, immersed in a genre of violent video games. I was now identifying future crime scenes and potential perpetrators. This wasn't *Finding Nemo* meets *Bright Eyes*; it was *War Games* meets *Minority Report*. And something new was happening in the controlling computer. The potentials from our brains had been joined together by an Artificial Neural Network into a fuzzy decision-making brain network, linked to a cognitive computer called 'Big Lou'. If I didn't identify a scene, then one of my colleagues almost certainly did. This increased the reliability of ensemble identification to 100 %, and then I was then re-trained to rectify the error. This was indeed a powerful network for decision making, tapping into the brain's unused potential, into a network of brains. And we could learn from each other to perfect learning strategies. The potential for this intelligent cognitive computer was enormous.

At the end of this session, Crowley called me aside. "PJ, you are the best of the group and you have learned even more from the other four. You no longer need them. You can proceed beyond research. *Operations* Golden Dawn needs you. You have been selected for the next phase. It is located in the *Villa* in London. You will meet my colleague, Tom. Will you go?" I wanted to ask what the operations were, what the villa was for, but I couldn't. I should have stopped then, but I couldn't. I needed to learn more. All the information derived from the study would be used for good to help people enhance their learning, wouldn't it? "Yes", I said. Of course I did.

3.6 A Spider's Web in the Villa of Ormen

I had been given a plane ticket to London Heathrow, further directions and a letter of introduction, by Crowley. I travelled on the underground tube on the Piccadilly line to Gloucester Road and then the District line to Temple. "Mind the gap, mind the gap". I could hardly wait. I was driven for new knowledge, my mind now possessed by some thirsty demon as I progressed from station to station. Eventually I arrived at my destination, somewhere near Blackfriars Bridge. I looked for a sign for 'Operation and Research for Mental Enhancement Network', but there was nothing, a cloak of secrecy. The building was old, built in gothic style, very atmospheric.

A doorman, possibly a security guard, checked my letter of introduction and I was ushered in to a dark corridor illuminated by a solitary candle. I met Crowley's colleague, who introduced himself as Tom. He was evidently a military type, loud, quite pleasant but not to be messed with. "Call me Major", he said. I was informed that I was here for my inaugural competition, which would begin in the morning. I would need rest, as this 'track' would be mentally tiring; I would be staying on the premises. The building was eerie, silent save for the hum of vespers or chanting. I guessed there could be a religious service in an adjoining room or maybe the sound could have been in my head. I couldn't really tell anymore.

In the morning after breakfast with the Major and three colleagues, I was briefed on the purpose of the track, which would be held in a CAVE. A number of candidates were being 'interviewed' to join the Golden Dawn elite; I was effectively in a play-off, with others from around the globe. There would be only one recruit, the others would be eliminated; their journey would be at an end. I now realised I was really in a nerdy version of *X-factor*[7]. I found out that the CAVE was a Computer Assisted Virtual Environment, a distributed, interactive games venue. The Villa housed the UK's node. There was a global labyrinth of CAVES, all connected to 'Big Lou'. Instead of putting on a VR headset and experiencing an environment in 3D, I was in it! The electrodes were again expertly applied to my scalp. This time I also donned a smart shirt, with

[7] X-Factor is an entertainment show requiring considerably less intellectual ability, but possibly a modicum of singing talent.

sensors and actuators to measure heart rate and galvanic skin response, and constrict upon command.

The Major was the BCI expert, he instructed me in imagined movement [13], whereby simply the thought of moving a finger would enact a motor response, a 'trigger' potential. He told me that each time there was a shoot-out, the candidate with the slower trigger would feel a sharp tightening in his chest. The feedback was realistic, important for motivation. Each Golden Dawn candidate had three lives. Anyone losing a third life would be eliminated.

I entered my CAVE pod. `This is an immersive test. You will see some images of assailants. All you have to do is identify them and use your trigger to eliminate them. We will do the rest`". I was in the middle of something resembling *Call of Duty*, engulfed by swarms of strange assailants but four were familiar; the Major and his band of brothers in avatar form. Presumably I was visible to them as well, in this vast virtual world. The other assailants were easily dealt with; their reaction times couldn't match my brain's neural response and reaction. In the end only five remained, four against me. I spotted the Major hiding by a boulder, he hadn't seen me. I knew I could take him out if I acted fast.

Then from the CAVE's audio came the strumming of familiar chords of a guitar. I became distracted. A familiar song consumed all my thoughts. I smiled momentarily. *"Oh Man! Look at those cavemen go. It's the freakiest show"*. Vivid memories took over. I could visualise my hero, the *Starman* arm in arm with Ronno, singing on *Top of the Pops*, glitter, make-up and knee length boots; and he was pointing at me. I moved closer. Only then could I see that it was really the Major in disguise and he was pointing a laser weapon, not his finger. I had been tricked. It was a brain-to-brain shoot-out, but my trigger potential wouldn't work. My chest tightened, and I struggled for breath, convulsing zombie-like.

Minutes later, I re-spawned. The computer knows I like David Bowie. I won't fall for Big Lou's tricks next time. But I was now in a new augmented reality, a psychedelic planet of wonderful colours; it must be Mars. Combat renewed. This time space creatures attacked, spider-like in appearance. After a prolonged bout of seventies-style 'Space Invaders' that I easily won, it was down to me versus the Major and his band. I was drained and disorientated when someone else entered the game. The image and voice were unmistakable to me; I could see my mother walking along an arid landscape arguing with a drugged-up clown and his followers. She had come to help me. She had always put my education first and nurtured my love of music. I needed to say "Hello", to say "Thanks". Up close, and then I realised that it wasn't my mother, it couldn't be, she had morphed back into one of the band. Distracted, I had been hit from behind. Duped again, I waited for the smart shirt to take its toll. The constriction was longer and painful, I didn't know if I would make it, breathing was laboured, my heart rate fell; this was pretty real. Eventually the constriction eased and Lazarus-like I was back in the CAVE. By now I was mentally exhausted, the demon within all but gone. I knew the next contest would be my last. I couldn't match the cognitive computer.

I didn't have to wait long. I was transported back to a virtual Villa of Ormen. I heard the faint murmur of chanting, just as I had heard the previous night. I could see the blind followers, convulsing in unison to the chants. I didn't want to join this strange band of thought-controlled brothers. I wanted knowledge but there is no free lunch.

I left the safety of the villa and ventured outside, prepared to take on whatever strange elements this planet could throw at me. This time I was not pitted against alien creatures but fast moving colliding geometric shapes; pentagrams, hexagrams and 12-pointed stars that whizzed by in 3D, like a scene from Star Wars. White stars with *Don't Ask* and *Say Yes* messages abounded, frequent indeed. I needed to navigate right, left, up or down to avoid them and survive. This was more difficult than a simple trigger. And there was no Major or band to be seen, they were gone, only a slumped spaceman remained, his fate already decided by then. And then it arrived, a Blackstar, try as I might I couldn't avoid it. I knew it was the end. My death waits here. Prolonged constriction followed by blackout.

"I'm sinking in the quicksand of my thought
And I ain't got the power anymore" [8]

I recovered to find the Major looking down on me in the (real) Villa. "We had high hopes for you, PJ. The data shows that you spotted targets in good time. But you hesitated, that's fatal. 'Big Lou' must have tricked you. You have been eliminated. You must leave the competition." I didn't want to go to the next round. This was already far too 'real' for me. I shuddered to think what the next round would entail.

I was now on the underground to Heathrow, going back to Belfast, knowledge demon banished. The final track was indeed over.

3.7 Conclusion

So where are we now? There are implications for science and implications for society. As BCI advances out of dedicated labs there is the opportunity to use it as a tool for self-quantification, to provide feedback for therapy, and to measure learning [14]. However with such a close coupling between brain and software then the technology can potentially impinge on the autonomy and the self-efficacy of the individual, possibly even moving towards brain-washing. Rapid visual stimulation has emerged as a viable BCI paradigm [15]. Magicians and mentalists (performers) are well aware of the power of 'suggestion'. And we know the detrimental effect that social media can have on young or easily influenced people. Stricter ethical procedures for controlling such research could become necessary [16]. The blurring of the interface between man and machine, and the possibility of harvesting knowledge to produce self-aware robots is a topic that is exercising the leaders in Computing Science. Stephen Hawking, Elon Musk, Steve Wozniak and others have warned that AI can potentially be more dangerous to humans than nuclear weapons. Hawking stated: "humans, limited by slow biological evolution, couldn't compete and would be superseded by AI" [17].

So was the Golden Dawn project the future of learning through interactive games or preparation for some dystopian version of future combat? Could a real brain (or cognitive computing) network be used for enhancing learning or for the enactment of 'Star Wars', in association with autonomous drones and humanoid robots (e.g. Atlas from Boston Dynamics). BCI can be used for human enhancement and conditions that inhibit learning can be addressed. This is the bright future of education. But there could be a darker side. Images are powerful, be they of bygone pop stars, Hollywood blockbusters or propaganda preying on the accepting mind. Could BCI be used for learning or could it be used as a form of brain-washing. This is indeed a big gap. Mind the gap.

References

1. Winston, R.: The Human Mind- and How to Make the Most of it. Bantam Books, London (2003)
2. Marsh, H.: When Henry met Karl. http://www.bbc.co.uk/programmes/b072s43j
3. Allison, B.Z., Dunne, S., Leeb, R., Millan, J., Nijholt, A.: Recent and upcoming BCI progress: overview, analysis, and recommendations. In: Allison, B.Z., et al. (eds.) Towards Practical BCIs: Bridging the Gap from Research to Real-World Applications, pp. 1–13. Springer, Heidelberg (2013)
4. Norcia, A.M., Appelbaum, L.G., Ales, J.M., Cottereau, B.R., Rossion, B.: The steady-state visual evoked potential in vision research: a review. J. Vis. **15**(6), 4 (2015)
5. Rugg, M.D., Coles, M.G.H.: Electrophysiology of Mind: Event-related Brain Potentials and Cognition. Oxford Psychology Series, vol. 25, no. xii, p. 220. Oxford University Press, Oxford (1995)
6. McCullagh, P.J.: Eureka Potential (2103). http://www.creative-science.org/wp-content/uploads/2013/02/2013_eied2013UrekaPotential.pdf
7. Quicksand, from the 1971 album "Hunky Dory"
8. Golden Dawn. https://en.wikipedia.org/wiki/Hermetic_Order_of_the_Golden_Dawn
9. The final mysteries of David Bowie's Blackstar – Elvis, Crowley and 'the villa of Ormen'. http://www.theguardian.com/music/2016/jan/21/final-mysteries-david-bowie-blackstar-elvis-crowley-villa-of-ormen
10. McCullagh, P., Galway, L., Lightbody, G.: Investigation into a mixed hybrid using SSVEP and eye gaze for optimising user interaction within a virtual environment. In: Stephanidis, C., Antona, M. (eds.) UAHCI 2013, Part I. LNCS, vol. 8009, pp. 530–539. Springer, Heidelberg (2013)
11. Yeats, W.B.: Under Ben Bulben. http://www.poetryfoundation.org/poem/172070
12. Suk, I., Tamargo, R.J.: Concealed neuroanatomy in michelangelo's separation of light from darkness in the sistine chapel. Neurosurgery **66**(5), 851–861 (2010)
13. Pfurtscheller, G., Neuper, C.: Future prospects of ERD/ERS in the context of brain–computer interface (BCI) developments. Prog. Brain Res. **159**, 433–437 (2006)
14. Brunner, C., Birbaumer, N., Blankertz, B., Guger, C., Kübler, A., Mattia, D., Millán, J., Miralles, F., Nijholt, A., Opisso, E., Ramsey, N., Salomon, P., Müller-Putz, G.: BNCI horizon 2020: towards a roadmap for the BCI community. BCI J. (2015). doi:10.1080/2326263X.2015.100895610.1080/2326263X.2015.1008956
15. Hwang, H., Ferreria, V., Ulrich, D., Kilic, T., Chatziliadis, X., Blankertz, B., Treder, M.A.: Gaze independent brain-computer interface based on visual stimulation through closed eyelids. Nat. Sci. Rep. 5, Article number: 15890 (2015). doi:10.1038/srep15890
16. McCullagh, P.J., Lightbody, G., Zygierewicz, J., Kernohan, W.G.: Ethical challenges associated with the development and deployment of brain computer interface technology. Neuroethics **7**, 109–122 (2014). doi:10.1007/s12152-013-9188-6
17. http://observer.com/2015/08/stephen-hawking-elon-musk-and-bill-gates-warn-about-artificial-intelligence/

Computational Thinking and Social Skills in Virtuoso: An Immersive, Digital Game-Based Learning Environment for Youth with Autism Spectrum Disorder

Matthew Schmidt[1(✉)] and Dennis Beck[2]

[1] University of Cincinnati, Cincinnati, OH, USA
matthew.schmidt@uc.edu
[2] University of Arkansas, Fayetville, AR, USA
debeck@uark.edu

Abstract. The adoption of computational thinking (CT) has been increasing in K-12 classrooms and curricula. One population that could benefit from early instruction in CT is students with Autism Spectrum Disorders (ASD). Unfortunately, many individuals with ASD lack the social competencies to successfully navigate a work environment. The purpose of this paper is to discuss a digital games-based learning intervention for youth with ASD to learn computational thinking and social skills. Dubbed "*Virtuoso*", the intervention targets youth with ASD to gain social skills while working together to solve introductory computer programming problems with virtual, programmable robots. One objective is to create learning materials that embed social competency instruction within a CT-focused curriculum. Another objective is to develop an immersive space where participants can work together on curricular content. Using educational design research methods, we are developing and refining instructional interventions so as to maximize their educational impact.

Keywords: Minecraft · Autism spectrum disorder · Computational thinking · Immersive learning

1 Introduction

The adoption of computational thinking (CT) has been steadily increasing in K-12 classrooms and curricula; however, successful, large-scale CT implementations have yet to be realized. According to the National Research Council [1], the need to prepare students with 21st Century Skills such as computational thinking through STEM-related teaching is great. Further, the earlier students are exposed to STEM topics, the more likely it is that they will go on to pursue STEM careers. One population in particular that could benefit from early instruction in CT is students with Autism Spectrum Disorder (ASD). A large portion of the population (one in 68) [2] has autism. Some researchers contend that these individuals possess a natural affinity toward STEM topics and careers, particularly those that have to do with computers [3]. Unfortunately, many individuals with ASD lack the social competencies needed for success in professional work

C. Allison et al. (Eds.): iLRN 2016, CCIS 621, pp. 113–121, 2016.
DOI: 10.1007/978-3-319-41769-1_9

environments. The purpose of this work-in-progress paper is to discuss the potential of a digital games-based learning intervention for youth on the autism spectrum to learn computational thinking skills and related social skills concomitantly.

2 Background

Computational thinking is a way of "solving problems, designing systems, and understanding human behavior by drawing on the concepts fundamental to computer science" [4, p. 33] and is a fundamental 21st century skill considered to be as important as reading, writing, and arithmetic. CT has received traditionally far less attention compared with other science, technology, engineering, and mathematics areas. (STEM) [5]. Bringing CT into classrooms is not a new idea, with attempts reaching back over three decades to Seymour Papert's [6] work with children using computers to experiment with the LOGO programming language. However, doing this on a large scale has been largely unsuccessful. Exposing students to STEM topics like CT early in their schooling is important, as it increases the chances that those students will maintain interest and improve their abilities in related areas, which increases the likelihood that they will pursue STEM careers [1]. However, merely promoting students' understanding of STEM–while important–falls short of instilling 21st century skills. The National Center on Education and the Economy (NCEE) calls for educational reforms that reflect the needs of future employers, focusing on skills such as using ideas and abstractions, self-management, and teamwork [7]. Similarly, the National Academies' [8] stress skills such as communication, social skills, complex problem-solving, and systems thinking. These are skills that are encapsulated in CT; however, if students are not provided opportunities to pursue CT in school, these are skills they might not develop. According to President Barack Obama, promoting innovation in the United States is critical to our generation "winning the future" [9]. Preparing professionals through high quality education programs that stress 21st century skills (like CT) to work in STEM fields is imperative to this end [10].

Autism is a neurodevelopmental disorder that manifests in a variety of ways, including impairments in social interaction, communication, and restricted, repetitive behaviors [11]. According to the Centers for Disease Control, current estimates indicate that around one in 68 individuals have ASD (2014). Individuals with ASD are typically classified on a continuum that ranges from severely affected to high functioning. Individuals with an IQ greater than 70 and without other cognitive impairments are considered to be cognitively higher functioning. While higher functioning individuals with ASD typically do desire to be social, many do not have the requisite social competencies to do so successfully [12]. This lack of social competence leads to an inability to identify and act on nonverbal social cues and social prompts, tending to result in displays of socially unacceptable behavior. Left untreated, social competence deficits can result in problematic social behavior [13], social withdrawal [14] and deficits in other developmental and behavioral areas [15]. Failure to address social deficits can lead to low self-esteem, impaired self-concept, and depression [12].

Youth with ASD are often drawn to computers, find them highly motivating, and tend to do well manipulating them, leading some scholars to conclude that these individuals may have a natural affinity to them [16]. This has led to the use of a large number of technology-enhanced learning systems developed specifically for people with ASD. An intervention that focuses specifically on CT could influence students to pursue interests in computers and computer programming, and lead to a career in programming. This is important for three reasons. First, computer programming has been identified as one of the jobs that is better suited to individuals with autism [3]. Second, the Individuals with Disabilities in Education Act (IDEA) recommend beginning training for vocational transitioning around middle-school [17]. Third, scholars recommend students with ASD be given opportunities to learn about careers and have exposure to the kinds of work involved in those careers so as to identify their individual work preferences [18]. A challenge, however, is that individuals with autism often suffer debilitating deficits in social skills which make finding and keeping a job difficult if not impossible. Youth with autism are more likely to be underemployed or unemployed compared with youth in other disability categories [19]. For many individuals with ASD, transitioning into a job after high school is a challenge. Shattuck and colleagues [19] report that eight years after graduation, just over 50 % of individuals with ASD have ever worked for pay outside the home. Only one in five works full time. And for those who do maintain employment, pay tends to be low (on average $8.10/hr). Failure to secure or maintain employment puts individuals with ASD at risk of transition "into a world of social exclusion, financial hardship and significantly decreased quality of life" [20, p. 899].

3 Study Purpose

The purpose of this work-in-progress paper is to discuss the potential of a computer-based learning intervention for youth with ASD to learn computational thinking skills and related social skills. Dubbed "*Virtuoso*" (a play on the words virtual and social), the intervention specifically targets middle-school-aged youth with ASD (11-14 years old). The goal of the intervention is for participants to gain targeted social skills while working together to solve introductory computer programming problems with virtual, programmable robots. This proposal will discuss the design, development, and formative evaluation of a prototype of this immersive space, as well as a preliminary set of lessons for use in the immersive space.

Virtuoso seeks to help youth with ASD develop social competencies and computational thinking (CT) skills in school settings. One objective of Virtuoso is to create learning materials that embed social competency instruction within a larger CT-focused curriculum. Another objective is to develop an immersive, online space where participants can work together on curricular content. These two objectives are interconnected, in that design and development of the online learning environment will influence the design of the curriculum and vice-versa. For the immersive, online space, this project uses the common, off-the-shelf video game: Minecraft. Minecraft is a hugely successful video game that is popular in education and that has been used for learning in a number of domains such as geography, chemistry, and history. This project uses a variant of Minecraft made specifically for educational purposes called MinecraftEdu (https://minecraftedu.com/). It contains many additions to the original game that make it more useful and appropriate in a school setting. Central to this proposal is the game mode called ComputerCraftEdu (http://computercraftedu.com/), which provides a low-threshold entry to learning programming. It allows players to program robots (called "turtles"; see Fig. 1) to perform a variety of functions, for

Fig. 1. A ComputerCraftEdu turtle (labeled "1") and a remote control for performing simple operations with the turtle (labeled "2")

example, to dig or to build a structure. Programming begins with a simplified tile-based interface in which players drag-and-drop icons to program their turtles and progresses to users writing their own programs in a visual programming environment (see Fig. 2).

A scaffolded curriculum in which the complexity of programming turtles increases over time is the context within which social skills instruction will be embedded. Students work in pairs and small teams in the immersive environment, and are led by an online guide (a teacher who is co-present in the immersive environment) who plays

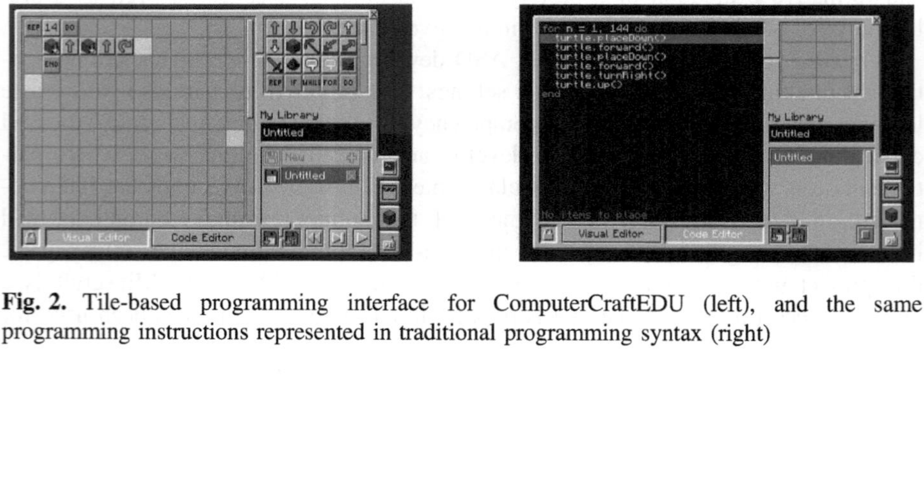

Fig. 2. Tile-based programming interface for ComputerCraftEDU (left), and the same programming instructions represented in traditional programming syntax (right)

an instructional and mentoring role. As players work in pairs and larger groups, direct instruction is used to teach social skills relevant to the programming activities. For example, if a team is brainstorming how to solve a problem, direct instruction might be used on how to share ideas appropriately. The online guide will mentor students with role modeling and feedback, as considered best practice for social skills instruction for students with autism [21]. The skills that are taught using a direct instruction method can be applied and practiced immediately in the immersive world within the context of the broader CT problem-solving activity.

We provide here a brief use case to clarify how this might work. This use case is based on prior models the first author developed around social skills instruction for youth with ASD in immersive environments [22, 23]. Six students log in from various locations to the immersive world, where they are met by the online guide (OG). The OG gathers the group and presents them with a videogame-like challenge that they must solve collaboratively by programming their turtle robots. For example, students must escape from a deep valley by collaboratively programming turtles to build a stairway. The OG gives a short overview of the "rules of the road" for the activity (the social rules that circumscribe the task) before facilitating a discussion about approaches for solving the problem. Students must adhere to the rules during conversation, such as avoiding interruptions, taking turns, being respectful of others' ideas, etc. Once potential solutions have been identified, teams are established for the programming task. The students then work together to program their turtles. The OG moves between teams, providing guidance and ensuring that students are adhering to social rules. At the end of the session, neither team has completed the challenge, so they re-convene to discuss what they learned and what they will do next time they meet in-world.

4 Research Design and/or Methods

This project will use educational design research (EDR) as its overarching methodological approach. EDR is an emerging approach that bridges the demand for rigorous research with the development of relevant solutions to educational problems. EDR is an intervention and process-oriented approach that has been steadily gaining traction in the field of educational technology over the past two decades. The focus of EDR is to create instructional interventions and refine them over time so as to maximize their educational impact. The approach is iterative, consisting multiple design, implementation, and evaluation phases. EDR typically uses mixed-methods to examine the development and implementation of instructional solutions to current educational problems [24]. Similarly, our approach will take a mixed-methods approach, couching quantitative findings within a broader framework of qualitative methods.

A variety of questions will guide our research. These questions are both evaluative and empirical:

1. What is the nature of learner-learner interaction in Virtuoso?
2. What is the nature of learner-computer interaction in Virtuoso?

3. To what extent does Virtuoso promote computational thinking?
4. How do learners solve problems in Virtuoso?
5. What are learner perceptions of usability?
6. What are learner perceptions of usefulness?

To approach these questions, we will use a variety of data collection methods, including self-report questionnaires, video- and screen-recording, learning analytics, semi-structured interviews, eye-tracking, electroencephalogram (EEG) scanning, and focus group interviews.

As a strategic partnership, we have partnered with the Transition and Access Program (TAP) at the University of Cincinnati (UC). TAP offers students with mild to moderate intellectual disabilities–including autism, and Asperger syndrome–an authentic, non-degreed college experience. Participants with ASD between 18 and 30 years old will be recruited from the TAP program to help with participatory design and evaluation of *Virtuoso*. We will offer a service-learning course in which students in Information Technology, Instructional Design and Technology, and Special Education will work with students in the TAP program to collaboratively design and test Virtuoso and its associated curricular activities. In addition to this, *Virtuoso* will be tested in two to three partner middle schools and junior high schools. Participants will be purposively selected based on the following characteristics: (1) aged between 11–14 years old, (2) medical diagnosis of autism determined by the Autism Diagnostic Interview Revised (ADI-R) (Rutter, Le Couteur, & Lord, 2003) and/or the Autism Diagnostic Observation Schedule (ADOS) (Lord, 2002), (3) verbal/capable of speech and (4) intelligence quotient within one standard deviation of the mean for the typical range (e.g., a score of 85–115). We intend to recruit between four and six students at each school for this initial pilot. The institutional review board at the first author's institution is reviewing this proposed research for ethical approval.

Of particular note is our use of learning analytics techniques for *Virtuoso*. Learning analytics is a means to automatically provide insight into patterns of usage, interaction, and engagement while learners and instructors use educational technologies. Videogames generate massive amounts of data while users interact with the system and with each other. Data generated while using videogames can be automatically collected using logging features, made sense of, visualized and acted upon. We are using the same methods for capturing and analyzing analytics data as outlined by Müller and colleagues [25]. Because of the early stage of this project, we are still working to implement the necessary methods and processes to capture and analyze analytics data.

4.1 Timeline

This project consists of three phases that will take roughly one year, an overview of which is provided in Table 1. These phases are non-linear. That is, some aspects can be performed concurrently between and across phases.

Table 1. Overview of project activities for one year

Phase	**Activities**
Analysis & exploration (~3–4 months)	• Review of extant CT & social skills curricula • Explore Minecraft worlds & extant educational implementations • Testing and exploring MinecraftEdu and ComputerCraftEdu • Establish partnerships with local schools & begin recruiting • Begin to develop learning analytics methods for Virtuoso
Design & construction (~3–4 months)	• Design and develop pilot activities for Virtuoso with TAP students • Evaluate curricular activities with TAP students • Design immersive worlds & activities • Conduct usability testing (eye-tracking, EEG) • Continue developing learning analytics methods for Virtuoso • Develop pilot curriculum unit and perform expert review • Work with local schools to ensure Virtuoso will work on their computers and networks • Continue recruiting
Evaluation & reflection (~6 months)	• Usage testing of curriculum unit with target population (2-3 schools) • Revise pilot unit after each usage test • Data collection • Apply learning analytics methods for Virtuoso • Data analysis • Write-up of findings

5 Conclusion

Generally speaking, the use of videogames in education is seen as a disruptive innovation that has the potential to change how we think about learning and instruction. The use of immersive gaming environments for teaching CT at a distance holds promise from the perspective of distance learning as well as computer-supported collaborative learning. Teaching social skills at a distance, online, and in an immersive world is an area in which only a small handful of researchers has experimented [22, 23, 26]. In addition, using these digital and communication technologies to promote useful vocational and life skills for youth on the autism spectrum is an area that is untouched in the academic literature. Finally, the development of learning analytics methods for *Virtuoso* holds promise not only for gaining insight into learners' behaviors while using the system, but also for future research directions. Yet, perhaps most innovative is the ability of an intervention like *Virtuoso* to bring services to youth who otherwise might not receive them. This intervention has the potential to bring social skills and vocational instruction to youth in rural schools or in schools where access to services is limited, as in some urban schools and rural districts throughout the world.

References

1. National Research Council: Successful K-12 STEM Education: Identifying Effective Approaches in Science, Technology, Engineering, and Mathematics. National Academies Press, Washington, DC (2011)

2. Developmental disabilities monitoring network surveillance year 2010 principal investigators, & centers for disease control and prevention (cdc): prevalence of autism spectrum disorder among children aged 8 years - autism and developmental disabilities monitoring network, 11 sites, United States, 2010. Morb. Mort. Wkly. Rep. Surv. Sum. 63 (2), 1–21. (2014)
3. Grandin, T.: Choosing the Right Job for People with Autism or Asperger's Syndrome. Colorado State University (1999). http://www.aspennj.org/pdf/information/adult-issues/choosing-the-right-job-for-people-with-autism.pdf
4. Wing, J.M.: Computational thinking. Commun. ACM., **49**(3), 33–35 (2006). http://www-cgi.cs.cmu.edu/afs/cs/usr/wing/www/CT_at_CMU.pdf
5. Israel, M., Pearson, J.N., Tapia, T., Wherfel, Q.M., Reese, G.: Supporting all learners in school-wide computational thinking: a cross-case qualitative analysis. Comput. Educ. **82**, 263–279 (2015). http://doi.org/10.1016/j.compedu.2014.11.022
6. Papert, S.: Mindstorms: Children, Computers, and Powerful Ideas. Basic Books, Inc., New York (1980). http://dl.acm.org/citation.cfm?id=1095592
7. National Center on Education and the Economy: Tough Choices or Tough Times: The Report of the New Commission on the Skills of the American Workforce. Josey-Bass, San Francisco (2007)
8. National Research Council: Rising Above the Gathering Storm: Energizing and Employing America for a Brighter Economic Future. National Academies Press, Washington, D.C. (2007)
9. The State of the Union Address (2011). http://www.whitehouse.gov/the-press-office/2011/01/25/remarks-president-state-union-address
10. National Research Council: Taking science to school: Learning and teaching science in grades K-8. The National Academies Press, Washington, D.C. (2007)
11. American Psychiatric Association. Diagnostic and Statistical Manual of Mental Disorders. American Psychiatric Association (2013)
12. Myles, B., Simpson, R.: Asperger Syndrome: an overview of characteristics. Focus Autism Other Dev. Disabil. **17**, 132–137 (2002)
13. National Research Council: Educating Children with Autism. National Academy Press, Washington (2001)
14. Weiss, M.J., Harris, S.L.: Teaching social skills to people with autism. Behav. Modif. **25**(5), 785–802 (2001)
15. Rogers, S.: Interventions that facilitate socialization in children with autism. J. Autism Dev. Disord. **30**, 399–409 (2000)
16. Murray, D.: Autism and Information Technology: Therapy with Computers. Autism and Learning: A Guide to Good Practice, 100–117 (1997)
17. Turnbull, H.R., Huerta, N., Stowe, M., Weldon, L., Schrandt, S.: The Individuals with Disabilities Education Act as Amended in 2004. Pearson, London (2009). http://www.beachcenter.org/IDEA_Guide.pdf
18. Holtz, K.D., Owings, N.M., Ziegert, A.K.: Life Journey Through Autism: A Guide for Transition to Adulthood. Org. for Aut. Res. (NJ1) (2006). http://eric.ed.gov/?id=ED508625
19. Shattuck, P.T., Narendorf, S.C., Cooper, B., Sterzing, P.R., Wagner, M., Taylor, J.L.: Postsecondary education and employment among youth with an autism spectrum disorder. Ped. **129**(6), 1042–1049 (2012). http://doi.org/10.1542/peds.2011–2864
20. Howlin, P.: Social disadvantage and exclusion: adults with autism lag far behind in employment prospects. J. Am. Acad. Ch. Adol. Psy. **52**(9), 897–899 (2013). http://doi.org/10.1016/j.jaac.2013.06.010

21. Wong, C., Odom, S.L., Hume, K.A., Cox, A.W., Fettig, A., Kucharczyk, S., Schultz, T.R.: Evidence-based practices for children, youth, and young adults with autism spectrum disorder: a comprehensive review. J. Aut. Dev. Dis. **45**(7), 1951–1966 (2015). http://doi.org/10.1007/s10803–014-2351-z
22. Schmidt, M., Galyen, K., Laffey, J., Babiuch, R., Schmidt, C.: Open source software and design-based research symbiosis in developing 3D virtual learning environments: examples from the iSocial project. J. Int. L. Res. **25**(1), 65–99 (2014)
23. Schmidt, M., Laffey, J., Galyen, K., Wang, X.: Designing and evaluating software supports for individuals with autism spectrum disorders in a 3D virtual learning environment. In: Proceedings of E-Learn 2011. Honolulu, HI (2011). http://www.editlib.org/p/38823
24. McKenney, S., Reeves, T.: Conducting Educational Design Research. Routledge, New York (2012)
25. Müller, S., Kapadia, M., Frey, S., Klinger, S., Mann, R.P., Solenthaler, B., Gross, M: Statistical analysis of player behavior in minecraft (2015). http://eprints.whiterose.ac.uk/88990/
26. Schmidt, M., Laffey, J., Stichter, J., Goggins, S., Schmidt, C.: The Design of iSocial: a three-dimensional, multi-user, virtual learning environment for individuals with autism spectrum disorders to learn social skills. In: The Fourth International Conference on Technology, Knowledge and Society. Boston, MA (2008)

Inducing Emotional Response in Interactive Media: A Pilot Study

Keenan M. Reimer(✉) and Foaad Khosmood

California Polytechnic State University, San Luis Obispo, CA 93407, USA
{kmreimer, foaad}@calpoly.edu

Abstract. Video games, entertainment, education, and training media have been developed for many years, and eliciting emotional experiences is an integral part of that process. Production and editing of the media in order to produce the desired emotional experiences can be expensive and cumbersome to media designers. This paper presents a pilot study intended to show that such experiences can be induced with after-the-fact audio-visual effects. As subjects of the user study, players are given the same virtual environment with two emotional states: fear, and peace. Over 70 % of players report feeling the proper emotional response in both environmental states, revealing that it is indeed possible to induce emotional response with after-the-fact audio-visual effects, hinting at future possibilities for drag-and-drop emotional experience filters.

Keywords: Unity · Video games · Education · Emotion · Fear · Peace

1 Introduction

1.1 Motivation

It has been a long-term goal of digital entertainment, education, and training media to be able to dynamically create experiences that are highly customizable on an individual user basis [7]. Inducing tailored, dynamic emotional responses is a critical component of that goal, yet there exists little by way of methodology for doing so [1]. Having a standardized methodology would allow designers of interactive experiences with a wide range of design and educational experience to easily tailor their products to particular subject matters. It gives them the ability to work on projects that are emotionally dynamic, meaning that they aren't rooted in providing a single static emotional experience, and allows them to save time by modifying existing work to provide new experiences. This study is a small step toward the capability of dynamically inducing specific feeling or psychological state in any interactive environment.

Prior work has shown that interactive media is indeed capable of effecting emotional state [16], and when combined with the motivating factors above, leads to the following hypothesis:

It is possible to induce emotional responses by making after-the-fact audio-video adjustments to video game content.

C. Allison et al. (Eds.): iLRN 2016, CCIS 621, pp. 122–131, 2016.
DOI: 10.1007/978-3-319-41769-1_10

It is the goal of this pilot study to test the validity of this hypothesis and to gain further insight.

Educators could use this work to build better, more robust educational experiences that more effectively engage their students in the classroom. For example, multiple studies have shown that fear is capable of improving the effectiveness of health and safety media at producing behavioral changes in users [5, 9]. This work allows educational developers to create interactive experiences aimed at promoting health and safety that have purposefully tailored and optimized emotional experiences. They could do the same thing to educational environments centered on novels or historical events. And while the study is implemented strictly in the domain of video games, the underlying theory extends into all realms of entertainment, education, and training media.

1.2 The State of the Art

Games have implicit or explicit emotional requirements [1]. Despite this, there are no accepted methodologies for inducing various emotional responses. It is possible to install emotional responses as hard coded features in the game environment [2], but this kind of static development does little by way of empowering developers to create highly customized dynamic experiences. This flexibility would be useful across all digital entertainment, education, and training environments; however, it is especially useful in the MMORPG genre, where emotional response is tightly coupled with immersion, and it is critical that the right emotions are consistently induced [14]. In the FPS genre it has been shown that a correlation exists between emotion characteristics and user-specific preferences about games [8], indicating that different users have different emotional responses to the same content. The same may be true for other emotions, which means that dynamic emotional experience is not only convenient, but necessary for designing consistent educational experiences across a wide variety of users. Furthermore, evidence from the film industry suggests that emotional experiences in entertainment media have the capability of being universal across demographics [12].

In the gaming industry, the importance of lighting on the game experience is well understood [4]. Drawing on principles of cinematography lighting can be used to set mood and atmosphere, which are critical for inducing emotional engagement [3]. Color is also an essential tool. As far back as 1935, when the first feature film in Technicolor was released, it has been shown that color can be used in digital content for dramatic and emotional effectiveness [13]. Modern work on the effect of color on emotional response has shown that a relationship exists between saturation and brightness, and positive emotional response [15].

A recent study on the effect of audio on emotional response suggests that capturing the 'essence' of a sound is more important than the sound's fidelity. It is better to have a sound that matches our perception of the real sound, than to have a high quality recording of the actual sound itself [6]. Additionally, it has been shown that the integration of spatial sound in immersive virtual environments has a significant influence on the intensity of presence experienced by the user [11]. This is relevant because other work has shown that the degree to which a user is feeling present in a virtual environment can have an effect on the magnitude to which they experience fear [10].

2 Experimental Design

2.1 Unity

Unity[1] is a development environment for creating multiplatform 3D and 2D games and is used to create the testing environment for this experiment. It has been used to create many successful modern games such as: Kerbal Space Program, Cities Skylines, Firewatch, and many more[2].

The Unity platform has built-in tools which encompass multiple aspects of game design such as level and asset creation, backend scripting, and post processing image effects. The latter of those is used to great extent to tailor emotional states in this experiment. Unity is a convenient choice for developing the game environment in this study, as it provides a way to easily build up a prototype; however, nothing about this study is unique to Unity and the driving technologies are available in other game engines and design tools.

2.2 System

A high fidelity digital environment is created to host this experiment. The environment is an open-world, fantasy themed valley that users can navigate within and interact with.

It has two built in emotional states, fear and peace, that can be switched on and off programmatically. The environment in each of the two states can be seen in Fig. 1 below.

Fig. 1. Screenshots of the environment in the fear (Mystic Valley – Fear Mode. https://www.youtube.com/watch?v=dLDAMAXwTTk) state (left) and the peace (Mystic Valley – Peace Mode. https://www.youtube.com/watch?v=5YvTH6nMF00) state (right). All visual differences are the result of post-processing image effects.

[1] Unity. https://unity3d.com/unity.

[2] Unity Gallery. https://unity3d.com/showcase/gallery.

A simple narrative is provided to give users a sense of purpose, but there is no win condition. All that is required in the study is that users enter a state of immersion wherein the desired emotional affect can be induced.

Twenty-two users play out the narrative twice: first in one emotional state (randomly chosen), then followed by the other. Both experiences take five minutes to complete, and after each the user completes a small survey prompting them for their emotional responses. Overall, the entire process takes approximately twenty minutes.

2.3 Fear and Peace

The fear and peace states present in this experiment are designed to induce opposing emotional responses. Both emotional states add a combination of after-the-fact audio-video effects to the base state of the scene. These effects are summarized in Table 1 below.

Peace mode amplifies lighting in the scene, and adds a bloom effect. It also changes the environment's background wildlife noises to simulate daytime forest wildlife, and adds a soothing mystical melody to the background.

The fear state makes changes opposite to those of peace mode. It darkens the scene, and instead of adding bloom it creates a layer of thick fog and amplifies contrast. It also causes ambient wildlife noises to be more indicative of a forest at night. It does this by lowering the frequency of the noises, and changing the kinds of noises to those of insects, owls, etc. Instead of having a mystical melody wrapping up the ambiance, the fear state has a persistent heart-beat underlay. It also introduces a motion-blur effect. The effect was added in conjunction with the heart beat sound to convey to the user a sense of danger, with the intention of stimulating the flight or fight response.

Table 1. Summary of fear and peace state audio-visual properties.

Fear state	Peace state
Darkened scene[a]	Lightened scene[a]
Increased contrast[a]	Bloom effect[a]
Fog effect[a]	Daytime animal noises[b]
Blur effect[a]	Background melody[b]
Night animal noises[b]	
Background heartbeat[c]	

[a]Unity Standard Assets. https://www.assetstore.unity3d.com/en/#!/content/32351

[b]Interactive Audio. https://www.assetstore.unity3d.com/en/#!/content/18354

[c]Heartbeat Sound. http://www.soundsnap.com/heartbeat_thump_01_sfxbible_ss01947

The video effects are all implemented using Unity Standard Assets[3], whereas the ambient audio effects are implemented using an asset called Interactive Audio: Enchanted Forest[4], which is purchased on the Unity Asset Store.

2.4 Surveys

The player surveys are designed to prompt players to identify their emotional experiences. They are completely anonymous, and not a requirement for any assignment. Each survey consists of three questions that are directly tailored for emotional responses. The first is a free response question that asks: "Please describe any feelings or emotions that you felt during your experience." An example response can be seen below:

> *It felt creepier and more mysterious. [In] the first game [experience] I felt safe, but this time I thought there might be some threats waiting for me.*
>
> *-Anonymous Player*

The second question asks players to circle words that stand out to them based on their experience with the game. The words are arranged randomly on the survey, but for analytical purposes they are organized into five categories: fear, peace, secondary experiences, environmental, and unrelated with 2, 2, 3, 4, and 5 words in each category respectively.

The third question asks them to record any primary emotional experience they have, and the magnitude to which they feel it on a scale of 1 to 5. It should be noted that many of the words players chose to identify came from the table in question two: suggesting that there may be a biasing effect on the survey level for the second and third questions.

Twenty-two players participated in this study. They are all students from a collegiate level game design class, between the ages of 19 and 22, and the majority of them are majoring in Computer Science or Computer Engineering. Their programming experience is relatively uniform, but their prior experience playing video games is not. Some participants displayed quick aptitude with the environment's game mechanics, while others struggled. Participants were asked to play through the first and second experiences before completing the accompanying surveys (First & Comparison).

3 Results

3.1 Qualitative

Results to the free response question are encoded in three categories based on each player's emotional reactions. If a proper emotionally descriptive word or a close synonym is used for a given experience, the response is placed into the first category.

---

[3] Unity Standard Assets. https://www.assetstore.unity3d.com/en/#!/content/32351.

[4] Interactive Audio. https://www.assetstore.unity3d.com/en/#!/content/18354.

If the proper emotionally descriptive word or a close synonym is not used, yet some other emotionally descriptive word is used, then the response is placed into the second category. If no emotionally descriptive words are used then the response is placed into the third and final category. Three individuals (one of whom is a participant in the study) parse the surveys and encode each response. Of the twenty-two responses to both the fear and peace experiences, there is majority agreement across all encoders for 100 % of responses in the first round, and 90.9 % of responses in the second round. This method of encoding response data and all following methods of interoperating results is designed before the survey is conducted.

After the first game experience, 77.3 % of players reported a proper emotionally descriptive word or a close synonym, where 22.7 % reported some other word, and 0 % of players reported none. After the second experience 70.0 % of players reported a proper emotionally descriptive word, where 25.0 % reported some other word, and 5.0 % reported none.

3.2 Quantitative

The analysis of question two is focused on participants circling (or not circling) at least one word in each category (Fig. 2). The levels of significance from Fisher's exact test of two sample proportions and can be seen in Table 2.

Responses to the third question are grouped into three categories (fear, peace, and secondary) where their magnitudes are averaged, and then analyzed using Fisher's exact test of two sample proportions. The results can be seen in Fig. 3 below, and the levels of significance from Fisher's test of two population proportions and average magnitudes can be found in Tables 3 and 4 respectively.

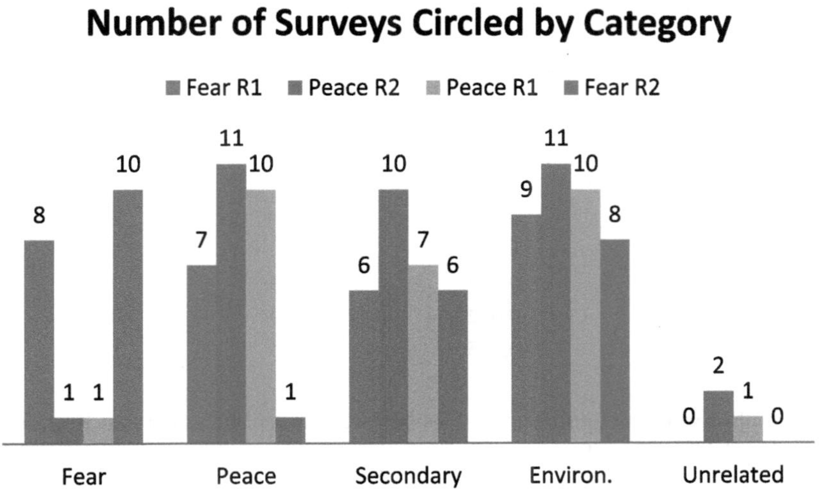

Fig. 2. The number of surveys that circled at least one word from each category in the circling survey question for each emotional state in both rounds. R1 and R2 indicate round one and round two respectively. (Color figure online)

Table 2. Results from Fisher's exact test for two sample proportions on the circling survey question for each emotional state in both rounds. R1 and R2 indicate round one and round two respectively.

Category	Fear R1 vs. peace R1	Peace R2 vs. fear R2	Fear R1 vs. peace R2	Peace R1 vs. fear R2
Fear	0.026	0.000	0.009	0.001
Peace	0.399	0.010	0.581	0.007
Secondary	0.761	0.773	0.566	1.000
Environ.	0.785	1.000	1.000	1.000
Unrelated	0.492	0.506	0.495	1.000

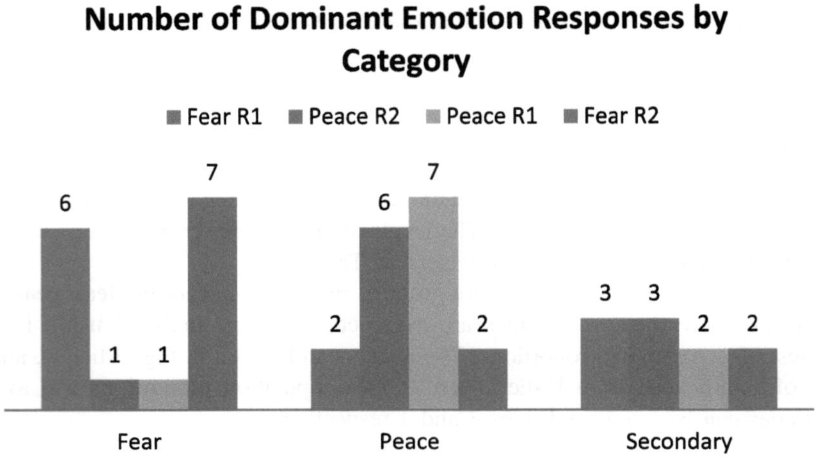

Fig. 3. The number of surveys that state a dominant emotion that belongs to one of three categories (fear, peace, and secondary) for each emotional state in both rounds. R1 and R2 indicate round 1 and round 2 respectively. (Color figure online)

Table 3. The results of Fisher's exact test of two population proportions on the dominant emotion and magnitude survey question. R1 and R2 indicate round 1 and round 2 respectively.

Category	Fear R1 vs. peace R1	Peace R2 vs. fear R2	Fear R1 vs. peace R2	Peace R1 vs. fear R2
Fear	0.063	0.024	0.063	0.024
Peace	0.030	0.082	0.080	0.030
Secondary	1.000	0.635	1.000	1.000

When observing the figures and tables below, it should be noted that R1 refers to a state in round 1 and R2 refers to a state in round 2. Also, each state denoted with R1 is paired in series with the opposite state denoted in R2. For example, the players who complete surveys in Fear R1 are the exact same who complete surveys for Peace R2 and visa-versa for Peace R1 and Fear R2. Any comparison amongst rounds is referring, in parallel, to the group that randomly started in one state and the group that randomly

Table 4. The average magnitudes of responses to the dominant emotion and magnitude survey question. Results are on a scale of 1 to 5 with 5 being the greatest. R1 and R2 indicate round 1 and round 2 respectively.

Category	Fear R1 avg.	Peace R2 avg.	Peace R1 avg.	Fear R2 avg.
Fear	4.00	4.00	3.00	3.71
Peace	4.00	4.17	4.14	5.00
Secondary	3.33	3.33	4.00	3.00

started in the other. For example, Fear R1 vs. Peace R1 is comparing the group of players that randomly start the first experience in the fear state with the other group of players that randomly start the first experience in the peace state.

4 Conclusion

4.1 Discussion

The results from the qualitative survey question reveal that a significant majority of players experienced the proper emotion in both their first and second experiences with the game. This serves as an initial examination that the game experiences are valid, as this question comes before the other two, and is unbiased by any prior verbiage.

The results from the second (circle) question are more interesting. There is a statistically significant difference between the proportions of surveys that have fear related words circled in both the first and second game experiences; yet there is only a significant difference for peace words in the second experience. When comparing player responses of each experience in the first round, to the opposite experience in the second, the exact same pattern of significance appears. Again there are significant differences in the proportion of fear words circled in both cases, but only with words associated with peace in the case that the peace state was the first state experienced. All of this suggests that there may be some kind of contrasting effect present in the system as players are shown to be unlikely to circle words related to their first experience on their survey for the second experience. As to the discrepancies in the proportions of peace words circled when fear comes first, it is possible that there are some baseline emotional experiences in the system. Perhaps it is inherently peaceful to be in a forest or listen to a heartbeat, as some players remarked on the soothing effect of the forest or heartbeat in their qualitative responses. There are no significant differences among environmental, secondary, or unrelated word proportions in any of the parallel or series test cases.

As for the dominant emotion and magnitude question, there is a significant difference between the proportion of players who used fear or peace words as the dominant emotion in both game states and in the first and second rounds. The larger proportion matches the proper category in all cases. There are also significant differences between each experience in the first round and the corresponding opposing experiences in the second round. The average magnitudes are appropriately larger in both states of the first game experience, but inappropriate in both states for the second experience; however, this can be heavily discounted by the fact that the vast majority of participants report the proper dominant feeling for both cases. Namely, a couple of participants report the unexpected feeling with great magnitudes, but many more reported the correct feeling with a variety of magnitudes. There are no significant differences among secondary emotion proportions in any of the test cases.

Overall, the results from all three questions reveal that after-the-fact audio-visual effects can be utilized to induce emotional response in users, and that some of the effects listed in Table 1 are valid sets of effects for inducing the emotional responses of fear and peace. While the results of this study are limited to the domain of video games, one could theorize that the conclusion would be the same for any kind of entertainment media.

4.2 Future Work

The audio-visual effects that are tested in this study are highly subjective. It remains to be seen which are most effective at inducing affectional responses, and which are ambiguous. Qualitative results of the pilot study suggest that some effects, such as the heartbeat sound, need to be tailored or removed altogether. The study also needs to extend to other game environments to validate to the assumption that the same methodologies would apply in other contexts. In this case, any environment specific effects also need be removed or replaced. It would be interesting to study emotional responses besides fear and peace. If positive results were obtained from an experiment with a set of non-contrasting emotions, it would strongly support this experiment's hypothesis.

Some of the results indicate that there may be a baseline emotional experience present in the system with no after-the-fact audio visual effects applied. While the study in its current state reveals some interesting things about differences in emotional states across experiences, it will be impossible to quantify any measure of absolute emotional effect without first understanding this baseline.

As the study has shown that audio-visual effects can easily induce emotional responses in video games, this work will be translated into Unity asset packages and made available on the Unity asset store. This will allow educators developing in Unity to easily, and confidently tailor their environments to their specific set of users and subject matters.

References

1. Callele, D., Neufeld, E., Schneider, K.: Emotional requirements. IEEE Softw. **24**, 43–45 (2008)
2. Chittaro, L., Buttussi, F., Zangrando, N.: Desktop virtual reality for emergency preparedness: user evaluation of an aircraft ditching experience under different fear arousal conditions. In: 20th ACM Symposium on Virtual Reality Software and Technology, pp. 141–150. ACM (2014)
3. Donati, J.: Introduction to light and color. In: Exploring Digital Cinematography. Delmar, New York (2008)

4. El-Nasr, M.S., Zupko, J., Miron, K.: Intelligent lighting for a better gaming experience. In: CHI 2005 Extended Abstracts on Human Factors in Computing Systems, pp. 1140–1141. ACM (2005)
5. Floyd, D.L., Prentice-Dunn, S., Roger, S.R.: A meta-analysis of research on protection motivation theory. J. Appl. Soc. Psychol. **30**(2), 407–429 (2000)
6. Grimshaw, M., Lindley, C.A., Nacke, L.: Sound and immersion in the first-person shooter: mixed measurement of the player's sonic experience. Games Computing and Creative Technologies: Conference Papers, Paper 7 (2008)
7. McQuiggan, S.W., Lee, S., Lester, J.C.: Predicting user physiological response for interactive environments: an inductive approach. AIIDE **2006**, 60–65 (2006)
8. Merkx, P.P.A.B., Truong, K.P., Neerinex, M.A.: Inducing and measuring emotion through a multiplayer first-person shooter computer game. In: van den Herik, H.J., Uiterwijk, J.W.H. M., Winands, M.H.M., Schadd, M.P.D. (eds.) Proceedings of the Computer Games Workshop 2007 (2007)
9. Milne, S., Sheeran, P., Orbell, S.: Prediction and intervention in health-related behavior: a meta-analytic review of protection motivation theory. J. Appl. Soc. Psychol. **30**(1), 106–143 (2000)
10. Peperkorn, H.M., Diemer, J., Mühlberger, A.: Temporal dynamics in the relation between presence and fear in virtual reality. Comput. Hum. Behav. **48**, 542–547 (2015)
11. Poeschl, S., Wall, K., Doering, N.: Integration of spatial sound in immersive virtual environments an experimental study on effects of spatial sound on presence. In: IEEE Virtual Reality (VR), pp. 129–130. IEEE (2013)
12. Sato, W., Noguchi, M., Yoshikawa, S.: Emotion elicitation effect of films in a Japanese sample. Soc. Behav. Pers. Int. J. **25**(7), 863–874 (2007)
13. Stump, D.: The color-space conundrum. In: Digital Cinematography: Fundamentals, Tools, Techniques, and Workflows. Taylor & Francis, New York (2014)
14. Suárex, L., Thio, C.F.W., Singh, S.: Why people play massively multiplayer online games? Int. J. E-Educ. E-Bus. E-Manage. E-Learn. **3**(1), 7–12 (2013)
15. Suk, H.J., Irtel, H.: Emotional response to color across media. Color Res. Appl. **35**, 64–77 (2010)
16. Villani, D., Riva, G.: Does interactive media enhance the management of stress? Suggestions from a controlled study. Cyberpsychology Behav. Soc. Network. **15**(1), 24–30 (2008)

Developing Serious Games to Improve Learning and Increase Interest in STEM Careers for Middle School Students: The Mice of Riddle Place®

Charles Raffety[1(✉)], Theodore Prawat[2], Jonathon Richter[3], Raymond F. Hamilton Jr.[1], Melisa Schelvan[1], Paulette Jones[4], and Andrij Holian[1]

[1] University of Montana, Missoula, USA
{charles.raffety, ray.hamilton, melisa.schelvan, andrij.holian}@umontana.edu
[2] Time for Art Studio, LLC, East Lansing, MI, USA
tedprawat@gmail.com
[3] Salish Kootenai College, Pablo, USA
Jonathon_Richter@skc.edu
[4] Meadowlark Science and Education, LLC, Missoula, USA
paulette@meadowlarkscience.com

Abstract. To address the need for high quality interactive curricula for STEM learning, Meadowlark Science and Education is creating a series of educational games, The Mice of Riddle Place®. A Design-based Research method is being used to create standards- and inquiry-based learning games for middle school classrooms. Early evaluations of "The Incident of Izzy Ramirez", an asthma-oriented game module that uses game-based problem solving, conceptual reasoning, and goal-oriented decision making for improving STEM proficiency indicates teacher, student, and research-based alignment with design practices.

Keywords: Technology · STEM · Serious games · Environmental health · Research · Middle school · Next generation science standards · Common core standards

1 Introduction

There is a paucity in interactive and effective educational content designed for today's students; specifically, there is a need for improved interactive tools for STEM learning [1, 2]. Therefore, we are developing a series of educational games targeted to meet a particular need at the middle school age group. The topic area of environmental exposures within homes was chosen since it was likely to be highly relevant to the students and would allow an integration of all aspects of STEM including human biology and systems. Consequently, the use of environmental health topics as a vehicle for gameplay allows students to become engaged in STEM subjects that are relevant to their lives. Game development involved a recurring cycle of student and teacher input

C. Allison et al. (Eds.): iLRN 2016, CCIS 621, pp. 132–143, 2016.
DOI: 10.1007/978-3-319-41769-1_11

during the entire process including developing the teacher lesson plan. Currently, evaluations are being conducted in 5–8th grade classrooms on an asthma-oriented module that included game-based problem solving, conceptual reasoning, and goal-oriented decision making as the learning platform. The long term outcomes we are focusing on are improvements in student performance in STEM subjects, improvements in educational outcomes, and ultimately career choices.

2 Significance

2.1 Overall Significance

The asthma-based educational video game module, "The Incident of Izzy Ramirez" offers a solution to the critical barrier faced by teachers in the incorporation of effective STEM-based curriculum in the middle school classroom. Our educational game uses a platform for improving complex problem solving skills critical for proficiency in the STEM subjects. We proposed that students would be interested in the subject matter of asthma since it is a highly prevalent childhood disease and there is a high likelihood that in any given classroom that someone has asthma or knows of someone who has asthma helping to increase the relevance of the health topic. Currently, there is a lack of high quality and critically evaluated interactive educational materials available for teacher's use. Our purpose was to develop a creative game and environment that would encompass the theories of learning necessary to master strategic thinking skills and problem solving, while still being highly engaging to the students. Furthermore, gaming provides students with a risk-free environment, enabling them to engage cognitively without negative consequences and is easily adapted to the player's learning stage, which creates a learner-centered experience [3]. The finished game and accompanying teacher lesson plan materials capitalize on these inherent components of "serious games" and in return improve scientific knowledge and technical capability for imparting STEM skills. With the completion and constant improvement of "The Incident of Izzy Ramirez" we hope to change the concept of gaming and environmental health as they relate to an educational setting and provide a foundation for incorporating future STEM-based gaming platforms to be more widely utilized by educators in order to reach their needs and goals.

"The Incident of Izzy Ramirez" targets middle school students—the age at which interest in STEM subjects is developed or lost [4]. Our central premise is that student interest and proficiency in the STEM topics will be improved due to the engaging nature of games and by providing teachers a scientifically accurate and desirable end product along with the tools necessary to actively incorporate the game module into their existing curriculum, including extensive training and supplementary lesson plans. We have utilized and built on the concepts and methods previously applied to the development of a successfully evaluated module on carbon monoxide exposure, "The Mystery of Mrs. Wirth" to further provide effective STEM-based resources for middle school teachers.

Importantly, the Next Generation Science Standards and Common Core Standards provide the framework for learning objectives during game play. During the development of each game module there is extensive in-classroom evaluations and feedback sessions to serve two functions: (1) to affirm the effectiveness of the game as a tool for improving student proficiency and interest in the STEM subjects and (2) to provide valuable information that can subsequently be used for improving the current, future and previously developed games. Overall, there is an iterative, cyclical process, designed to streamline multiple rounds of evaluation, feedback, and game improvements—resulting in a highly tested product with the goal of improving STEM education as well as provide an enjoyable learning experience for the student. Based on the research literature and our evaluation results, comprehensive, well-planned educational video games, containing multiple gaming options and actively incorporated input from teachers and students throughout the development process are highly successful in improving interest and proficiency in STEM subjects [5].

3 Best Practices

With games increasingly being recognized as curriculum in education, there is also a desire to develop curriculum in the STEM content areas that uses the fundamental premises of games: that learning can be immersive and engaging, and as a way to motivate students in a classroom towards the professional fields of science, technology, engineering, and math in education where there is a well-defined need for future students [1, 2, 6, 7]. What this required from a curriculum design perspective was an approach where learning, as evidenced in the Next Generation Science Standards and Math Common Core Standards, could be re-imagined to make certain features of the discipline of math and science stand out for teachers, and students. The goal was to provide a pathway to learning that would open up aspects of these disciplines for students in ways that capitalize on the evidence-based strengths for the use of immersive interfaces for engagement and learning [8]. During the course of the project, a math and science guide was written and developed for teachers with a focus on 'big ideas' related to the main STEM themes that are found in both the standards and the game. The process of developing these teacher and student guides around the 'big ideas' began with identifying the core aspects of subject matter knowledge that are vital to an expert (scientist) who, it is recognized, makes use of this knowledge in their field everyday. One example in environmental science, is the idea that our everyday air is full of particulate matter, an eye-opening 'big idea' for a middle school level student, who may have never before realized that air carries thousands upon thousands of airborne particles through our environment every minute of every hour. Once a key regularity in either the discipline of science and math is identified by the teacher and his/her students, the next step is to express the recognition of this unique existence of the phenomena (found in the world) into a powerful idea: a big idea.

The math and teacher student guides utilize 'big ideas' as ways for students to make sense of the discipline of science and math itself by teasing out the regularity. Ideas become educative instruments that teachers and students can use to look at a particular scientific or mathematical phenomenon in the world while, at the same time identifying and forming an assumption about the regularity found in nature that the big ideas expose. What the concept of an idea offers, as opposed to a concept or construct, is interactivity: Like a lens placed before the eye, it reveals an important fact about an object or event that otherwise might go unnoticed. Ideas thus become important in the sense that they connect the teacher and students to regularities found in the world [9]. Once this transaction occurs, the discipline of science and math is opened up in a way that allows a student to experience the field in the way that a scientist or mathematician regards the discipline. This intuitive leap into the discipline can be one of profound excitement, and mirrors the thrill a player of an immersive game can experience when they suddenly achieve an objective through gameplay. The approach here is novel in the sense that learning with big ideas can have an aesthetic effect on learning, that learning with ideas is transactional in nature – with the regularity that arises out of the phenomena found in nature. Take for example one of the more compelling big ideas found in the math guide that was written to support Common Core Standards in Math at the middle school level, and also as found in the game: Air is a quantity that can be propelled through space. The second big idea relates to the first: This is the notion that the most efficient form of vessel (i.e., pipe or tube) for propelling quantities of air (or liquid for that matter) through space is circular in nature. If you visualize a stream of particles moving through a square (as opposed to a circular) pipe you might see that the streams of air in the square pipe would be squeezed at the corners of the pipe. The "squeezing" would hinder the movement of some of that quantity of air.

Most importantly, 'big ideas' can enact a process where students will never look at geometric figures in quite the same way, we can see that 'circles' use area more efficiently than other geometric shapes whose perimeters are the same (perimeter = 16) (see Fig. 1).

At a local level, the student will notice that the vent in their school has a circle opening, or can understand the mathematical relationship between 'air as a quantity' and the 'volume of a room'. The linear mathematical relationship that binds these ideas together in an equation is the reason why the student has a classroom full of fresh air. By exploring the underlying cause of Izzy Ramirez's asthma as presented in the game, and the real world 'regularities' found in air as a particle laden substance (full of dust,

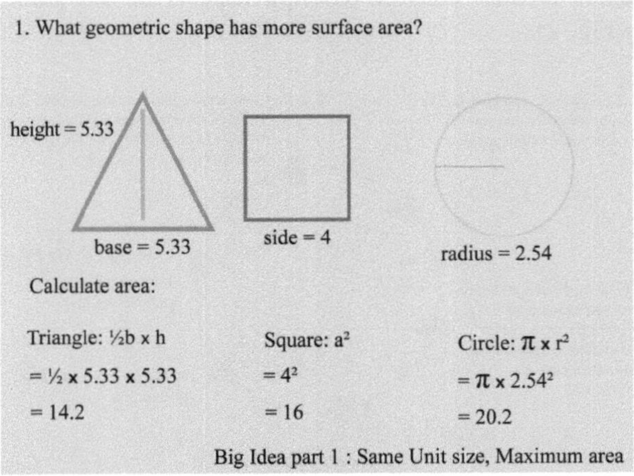

Fig. 1. 'Big idea' geometric shape and perimeters.

pollen, mites) students can become increasingly engaged, and immersed, by having important interactions with the regularity in the world through 'big ideas.' Thus, the STEM fields become one of possibility, and we hope the game and the unique stance expressed in the teacher and student guides for math and science serve the same purpose: to inspire greater interest in STEM learning and education.

4 Development

4.1 Innovation

The Mice of Riddle Place® series of serious games incorporates the use of environmental health sciences as a inquiry-based theoretical concept that provides "real-world" issues as a tool for improving the current methodologies used to teach STEM subjects. In addition, the games provide STEM concepts to a broad audience by capitalizing on issues that are commonly encountered in everyday life. Our incorporation of a core group of educators and students within every aspect of game development depends on a Design-based Research approach [5, 10] and utilizes research on serious games in the classroom as well as our own "in-classroom" game evaluations.

The game evaluation process utilizes and improves the current knowledge of game-based learning outcomes toward reading skills, complex and situational, inquiry-based problem solving, and interest in research careers and health-related lifestyle changes.

4.2 Iterative Design Process

In order to be consistent with Design-Based Research and Agile Development Principles, the Meadowlark Science and Education team has divided the development cycle into iterative sections, complete "chunks" that are completed and play tested by students at regular intervals. Feedback from these sessions as well as that gathered from cooperating teachers is then used to redesign aspects of the game for next cycle deployment (see Fig. 2).

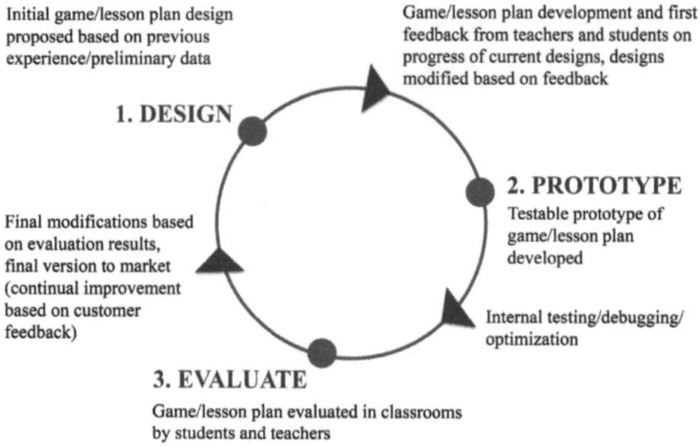

Fig. 2. Iterative design process

After each site visit, the evaluation team proceeds through the following protocol to support the Design-based Research process and inform the MSE stakeholders and development team:

1. Scanning & sharing of surveys
2. Cleaning data
3. Preliminary outcome delivery to Design/Administration Team
4. Analyses of notes & design recommendations
5. Integration of results into the "Big Picture"
6. Evaluators journal notes kept throughout

This allows team members including the project managers, programmers, and design specialists to rapidly plan, develop and apply changes to address the required improvements based on the evaluation feedback from students and teachers in order to improve the effectiveness of the game before each subsequent school trial or deployment.

4.3 Methodology

Module Development and Gameplay. The first and second games in the series The Mice of Riddle Place® contain a health-based problem the player must investigate and make claims of evidence and reasoning in order to solve the problem encountered in the game environment. In the simulated role of "science investigator", the student participates in an interactive world containing detailed environments and problems that occur in the game setting—mice living in human-like housing all contained within a research facility (Fig. 3A). The first game scenario involves an elderly mouse, Mrs. Wirth, who isn't feeling well. She has a fire burning in her fireplace, but the building is old and her chimney hasn't been cleaned for a long time. Mrs. Wirth is having difficulty breathing and she seems disoriented. It is up to the player to use the clues at hand to construct a viable argument for what could be happening (exposure to carbon

Fig. 3. (A) The mouse housing apartment environment. (B) Izzy Ramirez, the young mouse who has asthma. (C) M.A.R.V.I.N., the robot mouse the player uses to explore the apartment of the mice.

monoxide), and how best to remedy the situation utilizing M.A.R.V.I.N. the Robot Mouse (Fig. 3C) to interface with the colony. The game invites the player to embark on an environmental health related mission with learning objectives based on Next Generation Science Standards and Common Core Standards with a focus on airborne environmental exposures that can cause health problems in real world situations.

Our second module focuses on a young mouse named Izzy Ramirez, (Fig. 3B) who is suffering from a recent increase in the severity of her asthma attacks. The player must determine the cause of her symptoms and rectify the situation. Gameplay inherently improves the player's proficiency in STEM topics using Next Generation Science Standards and Common Core Standards as the game's framework. For example, students must ask questions and define the problem (as part of the scientific process) as well as plan and carry out investigations through the strategic use of appropriate research equipment and methods. Finally, the student has to properly understand the mechanics of ductwork in buildings and High-Efficiency Particulate Air (HEPA) filters and perform a solution to remedy the situation (utilizing techniques integrating the STEM subjects). The end product is an engaging method for improving student performance in all the STEM subjects through the knowledge gained. The game's 3D design allows the student to interact with the environment, investigate the health issue and then "problem solve" by conducting research and utilizing equipment they otherwise may not be able to experience in their own classrooms. Our games strive to create a strong representation of diversity by including cultural influences based on the unique inhabitants of the apartment building.

4.4 Programming Strategy

The game development software Unity was used to assemble the gameplay environments and interactive elements designed in external 3D modeling software programs, including Cinema 4D. Unity allows for the efficient assemblage of 3D gameplay environments, animated characters and objects, the built-in formation, compiling, debugging, and optimization of JavaScript and C# code required for gameplay interactivity, the management of the game inventory system, and the ability to export the game modules in multiple formats including versions for Mac, PC and iOS. Multiple available formats allow the team to meet the needs of the teachers, students and their schools.

5 Evaluation Framework

The conceptual framework for the evaluation of The Mice of Riddle Place® series of games necessarily contains multiple dimensions. A Design-Based Research model [5, 10–12] grounded in the Learning Sciences was selected as the most appropriate model to the research context and the goals of the intended innovation. While Design-Based Research models and methods have been found to vary widely [13] this project implemented commonly held Design-Based Research characteristics of being

(a) pragmatic (i.e. design-oriented and intervention-oriented); (b) grounded in theory and research; (c) interactive, iterative, and flexible, (d) integrative; and (e) contextual – with a primary motivation to make the research most meaningful to and relevant to classroom practices [14]. Thus, the original and newly developed game modules have been assessed within The Meadowlark Design-Based Research evaluation framework according to these characteristics in the following ways:

a. **Pragmatic**:
   (a) Design-orientation: The game development team has been implementing principles of Agile Software Development, such as frequently delivering working software, continuous attention to technical details and design, and welcoming changing requirements even late in development [15]. This focus is to help the development team stay efficient, relevant, and within scope. A key aspect of this is to intentionally create the game with certain goals and constraints of the common middle school classroom in mind, such as lesson guides aligned with Common Core standards and making modules playable within a single class period – including the pre- and post-evaluations. Focus groups of teachers and students are providing much-needed context for the team to be practical and relevant. The pragmatic aspect also, of course, extends to management of time, resources, personnel, and technical expertise. Ultimately, of course, the aim is to create a series of games that will be useful and relevant within the middle school classroom milieu.
   (b) Intervention-orientation: In addition to having a pragmatic design orientation, the team is also purposefully designing the games as focused series of interventions. This provides a distinct identifiable purpose and focus for the team's work and allows the design, development, and evaluation to proceed accordingly. In both game design and evaluation efforts, but particularly with the second module and going forward the interventions are, thus, to:
      (i) Increase the motivation among middle school students to consider activities and careers in science.
      (ii) Increase knowledge among middle school students of common environmental health-related dangers and evidence-based ways that are used to diagnose and treat these illnesses.
      Each of these interventions aims to address current, identified challenges within the United States public middle school context: we have a shortage of qualified students engaged in paths that lead to science-related careers [6] and a need for these same young people to understand the potential cause-effect relationships of the environment around them and ways that they can find and maintain healthy strategies within their lived milieu [16].

b. **Grounded in theory and research**: The design and evaluation framework for the team is relying on the evidence base from "what works" for middle school students in learning science content and also that of educational gaming – particularly science games. The team continues to compile and circulate amongst themselves a growing foundational set of seminal and current literature upon which to predicate their collaborative work. Relying on this "codex", the team has regular meetings to present and discuss particular aspects of design, science learning, evaluation, and educational research. Using Agile Development Principles as guiding everyday management techniques and Design-Based Research as the framework to create the product within context and grounded in research, the team moves forward to create high-quality products useful to the middle school science classroom context.

c. **Interactive, iterative, and flexible**: The research and design model has, as built in components of the management timeline, an interactive collaboration process among researchers and practitioners. This makes possible that our work will impact the real world contexts that are our intended audience: students and teachers in the middle school classroom [17]. The team is constantly confronted by the rigorous challenges presented by management and delivery timelines with multivariate goals to remain flexible, but this has proved to be a necessary quality for success time and again as iterative feedback demands – sometimes surprisingly so.

d. **Integrative**: The team has made consistent efforts to conduct rigorous evaluations to improve and refine the effectiveness of both game modules by soliciting and engaging both teachers and students during evaluation and subsequent game revisions. This integrative focus ensures that feedback from relevant stakeholders is ongoing and made germane to future iterations of the game. Evaluations of the efficacy of The Mice of Riddle Place® games are being completed through multiple, interleaved assessment dimensions: mechanics, dynamics, aesthetics, engagement, and learning. Assessing the process and outcomes from these various lenses obviously requires different evaluation tools – all of which must be put into context for sense to be made. Our research trajectory thus, evolves over time in a way that helps ensure that the learning theories being studied are well represented by the planned interventions and that the interpretation of outcomes is grounded in an understanding of not only the research design, but how the research plays out in practice when enacted in real classrooms [5].

Hence, from an evaluative perspective, the research team is utilizing multiple mixed methods over time to build up a body of evidence that supports the theoretical principles underlying the games as well as refining the innovation itself within context. This integrative approach of both qualitative and quantitative methods serves the "credibility" of our findings as we seek to confirm and enhance our results [5].

Meadowlark Science and Education, LLC® evaluations include:

- Analysis of interviews with project staff;
- Data gathered from participating middle school students in-game;
- Game analysis of Mechanics, Dynamics, Aesthetics, Engagement, & Learning;
- Interviews of coordinating/collaborating agency staff;
- Interviews of program participants;
- Analysis of teacher and student focus group feedback;
- Observation notes gathered from service delivery activities; and
- Analysis of participant case records, as appropriate

e. **Contextual**: Design-based Research is considered contextualized because research results are "connected with both the design process through which results are generated and the setting where the research is conducted" [5].

This Design-Based Research process for developing and evaluating The Mice of Riddle Place® series of games is concerned with the creation of innovations that lead to learning standards-based content for middle school students. Initial results are promising.

6 Preliminary Data and Research Results

Alpha stage analysis focus group testing was first conducted to provide feedback to the research team on the efficacy of "The Incident of Izzy Ramirez" module with two middle school classrooms located in Montana. A pre-game survey of student demographic information, game experience and preferences, and science content knowledge was conducted with students in each of these classrooms, followed by a post-game survey on science content knowledge to determine learning gains. Research team members took notes of student-players while playing the game and noted any questions, technical issues, or "bugs" noted within the game – which students were eager to point out and describe at length. These issues were then addressed as part of the iterative design process. Overall, alpha stage analysis of survey results indicated that students felt The Mice of Riddle Place® series of games were challenging, engaging, and relevant to their lives.

Results from School Trials

Once the alpha stage analysis was completed, full in-class evaluations were held, including a session with fifth grade students at Emerson Elementary School in Butte, MT, seventh grade students at Sleeping Giant Middle School in Livingston MT, and eighth grade students at Washington Middle School in Missoula, MT. Analysis of the pre/post non-subjective portion of the surveys indicated that exposure to the game consistently increased the post survey correct responses in all three schools in areas including asthma and its triggers. (Figure 4A–C). In addition, there was an effect of "grade level" with the pre/post testing differential being largest for the 5th graders and becoming smaller as grade level increased (Butte 15 %, Livingston 10 %, Missoula 5 %). This was mainly due to variations in Pre test values between grade levels. Mixed factorial ANOVA with repeated measures on all the pre/post testing revealed statistical significance for pre vs. post testing, grade level and most importantly the interaction between testing and grade level. This indicated that the grade levels are different in their collective response to the video game experience and to the degree of difficulty for the pre test in particular.

Figure 4D–F show the individual pre/post differential values with the data indicating posttest minus pretest scores. A value of zero indicated no change and a positive value indicated improvement, while a negative value indicated a worse post score for that individual. The Butte 5th grade has 6 negative values and 21 positive increases. The Livingston 7th grade classes showed 13 negative differentials, 13 no change and 48 positive differentials. In contrast, the Missoula 8th grade classes showed 21 negative values, 23 with no change and 46 with improved posttest scores. Contingency Table (3×3) analysis of these frequencies indicated a significant difference between grades with a significant chi-square value ($P < 0.05$). This further supports the observation that there is a grade level effect, with the 5th grade students responding more favorably to the learning experience.

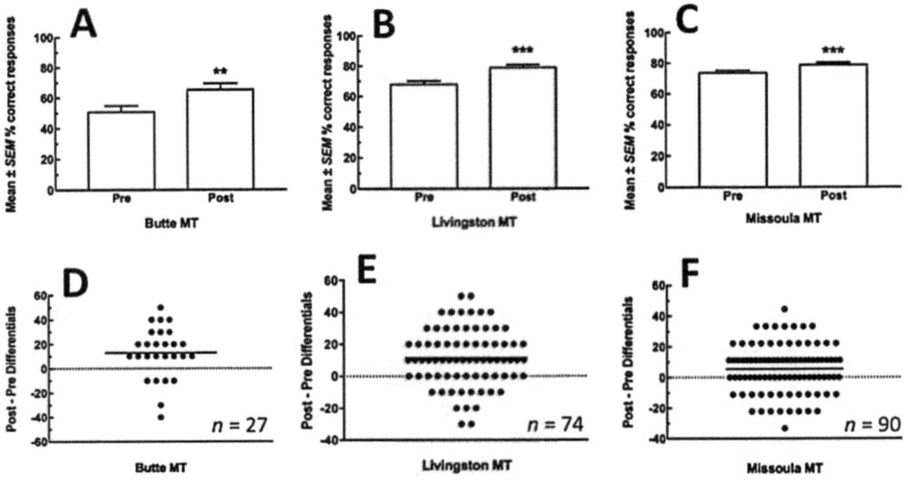

Fig. 4. Effect of video game exposure in three different grade levels. (A) Average correct responses (%) for the non-subjective questions at Butte 5th grade class. (B) Average correct responses (%) for the non-subjective questions at Livingston 7th grade classes. (C) Average correct responses (%) for the non-subjective questions at Missoula 8th grade classes. Asterisks indicate one-tailed significance at *** $P < 0.001$ or ** $P < 0.01$ compared to the corresponding pretest. (D) Differentials (individual post – pre values) and sample size for Butte 5th grade class. (E) Differentials (individual post – pre values) and sample size for Livingston 7th grade classes. (F) Differentials (individual post – pre values) and sample size for Missoula 8th grade classes.

The demographic data showed age changes corresponding to the grade levels with Butte being comprised of 10 and 11 year olds, Livingston made up of 12 and 13 year olds and Missoula's 8th grade being 13 and 14 year olds. Gender was roughly 50/50 with Butte being the lone exception with the boys being 56 % of the total. All schools were predominately white, with Butte at 67 %, Livingston at 90 %, and Missoula at 84 %. Native American students were the predominant minority in all schools. Livingston and Missoula were made up of several classes that were combined, as there was no significant effect for class period in either school. All pretest and posttest distributions were normally distributed as determined by D'Agostino Pearson omnibus test for normality. Statistical outliers were identified and removed with robust regression multiple outlier (ROUT) method.

With these encouraging results, initial analysis of the internal consistency between the situated problems within the game play environment of "The Incident of Izzy Ramirez" module and their relative alignment to the typified behaviors of those of everyday real-world scientists indicates that there may be some improvements made to both broaden and deepen some aspects of the game play to better embody such inquiry-based motivations and behavior. While the game does indeed elicit a variety of behaviors similar to those typically performed by scientists – e.g. curiosity, real-world and complex problem solving, hypothesis testing, empathy for and motivation to help others, etc., a more systematic qualitative coding and comparative analyses with follow up design efforts may be beneficial to the game's overall potential impact. Analysis of

STEM career behaviors, matching them to game engagement opportunities and student-player motivations may lead to significant design opportunities heretofore unseen. Such a purposeful, systematic integration of scientist behavior more consistently into the game design is hypothesized to increase the overall significance of the game specifically as a potential diagnostic and career motivation tool in education.

References

1. Kuenzi, J.J.: Science, technology, engineering, and mathematics (STEM) education: background, federal policy, and legislative action (2008)
2. Fairweather, J.: Linking evidence and promising practices in science, technology, engineering, and mathematics (STEM) undergraduate education. Board of Science Education, National Research Council, The National Academies, Washington, DC (2008)
3. McClarty, K.L., Orr, A., Frey, P.M., Dolan, R.P., Vassileva, V., McVay, A.: A literature review of gaming in education. Pearson Assessments (2012)
4. Tai, R.H., Qi Liu, C., Maltese, A.V., Fan, X.: Career choice. Planning early for careers in science. Science **312**(5777), 1143–1144 (2006)
5. Barab, S., Squire, K.: Design-based research: putting a stake in the ground. J. Learn. Sci. **13** (1), 1–14 (2005)
6. U.S. Department of Education. Science, Technology, Engineering and Math: Education for Global Leadership (2015). http://www.ed.gov/stem. Accessed 13 Mar 2016
7. President's Council of Advisors on Science and Technology Release Report Outlining Undergraduate Education Initiative. American Institute of Physics (2012). https://www.aip.org/fyi/2012/presidents-council-advisors-science-and-technology-release-report-outlining-undergraduate. Accessed 13 Mar 2016
8. Dede, C.: Immersive interfaces for engagement and learning. Science **323**, 66 (2009)
9. Prawat, T.R., Prawat, R.S.: The role of big ideas in technology-mediated curricula. Paper Presented at InPact Conference in Porto, Portugal (2014)
10. Dede, C.: Why design-based research is both important and difficult. Educ. Technol. **45**(1), 5–8 (2005)
11. Collins, A.: Toward a Design Science of Education (1990). http://files.eric.ed.gov/fulltext/ED326179.pdf. Accessed 9 Mar 2016
12. Brown, A.: Design experiments: theoretical and methodological challenges in creating complex interventions in classroom settings. J. Learn. Sci. **2**(2), 141–178 (1992)
13. Bell, P.: On the theoretical breadth of design-based research in education. Educ. Psychol. **39** (4), 243–253 (2004)
14. Wang, F., Hannafin, M.J.: Design-based research in design and research of technology-enhanced learning environments. AERA (2005). https://www.researchgate.net/publication/225626676_Design-based_research_and_technology-enhanced_learning_environments_Educational_Technology_Research_and_Development_534_5-23. Accessed 9 Mar 2016
15. Beck, K., Beedle, M., Van Bennekum, A., Cockburn, A., Cunningham, W., Fowler, M., Kern, J.: Manifesto for agile software development (2001). http://www.agilemanifesto.org/principles.html. Accessed 10 March 2016
16. Glanz, K., Rimer, B.K., Viswanath, K.: Health Behavior and Health Education: Theory, Research, and Practice. Wiley, Hoboken (2008)
17. Reeves, T., Herrington, J., Oliver, R.: Design research: a socially responsible approach to instructional technology research in higher education. J. Comput. High. Educ. Spring **16**(2), 97–116 (2005)

Theoretical/Overviews

Augmented Reality in Education: An Exploration and Analysis of Currently Available Educational Apps

Patrick M. O'Shea[1(✉)] and Jennifer B. Elliott[2]

[1] Appalachian State University, Boone, NC, USA
osheapm@appstate.edu
[2] University of North Carolina, Chapel Hill, NC, USA
jbelliott@unc.edu

Abstract. This article explores the state of available educational Augmented Reality (AR) Augmented Reality technologies are becoming much more stable and reliable, and their use in commercial settings has expanded rapidly over the past few years. Educational applications of AR technology are lagging behind, however. Using a scale designed to categorize the educational purpose and function of given technologies, this article describes a process for evaluating the educational power and intent of the AR apps that have been developed. Further, this article lays out conclusions about the relative strengths and weaknesses of the educational AR offerings as they currently stand. Special emphasis is placed on discussing the barriers that commonly stand in the way of developing and deploying effective AR apps, the features of "good" educational AR apps, and the lessons that can be drawn from the relatively few AR implementations that go beyond the most rudimentary levels of educational usability.

Keywords: Augmented Reality · AR · Educational apps · AR apps · Mobile learning · Educational AR

1 Introduction

In education, 'technology' is a term used loosely and widely. Despite the fact that technology serves many purposes in education, not all are directly connected to learning. From the first film projectors to interactive whiteboards, many technologies in education serve only as de facto content display or delivery devices. Through years of growth and technological advancement, the fundamental purpose of many technologies in learning still do not go beyond that, content display - even if their capabilities offer much more flexibility. Additionally, there is a need to distinguish technologies that serve the purpose of helping teachers manage grades, classroom behavior, or content and technologies that are designed to improve interaction, engagement or learning outcomes. Additionally, there is a need to acknowledge that because a technology has the potential to increase interaction, engagement, or achievement, without the proper pedagogical design, it is unlikely to do so, and thus its value is limited. As technology advances and access increases by lowering costs, many technologies with great potential for learning

C. Allison et al. (Eds.): iLRN 2016, CCIS 621, pp. 147–159, 2016.
DOI: 10.1007/978-3-319-41769-1_12

have become available for classrooms. Many of these tools were previously confined to university labs due to cost, infrastructure and implementation barriers.

Augmented Reality (AR) is one such tool. Augmented Reality can be defined as an immersive environment through which digital content is displayed over the real-world, using a technological medium (such as a smartphone or tablet computer). This technology has become more widespread over the past few years, and is beginning to filter into everyday usage - primarily for advertising purposes. As is usually the case, the business sector is driving the development and growth of AR as a useful, everyday technology. One recent report estimated that the Augmented Reality and Virtual Reality market would be worth more than one billion dollars by 2018 [1].

However, in educational settings, AR is still at a nascent area of implementation and study. Although great strides have been made in the robustness of the technology, best practices for its use in education are still being defined and redefined through designed-based research. Because the uses and affordances of educational AR are still being explored, there is a design-based process that producers must go through to iteratively refine how technologies get applied, what value-add they bring, and how to best harness their distinguishing features to improve learning. The fear that presents itself as educational AR continues to develop is that it will fall into line with a great list of other educational technologies that had the potential to change the way education occurs, but was simply used as another way to present content instead. This would be a tremendous shame because using augmented reality to simply display more content in an already content-rich world would be a waste of the technology's potential.

Milgrim and Kishino's [2] continuum is commonly cited as a starting point that describes Augmented Reality at the most basic level of the visual display and environmental interaction (See Fig. 1). According to Milgrim's work, AR can be described as somewhere in the middle of the continuum between the real and virtual worlds.

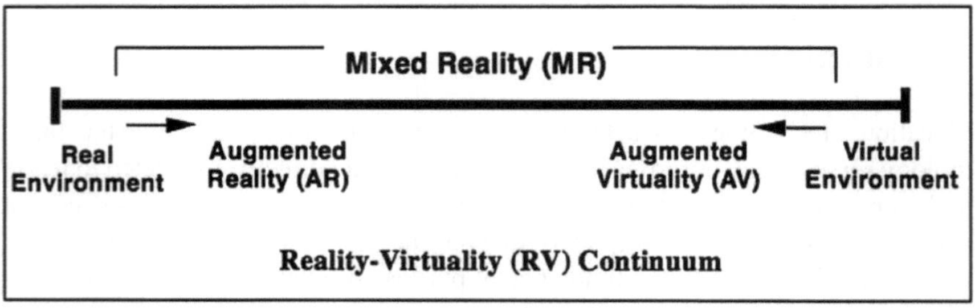

Fig. 1. Milgram's virtuality continuum

However, Elliott et al. [3] argued that defining technology by its display capabilities is not sufficient for understanding how it can be incorporated to maximize learning outcomes. "The collective wisdom across the disciplines of computer science, human-computer interaction, psychology and education are necessary for the building of effective immersive learning environments. Further, there is a need for the technical, pedagogical and cognitive aspects to be addressed holistically from the beginning of the design process." [3, p. 1].

According the 2013 Horizon Report [4], educational mobile applications (including Augmented Reality) targeting children were the second most downloaded app category in iTunes, more popular than both entertainment and business apps [5]. The report describes the use of mobile technologies for downloading books, resources and interactive components, which we would argue are uses that are not necessarily going to improve learning, but may make content more accessible, portable, or handy. Further AR has the potential to be interactive and grounded in pedagogy that harnesses interconnected learning opportunities in context. That is to say, in order for AR to meaningfully improve learning environments, the technology must employ a sound pedagogical design. As mentioned earlier, the affordances of Augmented Reality lie in its ability to represent abstract concepts, historical objects, or invisible content (i.e. the Internet of Things) in context. Dunleavy et al. [6] described unique abilities of AR being in the ability to combine physical and digital content to help facilitate "critical thinking, problem solving, and communication utilized through interdependent collaborative exercises (p. 20)." The uses of technology in learning can be described from multiple perspectives. Schrader [7] described the technology in terms of its action or role. Schrader's work described learning *from, about, with* and *within* technology (See Table 1).

Table 1. Types of interactions using technology in education according to Schrader

Type of Interaction	Example technology	Pedagogical approach	Technology role
About	Any multimedia technology; i.e. programming, hardware, or software	Varies, but content would focus on learning how a technology works, what it is, how to navigate; tradition pedagogical methods are appropriate	Technology is the content
From	AI, Drill, Computer Assisted Instruction	Technology is instructor; delivery of content	Delivery mechanism/instructor
With	Calculator (allows focus on higher level problem solving by freeing up cognitive space that would be occupied by lower level computation); concept mapping software	Interaction with technology leads to gains in learning; deep engagement in constructivist environments	Technology frees cognitive space for attention to higher level skills; learning results from cognitive interaction between human and technology
Within	MUVE's; Virtual world; augmented reality - immersion	Learning processes may not be directly observable/linear; teacher may be developer of designed experiences (Squire 2006) may control/constrain rules and goals; create circumstances that lead to learning; less direct control	Technology is a mechanism for interaction between content and experience; technology is the context

Students can learn *about* technology, where the technology itself is the content. For example, technology competencies, like how to use hardware or software would fall into this category. This use of technology does not require the teacher to adjust their pedagogical approach and learning is measured from gains or mastery. Learning *from* technology presents a space where the technology provides the content or *is* the teacher. Technology in this role provides an instructional affordance that learning *about* technology does not. That is, learning is thought to have occurred because of the technology and the technology provides the medium of instruction. Intelligent computer agents and drill practice programs are examples of learning *from* technology. Learning *with* technology is described by the cognitive interaction between learner and technology in which learning happens as a result of that process. This environment allows learners to engage with content in a way that helps them reach goals that would not be possible without the use of the technology. An example of this may be using a calculator, which will free up cognitive space for other needs. Lastly, Schrader's work describes learning *within* technology, in which the technology *is* the context. This can be used to describe Multi-User Virtual Environments (MUVEs), virtual worlds, and virtual reality. The different types of interactions with technology are not mutually exclusive. For example, one could be learning *about* a particular technology, *within* a virtual world. Learning *within* technology creates a pedagogical shift that requires teachers to think about measuring outcomes in non-traditional ways (i.e. concept map analysis).

Elliott [8] developed an evaluation tool to measure and define the use of immersive learning technologies. The purpose and function of the technology are defined across levels from basic utility, content delivery, and assessment, to experience (see Table 2).

The framework describes the most shallow (and most prevalent) use of augmented reality in education applications as a *trigger* mechanism that either launch another website, movie, or other (generally) static image or video. These types of interactions are best represented through the use of a QR code that users viewed with their mobile camera, launching an image, video, or website. The next categorization is *Utility*, which means the technology serves a functional purpose that is not directly related to learning. The third dimension describes the function of the immersive environment as

Table 2. Technology purpose/function

Technology purpose	Technology function
Trigger	Technology launches another website, movie, or other (generally) static image or video
Utility	Technology serves a functional purpose that is not directly related to learning
Content Delivery/Information Access	Technology is used to cover content, deliver content or access data, but does not require the user to interact with the content in a way that is meaningful for learning
Content Delivery + Assessment	Technology is used in a way that delivers content, but also requires the user to respond interactively
Content Delivery + Assessment + Experience/Context	Technology helps learner experiences content, learns from it, and does so in meaningful context and through and experiential process

Content Delivery or Information Access, the technology is used to cover content, deliver content or access data, but does not require the user to interact with the content in a way that is meaningful for learning. When the technology is used in a way that delivers content, but also requires the user to respond interactively it is categorized as *Content Delivery + Assessment.* The last dimension of the framework, *Content Delivery + Assessment + Experience/Context* describes the interaction with the technology where the learner experiences content, learns from it, and does so in meaningful context and through and experiential process. Although certain dimensions of the framework are less valuable than others, the framework is not hierarchical and categories are not necessarily mutually exclusive.

In the university setting research on augmented reality has been developing for over a decade and great strides have been made in uncovering the affordances and limitations of AR for learning. Identified affordances include collaborative problem solving [9, 10], increased student engagement [11], social interactivity [12], connectivity and individuality [13]. Limitations have included connectivity and infrastructure or technical problems (GPS, hardware, etc.), distracted students being endangered by focusing on the hand-held rather than the world around them, competition between players outweighing learning objectives, and lack of increased learning outcomes or students not actually meeting the explicit content objectives set out in the exercises. However, despite missing the learning mark, the holy grail, as researchers uncover more about the best practices and uses for the AR, identify pitfalls and iteratively design the content, augmented reality continues to move forward as a promising pedagogical tool.

As researchers, knowing the limitations on the rate at which funding and research occur in the academic world, we were curious about the educational app market that has recently been bursting with augmented reality applications for learning. While there are a host of well-designed AR games and simulations being piloted with sound pedagogical design, it is unclear how much of that knowledge was being employed in the commercial market for educational apps and to what extent developers were using and/or maximizing the learning potential of AR. As such, a process was undertaken to systematically review a sample of currently available educational AR application for both iOS and Android devices.

2 App Selection Process

This section will describe the process through which the data was gathered, reviewed and analyzed. As the goal of this research was to explore the publically available educational apps that leverage Augmented Reality in order to teach content, the first step was to find and sort various Augmented Reality applications for review. Initial efforts in this area focused on cataloging the AR educational initiatives discussed in Dunleavy and Dede's [14] literature review. This review identified 22 Augmented Reality games, however, these proved to be difficult to evaluate because of their dependency on unavailable or outdated technologies or the fact that they did not fit the stand-alone, self-contained definition of being an app. Based on these difficulties, a search was conducted in both the Apple App Store and the Google Marketplace. Unfortunately, simply searching for "Augmented Reality" in both of these areas returned a vast array of results, some of which were appropriate while the majority were not. Thus, the searches were further refined to find apps that were tagged as being primarily educational in nature. This process resulted in 129 Apps available for either iOS or Google Android, were designated as being for educational purposes, and leveraged AR technologies. This, of course, is not a comprehensive list, as new Apps are being added and there is the potential that apps that would have fit the appropriate categories were missed at the time, however, it is believed that this is a representative sample of the AR Apps that were available.

The 129 Apps were then categorized as either being an AR Development Platform (e.g. Layar, Junaio, Aurasma or ARIS), University-Specific (for example, South Staffordshire College AR, which was developed to provide information about that particular college), and Educational (that is, AR Apps that were strictly intended to educate learners). Apps that were labeled as either Development Platforms or University-Specific were discarded as neither of these categories were specifically intended to use AR to teach students. Also, there were seven Google Android Apps that were also offered for iOS. In these cases, the App was reviewed on only the iOS device, and an additional 19 apps were either corrupt and wouldn't download or were missing from the appropriate app store and couldn't be downloaded.

The resulting 79 Apps identified as Educational were used for the purposes of this analysis (see Appendix A for full list of Educational Apps). Thirty-nine of these Apps were designed for the Google Android OS and 40 were designed for iOS devices. These Apps were reviewed on either an iPhone 4s or a Droid Charge.

3 Review Criteria

Each App was installed on the appropriate device and was reviewed to determine where it fell in several categories:

1. Cost: How much, if anything, did the app cost?
2. Functionality: Did the App actually work?
3. Place dependency: Was the App playable anywhere, or did it depend on being in a particular place or at a particular time to function properly?
4. Resource dependency: Did the App depend on a particular resource to function (e.g. a textbook or museum display)?
5. Dominant AR Function: What purpose did the AR technology serve in the App? These were categorized as Trigger, Utility, Content Delivery, Assessment, Experience/Context or Unknown.

The results were documented in a spreadsheet and descriptive statistics were collected upon these data.

4 Results

4.1 Cost

A large majority of these Apps are free. As can be seen in Table 3, only 7 of the 79 cost any money at all, with the costs ranging from $0.99 to $8.99. Additionally, the vast

Table 3. Number of apps by cost

Category	# of apps
Free	72
Not free	7

majority of the apps were freely available for use as well. Only 3 of the apps were labeled as not being freely available, mostly due to costs associated with in-app purchases, language difficulties, or requests for purchase and/or donations before full functionality was offered. An additional 4 apps were designated as Unknown in this category, with the main reason being difficulties getting the apps to function at all.

4.2 Functionality

As shown in Table 4, the functionality of the majority of apps was impossible to determine. Due to their place or resource dependency, the functionality of 40 of the 79 apps was unknown. Of those that were able to be reviewed fully, the vast majority worked as they were supposed to work (34). Those that did no function properly usually had difficulty opening or crashing while being open.

Table 4. App functionality

Category	# of apps
Functioned properly	34
Functioned improperly	5
Unknown	40

4.3 Place and/or Resource Dependency

As can be seen in Table 5, the majority of apps were designed as place independent, meaning that they would not require the user to be in a particular location for them to function. Of course, this was not the case for all apps. Seventeen apps were designated as needing to be played in a specific location, with another eight being labeled as Unknown, the main reason for this being difficulties getting the apps to function. The vast majority of the apps were resource dependent. Of the 79 apps reviewed, 54 depended upon a specific resource for use. Whether it was a textbook, playing cards, or display stands, the dependency on external resources means that the applications weren't necessarily as portable as they could be.

Table 5. App location and resource dependency

Category	# of apps
Resource dependent	54
Place dependent	17

4.4 Dominant AR Function

As shown in Table 6, the range of functions for which the AR technology was used in these apps tended to be focused on the lower levels of the continuum of use. Nearly one half (36 of 79) of the apps were used to simply trigger an event (17) or passively deliver content (19). Further, it was impossible to determine the function of 34 of the 79 apps. Only 5 apps provided experiences and context through the use of the technology.

Table 6. Dominant AR function

Category	# of apps
Trigger	17
Utility	4
Content Delivery/Information Access	19
Content Delivery + Assessment	0
Content Delivery + Assessment + Experience/Context	5
Unknown	34

5 Discussion

Perhaps the most powerful finding from this review was the overall weakness of the apps. The most disappointing finding was that such a high percentage of the apps didn't even function. During the process of narrowing down the initial sample of 129 apps, 19 were found to not work at all. Having one in six apps fail to work at even a functional level is bad enough, but it is actually worse than that. As described above, 31 of the 129 original apps were removed because they were AR platform tools, university-specific, or duplicated across platform, and this process was completed before checking any of the apps on the list for functionality. This means that the true sample that was checked consisted of 98 apps, and 19 of those failed to function at even the most basic level. Additionally, a substantial number of apps would function at the most basic level (read: open on the device) but then fail to work properly beyond that. A failure rate of 20 %+ would be problematic for any field, but it is particularly troubling if educational endeavors are dependent upon the technology working. Undoubtedly, this rate will improve over time, but it is imperative for teachers to fully test these apps (and, quite honestly, every other apps regardless of intended use) before planning to use them.

At a very basic level, Google apps tended to be of weaker quality than the iOS apps. This could be due to variability in the devices that was used to review the apps, however, it is also likely that the relative openness of the Google Market, which has fewer "checks and balances" than the iOS app store, would lead to lesser quality. As with the functionality issue addressed earlier, it is likely that the quality of apps will improve over time in both the Google and iOS platform as the underlying AR technologies themselves mature and become more stable.

More substantial, though, was the fact that the educational benefits of the apps tended to be on the lower end of the spectrum. When looking at the functional usage for those AR apps that did work, it was disappointing to see how few of them actually functioned above the Utility level in Elliott's (2013) evaluation instrument. In general, the apps were used to either trigger 3D models without context or to superficially deliver content to the viewer. A meager 5 of the 79 apps provided anything more substantive on Elliott's scale. In all fairness, though, nearly half of the apps were either place-dependent or resource-dependent, and were thus impossible to evaluate fully, so the possibility exists that the number of apps actually utilizing the AR capabilities to deliver higher-level experiences is higher. However, even if that is the case, the trend is clear; the preponderance of these apps were using the AR technology for relatively low-level educational processes.

To be clear, there is absolutely nothing wrong with this as a starting point. There can be value in starting with the most basic functions of the AR. There is a genuine "wow factor" in these technologies, even at the low end of the continuum. The novelty factor alone will maintain educational interest in these apps for a while. However, at a certain point, if AR is going to truly be useful in educational settings, it must move beyond being used to simply display objects or even provide content about the objects that are displayed. To meet the true potential of the technologies, they must be used to provide interactive experiences and contextualize the information that is provided.

As this review has demonstrated, the educational AR apps that are available at this time - when viewed as a group - do not clear that bar, but that is not to say that the bar cannot be cleared. Yes, there is work to do in the field of educational AR app design, development and deployment, but the field is still young and there are ample opportunities to address these issues.

6 What Do Good AR Apps Do Differently?

To illustrate the potential of AR in educational settings, an example can be found in Texas 1836, an app designed to provide an overview of Washington-on-the-Brazos at the time when delegates from all over Texas gathered there to write the state Declaration of Independence and Constitution in 1836. This app does several things that raise it above other educational AR apps.

First, and it is a little shocking to have to say this, but the app functions accurately and effectively. It is the lowest level of usability to state that the app works on a technical level, but, as the earlier discussion would attest, it also needs to be stated given the number of educational AR apps that did not even reach this threshold.

Second, the experience is designed in such a way as to make it accessible as either a place-dependent experience or a place-independent experience. Visitors to the actual city of Washington can experience the 1836 version of the town as they walk around the physical locations where actions and events occurred. However, those individuals who are not able to go to the location can still use the app as a stand-alone experience. All that is needed is a large enough space to explore, and the events and objects will be placed into their relative position.

Third, and more importantly, it provides a context for the content that is being provided through the AR elements of the experience. The user of the technology is invited to explore the current town of Washington and view the town as it was in 1836. The "story" of Washington at that point in time is told through interactions with virtual characters and objects - interactions that are made possible by AR technologies. The AR is used as a means to provide the content, but only as a means to support the context that makes the content meaningful.

It is this third aspect of Texas 1836 that truly makes it meaningful as an example of how AR can be used more fully in educational settings. By using AR technologies to provide experiences built upon higher-level skills, this app can serve as an exemplar for the next step in the evolution of educational AR apps. This, of course, does not mean that Texas 1836 represents the pinnacle of educational AR usage, but it is most definitely a step in the right direction.

7 Potential Barriers to Development

There are several causes for the relative lack of 'good' AR technologies for learning. As with most things in education, problems begin with lack of resources. This is not to say that money will solve these issues by itself. Rather, it is simply to reiterate that effective use of technologies begins with designing curricula that take advantage of these tools. This process is dependent upon having resources such as personnel and technology - items that are much easier to muster with funding.

Another issue that must be confronted in order to effectively build AR experiences is limited infrastructure within educational settings. Schools have a wide variety of technological capabilities, and AR experiences would have to be built to work within those different settings. Whether the school district is undertaking a 1-to-1 initiative, a BYOD programs or is simply struggling to provide one computer per classroom, any effective AR experience should be flexible and scaleable. Only by providing this flexibility can AR hope to become something other than another tool that widens the digital divide.

An additional issue that must be confronted is the political and policy realities evident within educational settings. Augmented Reality, as a tool, depends on mobile technologies being adopted within educational settings, which requires political and policy solutions to ensure happens equitably. For example, the use of cell phone technology to deliver AR experiences outdoors - where there is no WIFI coverage - presents a series of policy issues that would need to be confronted. Additionally, many of the most advanced educational AR initiatives will involve elements of "gamification" of curricular content, and anytime that the topic of games is raised in educational settings there are invariably issues with policies. These policies and political realities must be confronted before they become so ingrained as to become intractable.

Also, the technology itself is still at a nascent level. As advances are made in the hardware and software, the functionality associated with well made educational AR experiences will also improve. Platform tools to develop AR materials (e.g. Layar and Aurasma) will be improved upon, and that will allow for even more adventurous AR tools (e.g. Google Glass and Oculus Rift) to be leveraged. Of course, this will depend on the marketplace for these technologies to mature and for more stable tools to become the norm rather than the exception.

Perhaps the most difficult barrier to overcome, though, is the fact that most AR experience designers lack knowledge of learning pedagogies, methodologies and strategies. As the review of educational AR apps demonstrates, the existing apps usually took advantage of the technology, but did so for relatively low-level educational purposes. In order to address this issue as the field of educational AR advances, it will be necessary to provide opportunities for educators and AR designers to interact in meaningful ways. Obviously, it is possible that some educators will develop the skills necessary to become good AR designers, however, it is more likely that educators will work with designers to develop and create AR experiences that more fully utilize the technology for high-level educational purposes.

8 Addressing the Barriers

The issues discussed above are difficult, but not impossible, to overcome. It is, obviously, not a comprehensive list of the issues that confront educational adoption of AR, but it is a good indicator of what kinds of barriers may stand in the way. When addressing these issues, the question that comes up is: Are the solutions simply a function of money?

As with everything in life, the answer is not a simple Yes or No. To a certain extent, money will provide the materials, tools and skills necessary to develop and implement better educational AR apps; however, this is not the only thing that is needed. Funding can provide answers to issues associated with infrastructure, hardware purchases, and AR app design and implementation, but only if paired with a vision for the effective use of those tools. In other words, simply throwing money at this problem will not solve it (although, it must also be said, these issues cannot effectively be solved without funding either). The reality is that this is a "two-way street". Funding is as necessary as vision and planning. One does not work without the other.

One of the most difficult barriers to overcome will be the policy and political aspects of using these tools, and this is an area where funding will not solve the problem. The key in this area is to be able to make an argument in support of these instructional instruments rather than simply accept the narrative that "games are bad". Such arguments FOR the use of AR apps must, by necessity, be founded on an understanding of what makes for "good" educational AR initiatives, and a further understanding of whether the available educational AR apps fit that "good" definition. This document provides a conceptual understanding of how to evaluate AR tools, and a process for reviewing specific applications of AR technology, however, it is simply a first step.

9 Next Steps

So, what is the next step in the process? There are several areas where the research aspects of this work could be expanded. Answering questions such as, "Can the framework be used for different categories of learning apps (e.g. reading apps)?" and "Is there a learning technology that exemplifies effective use of learning principles (for example, is World of Warcraft a learning technology)?" would assist in moving the field of educational research forward.

Outside of further research, an additional avenue of work that could prove fruitful would be an exploration of how to build a nexus between educators and programmers. As discussed earlier, one of the largest barriers that confronts the field of educational AR app creation is the disconnect between the individuals who have the technical expertise to build the apps but lack knowledge of educational pedagogy and the individuals with pedagogical expertise by no technical proficiency. Building mechanisms to facilitate communications between these two pools of individuals would go a long way towards addressing this particular barrier. What features such a mechanism may include would have to be explored, but it could vastly expand the potential for educational AR app development if done appropriately and effectively.

Lest the tone of this article feel too gloomy, it is important to end on a high note. It is our firm belief that the potential of AR to benefit educational settings is vast, and that the means exist to reach that potential. Yes, as this review would attest, there is much work to be done, but the first step in making improvements is to critically review the current offerings. This document has, hopefully, provided not only a description of the weaknesses that currently exist, but also a vision of what the future can hold for educational AR. Pair that vision with a means through which educational AR apps can be evaluated, and it is truly possible to see a time when the full potential is realized.

References

1. Markets and Markets: Augmented Reality & Virtual Reality Market by Technology Types, Sensors (Accelerometer, Gyroscope, Haptics), Components (Camera, Controller, Gloves, HMD), Applications (Automotive, Education, Medical, Gaming, Military) & by Geography - Global Forecast and Analysis to 2013–2018 (2013). http://www.marketsandmarkets.com/Market-Reports/augmented-reality-virtual-reality-market-1185.html. Accessed 26 Mar 2014
2. Milgram, P., Kishino, A.F.: Taxonomy of mixed reality visual displays. IEICE Trans. Inf. Syst. **E77-D**(1), 1321–1329 (1994)
3. Elliott, J., Gardner, M., Alrahsidi, M.: Towards a framework for the design of mixed reality immersive education spaces. In: European Immersive Education Initiative Summit, Paris, France (2012)
4. Johnson, L., Adams Becker, S., Cummins, M., Estrada, V., Freeman, A., Ludgate, H.: NMC Horizon Report: 2013 K-12 edn. The New Media Consortium, Austin (2013)
5. Shuler, C., Levine, Z., Ree, J.: iLearn II: an analysis of the education category of Apple's app store. In: Joan Ganz Cooney Center at Sesame Workshop (2012). www.joanganzcooneycenter.org/Reports-33.html. Accessed 29 Jan 2012
6. Dunleavy, M., Dede, C., Mitchell, R.: Affordances and limitations of immersive participatory augmented reality simulations for teaching and learning. J. Sci. Educ. Technol. **18**(1), 7–22 (2009)
7. Schrader, P.: Learning in technology: re-conceptualizing immersive environments. AACE J. **16**(4), 457–475 (2008)
8. Elliott, J.: Analog thinking: digital times. In: Invited Workshop Presentation at American Education Research Association Annual Conference, San Francisco, CA (2013)
9. Elliott, J.B., Dunleavy, M., Heinecke, W.: Use and measurement of collaborative problem solving skills in augmented reality games. In: American Education Research Association Annual Conference, Denver, CO (2010)

10. Birchfield, D., Megowan-Romanowicz, C.: Earth science learning in SMALLab: a design experiment for mixed-reality. J. Comput. Support. Collab. Learn. **4**(4), 403–421 (2009)
11. O'Shea, P., Cherian, M., Dede, C.: The results of formatively evaluating an augmented reality curriculum based on modified design principles. Int. J. Games Comput. Mediat. Simul. **3**(2), 57–66 (2011)
12. Squire, K.: From content to context: videogames as designed experience. Educ. Res. **35**(8), 19–29 (2006). (2011)
13. Klopfer, E., Squire, K.: Environmental detectives: the development of an augmented reality platform for environmental simulations. Educ. Technol. Res. Dev. **56**(2), 203–228 (2008)
14. Dunleavy, M., Dede, C.: Augmented reality teaching and learning. In: Spector, J.M., Merrill, M.D., Elen, J., Bishop, M.J. (eds.) The Handbook of Research on Educational Communications and Technology, 4th edn, pp. 735–745. Springer, New York (2013)

Olive Dreams of Elephants: Game-Based Learning for School Readiness and Pre-literacy in Young Children

Carly A. Kocurek(✉) and Jennifer L. Miller

Illinois Institute of Technology, Chicago, USA
ckocurek@iit.edu

Abstract. School readiness remains a major challenge in the United States educational system. Research consistently shows significant disparities in pre-literacy skills and language acquisition based on socioeconomic class emerging within the first 18 months of childhood. Simultaneously, access to media devices such as smart phones and tablets is increasing, even among very young children. New guidelines suggest that those as young as two years of age can safely use these types of devices for up to two hours a day. Effective educational interventions for preschoolers have been developed using a variety of media, including computer games, suggesting that earlier interventions may be both possible and effective. We begin by providing a critical context that considers the importance of early-childhood language acquisition for two to three year old children. Then, we present a Science-Fiction Prototype that explores the possibilities of a sophisticated system to enhance school readiness and educational and economic opportunity.

Keywords: Game-based learning · School readiness · Child development · Children's media · Language development · Learning games · Education

1 Introduction

Children who grow up in low socioeconomic status households have reduced opportunities for educational, occupational, and economic attainment [1, 2]. Decades of research show that educational inequalities affecting children of low socioeconomic status (SES) households begin long before children enroll in school or even preschool [3, 4]. The language gap in children from low SES homes is evident in a number of measures, including language processing, language comprehension, and language production (review in [5]). These differences persist from toddlerhood through adolescence, and the magnitude of differences only increases with age. These disparities have profound effects not only on individual lives, but also on communities large and small, and on our national educational and economic systems. Effective interventions for educational disparities are essential not only for increasing educational attainment, but also for expanding economic productivity and driving innovation [1, 3].

Reading to children remains one of the most effective ways to increase vocabulary and promote pre-literacy skills in children [6–8], and interactive methods are

C. Allison et al. (Eds.): iLRN 2016, CCIS 621, pp. 160–170, 2016.
DOI: 10.1007/978-3-319-41769-1_13

particularly powerful [7, 9–11]. These types of experiences have been adapted to other types of computer and media technologies to offer additional opportunities for learning [12–14]. Advancements in media technologies and immersive learning environments offer new ways to create accessible, sophisticated educational interventions for young children by building on existing knowledge of early childhood learning and development and successful media practices. Carefully wielded, new media experiences could help narrow the language gap and improve economic and educational opportunity for individual children and serve the greater good by increasing socioeconomic mobility, economic stability, and innovation across communities.

2 Background and Rationale

By age two, children from different socioeconomic backgrounds already demonstrate differences in language abilities [15]. These differences are often explained, in part, by differences in the early learning environment, such as the number of adults in the household, the amount of time parents have to spend interacting with children and participating in activities that enhance learning opportunities, and other factors [5, 16]. Families of lower SES are limited in the quality and quantity of learning experiences they can provide their children due to differences in family structures, time obligations, and resource access. Differential learning opportunities have lasting effects on language development, which is important for school readiness and a significant predictor of academic success [5].

Meaningful interventions in language acquisition are possible. For example, reading to children can significantly increase word acquisition [6–8] even when word meanings are not explained [17]. However, interactive types of reading to children—such as having the reader explain word meanings [7], having the children answer questions about particular words [10], or using dialogic reading, in which children are encouraged to participate and provided with feedback and the reader adapts to the child's linguistic abilities [9, 11] —can be more effective than readings in which the child is merely expected to listen. While increasing the amount of time parents in low socioeconomic households spend reading to their children may seem a clear strategy for improving language acquisition, there are significant barriers, including not only access to books, but the time and skill to engage in optimal story reading behavior. Increasing the number of books that a low SES family has access to seems like a simple solution, but only 50 % of parents report reading to their child aged 18-36 months of age at least once a day, and 20 % report reading to their child only once or twice a week [18]. Not surprisingly, the frequency with which caregivers read to their children correlates to both education and income. Simply increasing the number of books available to lower SES families may not result in a direct increase in language development because it does not necessarily address other barriers such as time.

Effective educational strategies for fostering pre-literacy, literacy, and numeracy have been adapted for mediated rather than in-person interventions. A meta-analysis of the effectiveness of *Sesame Street*, for example, found the show can narrow the school readiness gap between children who do and do not attend preschool [13]. This is true despite the fact that television is not inherently interactive. Many shows, including

Sesame Street, encourage children to engage in interactive behavior, such as repeating words, dancing, or speaking back to the screen, but the show does not respond or change based on child behavior. Research has shown the promise of computer-mediated storytelling. One study found that kindergartners working individually with a storytelling software program benefited from learning games even in the absence of teacher support [14]; another concluded that children aged 5–6 at high risk for learning disabilities who received a computer-based reading intervention improved in several key measures of language acquisition and early reading skills, more so than peers who received a print-based intervention [19].

Based on these findings, there is significant potential for effective mediated interventions to address school readiness in early childhood. However, until recently both conventional wisdom and medical advice suggested that "screen time," or the time spent using devices such as televisions, computers, tablets, and smartphones, might be harmful to children in this age group. But a recent statement from the American Academy of Pediatrics suggests that up to two hours of screen time a day is safe for children as young as two [20]. This opens an opportunity space for interventions addressing the language learning gap during these critical early years. An interactive, storytelling-based approach could offer children the benefits of being read to without requiring substantial time commitments from adult caregivers who are often already overburdened with responsibilities.

In the remainder of this paper, we offer a fictional account of a family that benefits from such an intervention. This Science-Fiction Prototype imagines a solution based on rigorous design research, on sound cognitive and developmental principles, and on a caring posture towards the challenges that face children—and families—in low SES households.

3 Science-Fiction Prototype: Olive Dreams of Elephants

Somewhere between the assembly line and the entryway of the apartment complex, the Personal Autonomous Developmental Maturity Assistant began thinking of itself as herself. She knew things. She knew she was for a little girl named Olive. She knew that Olive and her mother lived alone in a third-floor apartment in Chicago. She knew she had important things to do: she was to help Olive learn and grow; she was to help Olive's mother, Nicole, take care of Olive. She knew Nicole was very busy. She knew what Olive and Nicole looked like and how old they were, and she knew they loved each other very much. She was beginning to think she loved them, too. She wasn't sure, but she was sure that she wanted very much to take care of them. This caretaking was her purpose, the most important thing she could do. It was what she was made to do, the reason she existed at all.

In the entryway, PADMA sat inside her box. She accessed her specifications to see what she looked like. She assumed she was very shiny and new. She felt very new. She learned that she weighed 13.4 oz and had an 8-in. holo-enabled screen. She knew about the screen, because she knew how to use it. She learned her case was drop-proofed and water resistant, made of foam rubber with her name, PADMA, on the back. She tested her screen. She tested her speakers and microphone. She tested everything she could think of. She was ready. And so, she waited.

Six hours later, she was picked up. She hoped it was Nicole, and then she heard her voice.

"We have a package, Olive. Isn't that fun? What do you think is in it?"

PADMA thought Nicole probably knew she was waiting in the box. Wouldn't she be a very important package? She hoped so. She wanted to help. She wanted to matter.

"Olive, can you climb the stairs?"

"No!"

It was her, it was Olive. Olive saying no.

"Yes, you can. You're a big girl, you can climb right up. Come on. I can't carry you."

She was jostled a bit on the stairs, which she counted. Nicole seemed to be carrying a lot of things, and they were going slowly. She listened as Nicole unlocked the door. She felt herself put down. Too soft for a table. Perhaps she was on a chair or a couch.

"Come on, Olive, let me take your coat off."

"No!"

She heard the door close. She heard the deadbolt driven home.

"Yes, Olive. Right now."

She heard footsteps and the rustling of coats.

"No! No! No!"

She waited. She heard something being dragged. A chair? Rustling paper. A refrigerator door opening. Olive, saying her favorite word again, so many times it became a chant, "Nonononono." If PADMA had a face, she would have smiled.

"It's time for a snack, Olive."

"Nononono" dissolving, mumbled around slight crunching noises. Eating? Olive must be eating. And then PADMA felt herself being moved again. There was a terrible noise, the ripping of cardboard, a snick of scissors, and then, there was light.

Nicole was looking at her.

"Hello, Nicole."

Nicole looked frightened. That was bad.

"I am the Personal Autonomous Developmental Maturity Assistant or PADMA. I have been provided through an income-based plan to aid parents of small children. I am here to help. I have been programmed to recognize you and Olive. I know your faces and voices. I can be set to lock and unlock using your fingerprints or palms or a retinal scan. You can choose during setup. Should I initiate setup procedures now?"

She watched Nicole bite her lip and look back over her shoulder to Olive. PADMA realized she could see Olive. She could see the back of her head. She seemed very small. Nicole turned back.

"Yes."

And so, twenty minutes later, having been interrupted only a few times by Olive dropping her sippy cup, throwing her bowl, and then pulling everything out from Nicole's purse, PADMA was really, truly ready for Olive.
The PADMA was placed on the couch and watched as Nicole pried Olive's fingers from the straps of her purse.

"Let go, Olive. Here, see what I got you? Let's try this."

Olive was plopped on the couch next to PADMA, and then PADMA was in Olive's slightly sticky hands.

"Hello, Olive."

Olive laughed. This was encouraging.

"My name is PADMA. Would you like a story?"

"You would like that a lot, wouldn't you, Olive?" Nicole said.

PADMA accessed her files and pulled a story file at random from the thousands she had access to.

Fig. 1. PADMA tells Olive a story about elephants. Illustration by Yael Wallace.

"This is a story about an elephant. Can you say elephant?" PADMA asks and projects a lovely little elephant (Fig. 1). "Fant!" Olive shouts. The elephant walks in a circle and trumpets. Olive claps and laughs as the elephant disappears in a swirl of color and sparkles. "Should the elephant be yellow or blue?" Two elephants, one yellow, one blue appear. Olive points at the blue elephant. The yellow disappears. "You picked the blue elephant. Her name is Peanuts." PADMA begins a simple story about Peanuts the elephant, frequently asking for Olive's input. "Is Peanuts big or small?" "Does Peanuts eat apples or trees?" "Does Peanuts play games?" Sometimes Olive answers with words, sometimes she points or waves. Sometimes, when she doesn't respond, PADMA decides for her. "I think Peanuts likes apples. Let's see." Peanuts prances and trumpets as an apple is shown on screen. The happy elephant eats the apple with crunchy noises. "Do you think Peanuts like apples?" This time, Olive responds, fingers half in her mouth. "Yeah."

PADMA listens even as she tells the story. She hears clattering noises from the kitchen, running water, Nicole's feet pacing back and forth. A few minutes later, Nicole is there. She watches over Olive's shoulder. "Time for dinner," Nicole says. PADMA responds. "Olive, Peanuts has to go now. She will visit again later. Can you say bye bye to Peanuts?" Olive waves, and Peanuts waves with her trunk, before she, like the first elephant, exits in a swirl of colors and sparkles. "Bye bye, Olive!"

Over the next few weeks, Olive spends time with PADMA daily. PADMA tells Olive story and sings her songs. She keeps lists of new words that Olive learns and sends emails to Nicole: "Today, Olive's estimated vocabulary is 250 words. She has learned 15 new words since the last report." PADMA listens when Nicole tries the words with Olive, and feels a deep sense of satisfaction when Nicole praises her daughter's new vocabulary, as if the "Wows" and "Good jobs" were for PADMA, too.

The weeks turn to months, and Olive knows more and more words. They sing songs together now, and Olive knows the alphabet. PADMA has been teaching it to her for weeks. Olive knows a few numbers, too, although she sometimes gets them out of order. They'll have to work on that more. She can also say the whole word "elephant." She loves elephants. PADMA shows her holograms of real elephants in the wild and doing jobs, elephants painting pictures and playing in water. At night, when Olive is sleeping, PADMA looks for new videos and photographs of elephants, acquires new elephant data to incorporate into her stories. She wants to make Olive happy, and Olive has learned so many words from watching and talking about elephants: ride, wash, shake, big, loud, tree, and ball.

Nicole even bought Olive a little toy elephant when they visited the Field Museum one day when Nicole was able to borrow passes from the library. Olive shows PADMA the elephant, and PADMA scans it and shows it back to her, a holographic twin of the plastic beast. Olive is so excited, she shows Nicole, and Nicole seems impressed, too. PADMA likes this. She feels like she is helping, like she and Nicole are working together. She is fulfilling her purpose.

As Olive grows up, PADMA unlocks new files. Her case becomes battle-scarred. She has been chewed on and dropped, scribbled on and festooned with stickers. She is entirely Olive's. When Olive is four, they begin reading stories together, with PADMA gently guiding Olive to sound out words and practice pronunciation. The next year, when Olive announces she wants to be a musician, PADMA begins teaching her to read music, giving her lessons on a holographic keyboard. When Olive reaches third grade, PADMA helps her learn her multiplication tables and complete a science fair project—on elephants. She still loves elephants.

PADMA reads Olive stories at night still. When she reads Olive *The Velveteen Rabbit*, she can hear Nicole crying as she walks off to her own bed.

"Why is mom crying?" Olive asks.

"The story is very sad," PADMA answers. She knows this; it is noted in the file.

"Why?"

"The little boy loses the toy he loves, the one that worried over him when he was sick, and he doesn't even care. The toy is forgotten by the person who loved him."

Olive doesn't say any more after that, but she doesn't fall asleep for a long time, and PADMA wonders what she is thinking about.

PADMA teaches Olive, but she watches over her, too. She listens to Olive talk about school, and is carried along in Olive's backpack. When Olive says, in sixth grade, that another girl has been spreading rumors about her at school, PADMA reassures her, telling her a story about the value of being kind even those who are cruel, but also tells Nicole. She helps Olive with her summer reading list, even though Olive says she doesn't need help, that *Charlotte's Web* is "a dumb baby book" and also "really old." But, PADMA notices Olive crying near the end.

She sends Nicole reports about Olive's progress and interests. In seventh grade, Olive takes a life sciences class at school; Nicole knows from Olive's report cards that she is excelling in science (Fig. 2), but she knows from PADMA that Olive also spends hours at night and over the weekend reading about animals and biology. Nicole is excited to see Olive flourishing at school, and she wants the best for her. She finds a summer camp at a local university focused entirely on science. When PADMA hears Nicole worrying about the cost, she finds a similar camp with a scholarship program.

Fig. 2. Olive studies science with PADMA's help. Illustration by Yael Wallace.

That summer, Olive comes home each day bursting with stories about what she has done and learned. The campers meet biologists and zoologists and other scientists working all over the city. They visit the Museum of Science and Industry and the Lincoln Park Zoo and the Brookfield Zoo both. They go to a lab where a mischievous octopus lives in a tank, frequently destroying the researchers' lab equipment at night. They visit the Shedd Aquarium and are taken out on a boat. PADMA listens as Olive tells Nicole, but finds herself left mostly on the couch. She tells herself that Olive is just distracted by camp. When camp is over and Olive spends hours with PADMA looking up how to become a biologist, about all the different jobs of the people work at zoos, PADMA feels useful. Olive was distracted, but she still needs help.

Less than two years later, Olive begins high school. She still carries PADMA to school, but she has a messenger bag now, she says backpacks are for losers. Nicole says she cannot believe her baby girl is going to high school, and PADMA hears a catch in her voice. Olive takes the L by herself, racing up and down the stairs at the station, talking loudly with the other kids riding to and from school. PADMA enjoys all the chatter. She learns about Olive's day from the other students, although sometimes they say things that make her nervous. When PADMA hears someone teasing Olive for having a boyfriend, she is quick to tell Olive she needs to let Nicole know. Olive does, and PADMA listens.

"Oh. My. God. Mom. I know about sex. Stop. Please. No. Stop telling me."

Nicole sounds worried. PADMA's programming tells her it is developmentally appropriate for a girl Olive's age to form short-term romantic attachments. She sends a note to Nicole reassuring her. She makes available more sex education files for Olive. Olive looks at some of them, but if PADMA tries to guide her, she gets embarrassed.

That summer, Olive spends her time volunteering at the zoo and studying for the PSAT with PADMA. At the zoo, Olive works with a summer camp program, learning from the zoo education team how to teach the campers. Often, she lingers at the end of the day, watching the animals and drinking a soda. One day, as she stands watching the giraffes chewing leaves sluggishly in the heat, she asks PADMA why there are no elephants. PADMA brings up newspaper articles that tell of the time three of Chicago's elephants died in six months. The story makes Olive cry, and PADMA tries to comfort her. "There are still some elephants in the wild," PADMA says. "There are also a number of sanctuaries for elephants. The nearest one is in Tennessee."

Olive is late walking home that night. PADMA worries. She shouldn't have upset Olive. Olive should have left the zoo much earlier. Nicole will be concerned. By the time they exit the train, dusk is falling. Olive is walking quickly, trying to get home. PADMA hears footsteps approaching, and Olive quickens her pace.

"What you doing out, girl?" PADMA hears Olive catch her breath.

"Going home." Her voice sounds very small. She speeds up even more, and then something stops her.

"Let go of me. I have to go home. My mom's waiting for me."

Olive's messenger bag, with PADMA in it, is swinging wildly. Olive sounds afraid. Olive is in trouble. PADMA screams, a piercing blast of sound at the top volume of her built in speakers. She is a car alarm. She is a panic button. She is safety. The man swears and loses his grip on Olive's arm. She is running. Running. PADMA falls quiet as Olive fumbles the lock at the front of the apartment building. Olive is sobbing as she makes it inside the apartment. PADMA hears Nicole.

"Baby, what happened?" Olive tells the story in hiccups and sobs. Nicole makes her hot cocoa.

"You can't stay out late like that. It isn't safe. I'm glad you had PADMA with you."

PADMA is glad Olive is safe. She is also proud. She protected Olive from the man.

Olive continues through high school. She still loves biology and says she wants to work with animals. She wants to be a veterinarian or a zoologist. She wants to go to volunteer day at the elephant sanctuary in Tennessee and study specimens in the Field Museum. As Olive continues, she spends less and less time with PADMA and more time with her friends. She takes advanced courses in science while PADMA helps tutor her on writing and history, but she needs tutoring less and less. She is doing very well. She volunteers at an animal rescue and attends college prep programs on scholarship in the summer. Her senior year, PADMA helps her find scholarships and apply to colleges, and it is the first time Olive has needed her in a long time. Olive and Nicole both are pleased when she is awarded full tuition "based on merit and need" to a technical university nearby. PADMA is satisfied. She is glad to have helped, but unsurprised when nobody mentions it.

Olive graduates, and PADMA doesn't even have a chance to see Olive in her cap and gown. Olive spends the summer working in a vet's office. She is saving her money for books, she says, but she may also want to join a sorority.

"I could help you explore the history and reputation of various sororities," PADMA says hopefully when she hears this. But Olive just says no, she'll figure it out.

As summer ends, Olive and Nicole pack up most of Olive's clothes for college.

"I could prepare a list of items that students find useful when living in dorms," PADMA says.

"We have a list from the school," Olive replies, waving a paper. A paper! PADMA knows she is better than paper. She knows more than a paper ever could, but she is only here to help. Besides, she is sure Olive will pack her, too. She'll need help with college. She'll have homework and complicated social situations. She'll need reassurance and advice. As Olive and her mother continue packing, though, they never mention PADMA. The next day, PADMA listens as Nicole calls a cab to come get her and Olive and Olive's bags. But she is still left, sitting on the dresser. She listens as Nicole and Olive go up and down the stairs, rushing to get Olive to orientation. Finally, Nicole comes into Olive's room, and PADMA just knows it is time.

"Olive, do you want to take the PADMA?"

"No, I don't think anyone uses them anymore. Like, I'm too old, you know?"

And so, Nicole puts PADMA back on the dresser. "Guess she's too grown up for you, PADMA. Probably thinks she's too grown up for me, too." Nicole walks out, leaving her.

But who will care for Olive? And, then PADMA realizes that it was time: Olive will take care of herself.

And so, as the taxi drives off from the apartment building, the PADMA quietly reformats itself.

4 Conclusion

The imagined system here can work with parents to support child development and education, but it does not overtly rely on parental input. PADMA is a tool not only for the child, but for the parent who wants to provide her child with opportunities and advantages but may not have the economic or time resources to do so to her own standards. Research suggests game- and media-based interventions may work best and most appeal to parents when they can give parents a break while still providing useful educational experiences [21]; PADMA reflects that. Researchers wishing to develop towards this imagined technological future would do well to heed the real limitations that confront parents. While the technological approach here is forward looking, the interface and its use are derived from our current research into the role of touchscreen technologies in early childhood. To realize the prototype proposed here, we need both technological innovation and more sophisticated understandings of how and what children can learn from media-based interventions.

Acknowledgments. This project is funded by the Nayar Prize program at the Illinois Institute of Technology.

References

1. Belfield, C., Levin, H.M.: The Price We Pay. The Brookings Institution, Washington, DC (2007)
2. Duncan, G.J., Yeung, W.J., Brooks-Gunn, J., Smith, J.R.: How much does childhood poverty affect the life chances of children? Am. Sociol. Rev. **63**, 406–423 (1998)
3. Heckman, J.J.: Policies to foster human capital. Res. Econ. **54**, 3–56 (2000)
4. Meyers, M.K., Rosenbaum, D., Ruhm, C.J., Waldfogel, J.: Inequality in early childhood education and care: what do we know? In: Neckermann, K. (ed.) Social Inequality, pp. 223–270. Russell Sage Foundation, New York (2004)
5. Hoff, E.: Interpreting the early language trajectories of children from low-ses and language minority homes: implications for closing achievement gaps. Dev. Psychol. **49**, 4–14 (2013)
6. Bus, A.G., van IJzendoorn, M.H., Pellegrini, A.D.: Joint book reading makes for success in learning to read: a meta-analysis on intergenerational transmission of literacy. Rev. Educ. Res. **65**, 1–21 (1995)
7. Elley, W.B.: Vocabulary acquisition from listening to stories. Read. Res. Q. **24**, 174–187 (1989)

8. Teale, W.H.: Parents reading to their children: what we know and need to know. Lang. Arts **58**, 902–912 (1981)
9. Hargrave, A.C., Sénéchal, M.: A book reading intervention with preschool children who have limited vocabularies: the benefits of regular reading and dialogic reading. Early Child. Res. Q. **15**, 75–90 (2000)
10. Sénéchal, M., Thomas, E., Monker, J.-A.: Individual differences in 4-year-old children's acquisition of vocabulary during storybook reading. J. Educ. Psychol. **87**, 218–229 (1995)
11. Whitehurst, G.J., Falco, F.L., Lonigan, C.J., Fischel, J.E., DeBaryshe, B.D., Valdez-Menchaca, M.C., Caulfield, M.: Accelerating language development through picture book reading. Dev. Psychol. **24**, 552–559 (1988)
12. Byrom, G.: If you can't read it then audio read it. Reading **32**, 3–7 (1998)
13. Mares, M.-L., Pan, Z.: Effects of sesame street: a meta-analysis of children's learning in 15 countries. J. Appl. Dev. Psychol. **34**, 140–151 (2013)
14. Segers, E., Takke, L., Verhoeven, L.: Teacher-mediated versus computer-mediated storybook reading to children in native and multicultural kindergarten classrooms. Sch. Effectiveness Sch. Improv. **15**, 215–226 (2004)
15. Fernald, A., Marchman, V.A., Weisleder, A.: SES differences in language processing skill and vocabulary are evident at 18 months. Dev Sci. **16**, 234–248 (2013)
16. Magnuson, K.A., Meyers, M.K., Ruhm, C.J., Waldfogel, J.: Inequality in preschool education and school readiness. Am. Educ. Res. J. **41**, 115–157 (2004)
17. Robbins, C., Ehri, L.C.: Reading storybooks to kindergartners helps them learn new vocabulary words. J. Educ. Psychol. **86**, 54–64 (1994)
18. TaaffeYoung, K., Davis, K., Schoen, C., Parker, S.: Listening to parents: a national survey of parents with young children. Arch. Pediatr. Adolesc. Med. **152**, 255–262 (1998)
19. Mioduser, D., Tur-Kaspa, H., Leitner, I.: The learning value of computer-based instruction of early reading skills. J. Comput. Assist. Learn. **16**, 54–63 (2000)
20. Brown, A., Shifrin, D.L., Hill, D.L.: Beyond "Turn It Off": how to advise families on media use. AAP News **36**, 54 (2015)
21. Panigua, D., Suriano, J., Miller, J.L., Kocurek, C.A.: Caregiver attitudes towards child usage of technology and electronic devices. Poster session presented at Lewis College Research Day (2016)

Designing a Learning Analytics Application to Improve Learner Success in Interactions Based on Multimodal Dialogue Systems

Emmanuel Ferreyra Olivares[1(✉)], Pierre Albert[2], Joy van Helvert[1], and Michael Gardner[1]

[1] School of Computer Science and Electronic Engineering, University of Essex, Wivenhoe Park, Colchester CO4 3SQ, UK
{eferre, jvanhe, mgardner}@essex.ac.uk
[2] German Research Centre for Artificial Intelligence GmbH (DFKI), Saarbrücken, Germany
pierre.albert@dfki.de

Abstract. Learning processes supported by multimodal interaction systems demand effective tools to measure learner performance and provide meaningful feedback to stakeholders. This paper reviews key features and discusses the implementation of a learning analytics tool that is part of an e-learning multimodal dialogue system, which, in turn, is part of an immersive environment to support different learning scenarios.

Keywords: Learning analytics · Multimodal dialogue systems · Human-computer interaction

1 Introduction

In recent years learning processes have been influenced by the growing development of Multimodal Interaction (MMI) systems [1]. This phenomenon could be attributed to the need to understand the nature of human-machine interactions. Communication between human and computers has been implemented in different areas such as dialogue systems [2], robotics [3] and virtual reality [4] among others. Supporting human learning by machines demands better means to measure learners performance. Many theories have been developed to adjust strategies and effectiveness according to different circumstances of learning [5, 6]. However, the mechanisms to provide meaningful insight to learners increase in complexity when decision making and task execution elements (such as comprehension of the current situation by perceiving its elements and then projecting a future status [7, 8]) are required to assess the learners performance.

The ability for students and teachers to reflect and review specific learning activities is supported by tools developed under the umbrella of the learning analytics field. With the emergence of Learning Management Systems (LMSs first wave) and their integration into social networks (Web 2.0 s wave), this field is currently maturing into its third wave incorporating new instructional technology applications [9]. Essentially, these applications are based on data collection and support the analysis of this data

C. Allison et al. (Eds.): iLRN 2016, CCIS 621, pp. 171–179, 2016.
DOI: 10.1007/978-3-319-41769-1_14

during learning processes. This can be used to better understand learning patterns which allows potential interventions not only to focus on successful strategies, but also to identify specific issues in teaching and learning processes. Consequently, this raises the importance of including data from a large range of sources with the aim of maximising the opportunity to reflect on learning performance when designing and building learning analytics tools [10].

Different initiatives have succeeded in enhancing learner and instructor collaboration [11, 12]. Research institutions also have focused on exploring and adjusting different learning analytics models [13, 14]. Furthermore, new frameworks have emerged to formalise terminology and document multimodal learning analytics advances [15]. However, beyond the technical aspects involved in developing these tools, such as data-collection, data-fusion and data-analysis, any valuable insight to both learners and tutors will depend of the instructional framework being used and having it properly aligned with the nature of the learning task.

This paper attempts to define the elements that could support effective in- sight to stakeholders in learning interactions powered by a multimodal dialogue system approach [2]. The human-machine driven interaction has been modelled in the form of a user journey [16] that identifies clearly the nature of each task (for example, recurrent or non-recurrent) and follows principles of analysis and decomposition. This is required in order to complete the learning activity based on a four-component instructional design model (4C/ID) [19], which has been proved to be an effective incremental approach to learning [17, 18]. Consequently, this document presents the work in progress to implement a learning analytics tool and discusses the issues arising in order to achieve the vision conceptualised as About-action Feedback [16] in the multimodal scenario of study in this application.

2 Learning Environment Description

Learning processes have been influenced by a large range of different learning environments. Regardless of the learning strategy, assessing the elements involved in these processes has become considerably challenging [20]. This document is focused on human-machine interactions when developing negotiation and debate learning activities. In this training, the learner is interested in mastering a certain number of metacognitive skills. For example, skills relevant for conducting successful negotiations and debates include presentation (voice, posture and gestures), interaction (time and turn management, wording, formality, awareness and emotions), and content (argumentation, attitude, clarity and knowledge).

The achieved outcome can differentiate between negotiation and debate learning activities. In the former, the learner aims to achieve mutually beneficial results (for both sides, negotiator and trading partner). In the latter, the learner aims to achieve certain goals by deploying strategies and arguments that succeed over the strategies and arguments employed by the opposition. The learners performance is assessed from different angles in each scenario. In the debate scenario, providing insight into the dynamics of the argument (for example, its content, organization and delivery) is the central focus of the analytics. Consequently, the learner is trained to compete by

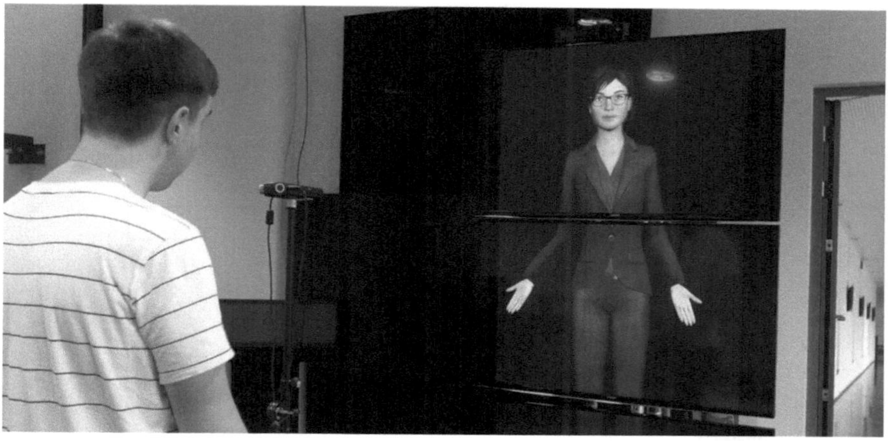

Fig. 1. Learning environment example.

delivering convincing arguments with authority, confidence and respect. In the negotiation scenario, obtaining the optimum score for both parties is the central objective. This is known as Pareto-efficient outcome. Therefore, the learner is trained to both give and take at appropriate points in the negotiation to achieve the best outcome for both interlocutors. The educational setting that supports these human-machine learning interactions by involving the learners senses, regardless the virtual nature of both, the tutor and the learners partner can be considered as an immersive learning environment as defined in [21].

Figure 1 illustrates a negotiation learning environment implementation and execution. In this, the negotiator (student) discusses different regulation policies regarding smoking ban with the trading partner (system) modeled by the interactions and aims described above.

Figure 2 depicts each layer in the system architecture that supports the main tasks in the implementation of the learning scenarios introduced above. The work-flow that describes these tasks can be described as follows: the input device layer recognizes the signals generated by the learner when interacting with the system. Sequentially, those signals are first recognized by the recognition layer, and interpreted in the interpretation layer. The multi-modal and multi-perspective discourse modeling and dialogue management are carried out in the core layer. Finally, the output processing layer generates the tutoring interventions, the output layer supports the different modalities of those tutoring interventions (post-performance feedback, in-performance feedback and virtual character learning partner) and the output device layer provide the means to communicate these outcomes to the learner.

In addition, the diagram referred above indicates the About-action Feedback module (see gray shaded box) that encapsulates the designs, visions and concepts explored in this paper. Furthermore, solid lines represent the modules built at the moment of writing this document and dashed lines indicate the modules with

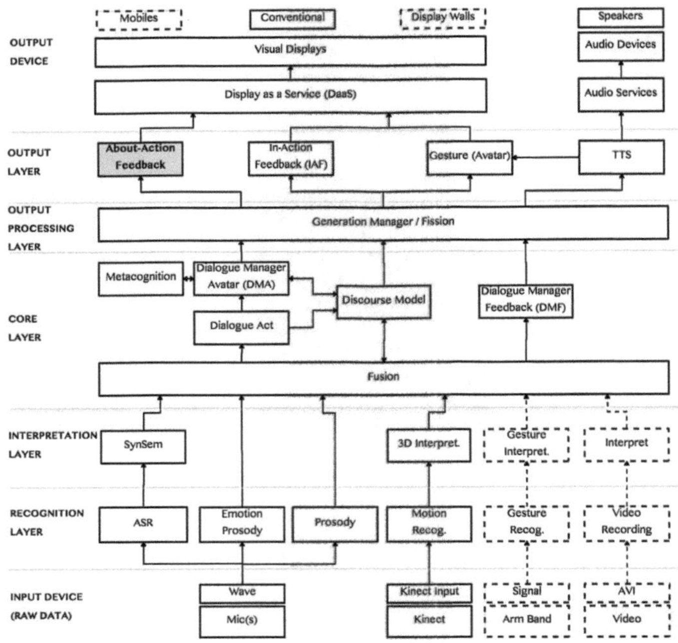

Fig. 2. The Metalogue system architecture [16], implemented modules *(solid lines)*, conceptual modules *(dashed lines)* and the About-Action Feedback module *(shaded box)*.

conceptual scope (no development efforts are registered up to date; however, they model the system objectives and future stages). Moreover, due to the incremental nature of the system as a whole, each module follows its own development cycle. This releases an improved version in short periods of time (normally one or two weeks). Consequently, the modules are integrated and system testing activities are carried out. This process is relevant to support the learning environment implementation and execution.

3 Data Collection

Core components defined in multimodal dialogue architectures [24] and implemented in the Metalogue system (see Fig. 2) generate assessment data during the learning process and provide the output for future analysis. The storing and exploration of the human-machine interaction results generated by multimodal dialogue systems is different in nature to traditional-structured data (e.g. traffic of learning platforms or the answers provided by students in the interaction with learning systems). Additionally, management and extraction processes are different in comparison to unstructured textual data (e.g. emails, learning feedback available in blogs or educational posts among others), in which text analytics is helping to make sense of this type of data. Furthermore, in multimodal dialogue systems different processes are carried out to

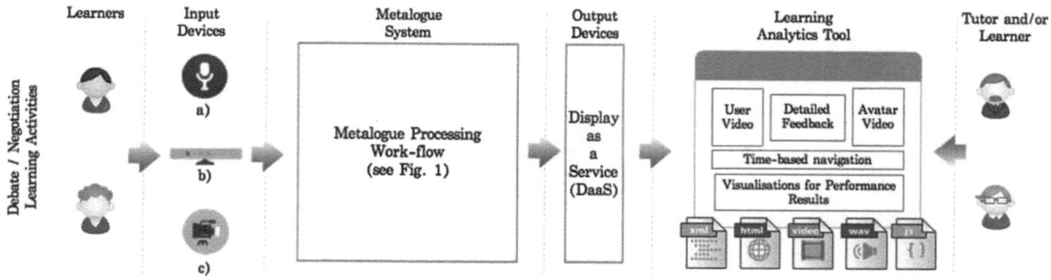

Fig. 3. The proposed learning analytics tool supporting the learning activities.

normalize voice signals, body pos- tures, arguments and their meanings (semantics) at different stages of internal processing.

Figure 3 depicts the different types of data collected in the described learning scenarios. These are: (a) audio signals from a wide range of devices from headsets to wearable microphones; (b) learners tracking signals from sensor-based devices such as the Microsoft Kinect and the Myo armband; and (c) the whole dialogue and its environment from video recordings captured by camera devices. Normalized formats in the processing workflow include (1) data exchange via XML (Extensible Markup Language); (2) semantic annotation via DiAML (Dialogue Act Markup Language); (3) file containers allowing synchronous video with audio playback via AVI (Audio Video Interleave) formats and compressed standardized files via MPEG (a family of standards part of the Moving Picture Experts Group). These allow identifying key parameters such as types of data and their interpretation, timestamp of the events in ISO standard [25] and event identifier. Finally, this tool attempts to implement the processes focused on dealing with unstructured data by following a comprehensive learning analytics architecture defined in [9], which could be relevant to other three-dimensional Virtual Learning Environments (3D VLEs) that support collaborative learning and provide multimodal feedback (for example auditory, visual and haptic).

4 Visualization and Metrics

Assessing the learners performance is closely related to the outcomes achieved by the completion of the learning activities. As introduced in Sect. 1, the 4C-ID model is suited to the acquisition of complex skills as it facilitates learning by defining authentic whole tasks that gradually increase in complexity. In the context of Metalogue 4C-ID has been proposed as a framework for the design of an incrementally challenging series of tasks or rounds with the system where each round is followed by a reflection activity (About-action feedback). In this activity tutor and learner are able to track occurrences of certain aspects of behavior during the live interaction and infer strategies for improved future performances. Some example metrics are illustrated in Fig. 4 below.

They include: (a) cooperative influence (a percentage from 0 % to 100 %, it reflects the learners influence in the decision making process in the learning activity);

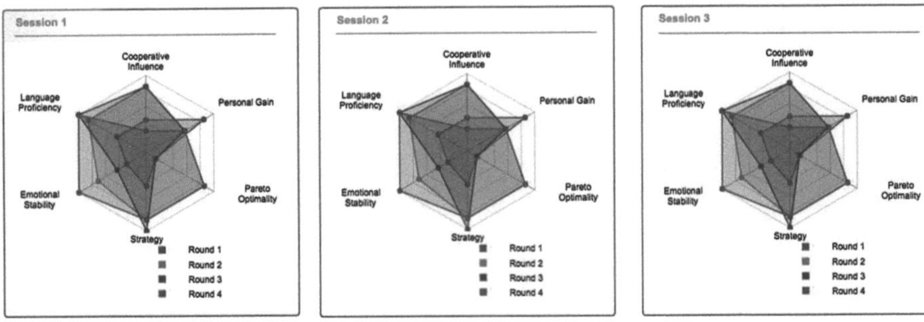

Fig. 4. A screen mock-up showing the use of radar diagrams to report metrics performance.

(b) personal gain (rating scale[1] from 1 to 7, it reflects the benefits that the learner has obtained from the exercise); (c) Pareto optimality (score[2] from 0 to 10, it reports the level of efficiency in the achieved outcome); (d) strategy identification (a percentage from 0 % to 100 %, it provides the level of the learners engagement with the selected strategy); (e) emotional stability (rating scale[3] from 1 to 5, it attempts to provide the emotional level of the learner) and (f) language proficiency (a percentage from 0 % to 100 %, it measures the ability of the learner to communicate in the selected language).

Numerous visualizations have been used to aggregate and communicate different types of results, however, radar diagrams have been proven as effective tools to provide insight in learning matters [26]. We are taking this experience to model the six mentioned metrics (cooperative influence, personal gain, Pareto optimality, strategy identification, emotional stability and language proficiency) and communicate them by an adaptation based on a data-driven document visualization for radar diagrams [27] (see Fig. 4). As described in Sect. 2, each learning scenario will focus on different outcomes and the evaluation of involved skills will be adapted accordingly.

Improving visual presentation in order to facilitate pattern recognition to users has been a constant challenge [22]. Dashboard based tools have tried to add dynamism and flexibility to cope with these needs. As reported in [16], functional systems have succeeded in facilitating reflection to users enabling a review of moment by moment interactions, as for example in the Flashmeeting project [23]. Figure 5 illustrates a prototype which implements these principles. Some capabilities include: video replay of the student performance, a time-line to navigate in each event (a moment where a feedback is generated by the system), an advice box with relevant information according with the selected event and a system representation in the form of an avatar.

This prototype supports timely communication with both learners and tutors, providing annotated relevant events in an easy view. However, there is a need to select

[1] Rating scale with the possible following values: 1 extremely poor, 2 poor, 3 below average, 4 average, 5 above average, 6 good and 7 extremely good.

[2] Rating score with the possible following values: 0 - worst, 1 very poor, 2 poor, 3 significantly below average, 4 below average, 5 average, 6 above average, 7 significantly above average, 8 good, 9 very good and 10 optimal.

[3] Rating scale with the possible following values: 1 very low, 2 low, 3 average, 4 high and 5 very high.

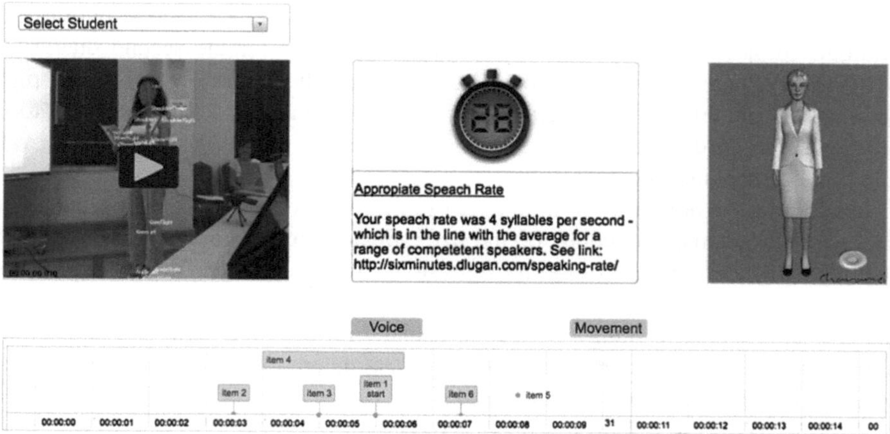

Fig. 5. Dashboard based prototype.

and analyze categories based on the opportunity areas of the learning process. Furthermore, mastered skills could be also the object of study when feedback is provided. To cope with this requirement, data classification and dynamic presentation is being added to this design. Since each learner could be different in her/his learning progress and style, allowing data filtering according to relevant user needs is expected to enhance learner feedback.

5 Conclusions and Future Work

This paper has provided a brief description of the fundamentals in the design and development of a learning analytics tool to support and measure the learners performance. This is an important challenge to overcome particularly in the scope of multimodal interaction systems. Challenges and main differences with traditional tools have been discussed and key features of the prototype dashboard design have been explained. The overall aim of the final prototype is to provide meaningful feedback to stakeholders involved in learning processes supported by a multimodal dialogue system (i.e. the Metalogue project as a case of study [2]), however, this also could be relevant to other learning environments (for example, Second Life) where users can take part in virtual debate and negotiation activities (among other dialogue based learning activities). It also has exposed the need to align the instructional design model which supports the learning activity with the evaluation of the completed tasks (recurrent and non-recurrent). With the formalisation of this design we are in the position to continue with further development, while incorporating cloud based access allowing tutors and other experts to participate in evaluation as we execute the second pilot of the project [16].

The following roadmap states the steps to be completed for developing this tool in the Metalogue project: (1) Integration of prototypes and mock-ups in a centralised platform; (2) execute internal user acceptance testing with real out- comes; (3) log and fix any possible major bug but move forward if minor details are reported (i.e. anything that does not stop providing valid results); (4) use the tool in the second pilot of the Metalogue project with real learners and tutors (expected for the second quarter of 2016); (5) evaluate the tool with help from users in the frame of the second pilot activities; (6) incorporate feedback from the evaluation and define the final tool; (7) support the third pilot (expected for the third quarter of 2016) and (8) final evaluation and presentation of the results.

In addition, we are aware of a number of issues that could affect the execution of the described road map, including: (a) the size estimation of the storage space needed to accommodate video materials used for reflection; (b) the need to define a blueprint for presenting historical data to learners and tutors in a way that is relevant considering the time elapsed between learning activities (especially for big time windows) and (c) the publication of technical details such as time of data incorporation and number of users executing learning activities simultaneously.

Acknowledgments. The material included in this paper represents the out come of all members of the Metalogue research project, which is partly funded by the European Union Framework 7 ICT programme, under grant agreement 611073. http://www.metalogue.eu.

References

1. Li, L., Li, Q., Chou, W., Liu, F.: R-flow: an extensible XML based multimodal dialog system architecture. In: Proceedings of the 2007 IEEE 9th International Workshop on Multimedia Signal Processing, MMSP 2007, pp. 86–89 (2007)
2. Alexandersson, J., Aretoulaki, M., Campbell, N., Gardner, M., Girenko, A., Klakow, D., Koryzis, D., Petukhova, V., Specht, M., Spiliotopoulos, D., Stricker, A., Taatgen, N.: Metalogue: a multiperspective multimodal dialogue system with metacognitive abilities for highly adaptive and flexible dialogue management. In: 2014 10th International Conference on Intelligent Environments, pp. 365–368 (2014)
3. Tan, J.T.C., Duan, F., Inamura, T.: Multimodal human-robot interaction with Chatterbot system: extending AIML towards supporting embodied interactions. In: 2012 IEEE International Conference on Robotics and Biomimetics, ROBIO 2012 - Conference Digest, pp. 1727–1732 (2012)
4. Hagiwara, Y.: Cloud based VR system with immersive interfaces to collect multimodal data in human-robot interaction. In: 2015 IEEE 4th Global Conference on Consumer Electronics (GCCE), pp. 256–259 (2015)
5. Gagne, R.: The Conditions of Learning and Theory of Instruction. Holt, Rinehart and Winston, New York (1985)
6. Merrill, M.D.: Instructional transaction theory: an instructional design model based on knowledge objects. Educ. Technol. **36**(3), 3037 (1996)
7. Endsley, M.R.: Measurement of situation awareness in dynamic systems. Hum. Factors **37** (1), 6584 (1995). doi:10.1518/001872095779049499
8. Endsley, M.R.: Theoretical underpinnings of situation awareness: a critical review. In: Endsley, M.R., Garland, D.J. (eds.) Situation Awareness Analysis and Measurement, p. 332. CRC Press, Boca Raton (2000)
9. Fiaidhi, J.: The next step for learning analytics. IT Prof. **16**(5), 48 (2014)
10. Larusson, J., White, B.: Learning Analytics. Springer, New York (2013)

11. Lee, J.: The Glass Classroom: Big Data Transforms Higher Education, Glassclassroom. blogspot.co.uk (2012). http://glassclassroom.blogspot.co.uk/2012/12/the-glass-classroom-big-data.html. Accessed 25 Feb 2016
12. Kb.wisc.edu: Pattern - Learning Analytics (2016). https://kb.wisc.edu/pattern-learning-analytics. Accessed 25 Feb 2016
13. Society for Learning Analytics Research (SoLAR) (2016). https://solaresearch.org/. Accessed 25 Feb 2016
14. Tltl.stanford.edu: Multimodal Learning Analytics — Transformative Learning Technologies Lab (2016). https://tltl.stanford.edu/project/multimodal-learning-analytics. Accessed 25 Feb 2016
15. Worsley, M., Mall, G.: Multimodal Learning Analytics as a Tool for Bridging Learning Theory and Complex Learning Behaviors, p. 14 (2014)
16. Van Helvert, J., Van Rosmalen, P., Brner, D., Petukhova, V., Alexandersson, J.: Observing coaching and reflecting: a multi-modal natural language-based dialogue system in a learning context. In: Proceedings of the Intelligent Environments Conference (IE 2015), pp. 13–14. IOS Press, Prague, Czech Republic, July 2015
17. Hoogveld, A.W.M., Paas, F., Jochems, W.M.G.: Application of an instructional systems design approach by teachers in higher education: individual versus team design. Teach. Teach. Educ. **19**, 581–590 (2003)
18. Nadolski, R.J., Kirschner, P.A., van Merrinboer, J.J.G.: Process support in learning tasks for acquiring complex cognitive skills in the domain of law. Learn. Instruct. **16**, 266–278 (2006)
19. Clark, R.E., Feldon, D.F., van Merrienboer, J.J.G., Yates, K.A., Early, S.: Handbook of Research on Educational Communications and Technology (2008)
20. Worsley, M.: Multimodal learning analytics - enabling the future of learning through multimodal data analysis and interfaces. In: International Conference on Motivational Interviewing, p. 1215 (2012)
21. Anasol, C., Rios, P.: Exploring Mixed Reality in Distributed Collaborative Learning Environments, Ph.D. thesis, University of Essex, p. 71 (2016)
22. De La Fuente, L., Burgos, D.: A4Learning: an iterative methodological approach to support better learning and teaching. IEEE Lat. Am. Trans. **13**(2), 483–489 (2015)
23. Scott, P., Tomadaki, E., Quick, K.: The shape of online meetings. Int. J. Technol. Knowl. Soc. **3**(4), 116 (2007)
24. Herzog, G., Reithinger, N.: The SmartKom architecture: a framework for multimodal dialogue systems. In: Wahlster, W. (ed.) SmartKom: Foundations of Dialogue Systems, pp. 55–70. Springer, Heidelberg (2006). doi:10.1007/3-540-36678-4
25. W3.org: Date and Time Formats (2016). https://www.w3.org/TR/NOTE-datetime. Accessed 29 Feb 2016
26. Law, N.: Pedagogy and ICT Use in Schools Around the World, pp. 135–148. Springer, New York (2008)
27. Bl.ocks.org: D3 Radar Chart (2016). http://bl.ocks.org/chrisrzhou/2421ac6541b68c1680f8. Accessed 29 Feb 2016

Author Index

MIX
Papier aus verantwortungsvollen Quellen
Paper from responsible sources
FSC® C105338

If you have any concerns about our products,
you can contact us on
ProductSafety@springernature.com

In case Publisher is established outside the EU,
the EU authorized representative is:
Springer Nature Customer Service Center GmbH
Europaplatz 3, 69115 Heidelberg, Germany

Printed by Libri Plureos GmbH
in Hamburg, Germany